WITHDRAWN

THEORIES OF C[RIME]

Presenting a clear, comprehensive review of theoretical thinking on crime, this book encourages students to develop a deeper understanding of classic and contemporary theories, and provides an interdisciplinary approach to criminology through the contributions of sociology, psychology and biology. Chapters cover:

- Crime: the Historical Context
- Biological Explanations for Criminal Behaviour
- Psychological Explanations for Criminal Behaviour
- Sociological Explanations for Criminal Behaviour
- Explaining the Criminal Behaviour of Women
- Explaining the Criminal Behaviour of Ethnic Minorities

By adopting an interactive approach to encourage students to react to the text and think for themselves, this book distinguishes itself from others in the field and ensures its place as a valuable teaching resource. The student-centred nature of the book is further enhanced by reflective question breaks throughout the text, chapter summaries and suggested further reading and websites.

Theories of Crime is a key text for any undergraduate student following programmes in Criminology and Criminal Justice.

Ian Marsh is Course Leader for Criminology at Liverpool Hope University and is a widely published textbook author. His recent publications include *Criminal Justice: An Introduction to Philosophies, Theories and Practice* (2004) (with John Cochrane and Gaynor Melville), *Sociology: Making Sense of Society* (3rd ed.) (2005) and *Theories and Practice in Sociology* (2002). **Gaynor Melville**, **Keith Morgan** and **Gareth Norris** are lecturers in Criminology at Liverpool H   University. **Zoe Walkington** is lecturer in Psychology at Sheffield Hall

THEORIES OF CRIME

Ian Marsh,
with Gaynor Melville,
Keith Morgan,
Gareth Norris and
Zoe Walkington

Routledge
Taylor & Francis Group

LONDON AND NEW YORK

First published 2006
by Routledge
2 Park Square, Milton Park, Abingdon, Oxon OX14 4RN

Simultaneously published in the USA and Canada
by Routledge
270 Madison Ave, New York, NY 10016

Reprinted 2007

Routledge is an imprint of the Taylor & Francis Group, an informa business

© 2006 Ian Marsh, with Gaynor Melville, Keith Morgan,
Gareth Norris and Zoe Walkington

Typeset in Garamond by Keystroke, 28 High Street, Tettenhall,
Wolverhampton
Printed and bound in Great Britain by TJ International, Padstow,
Cornwall

British Library Cataloguing in Publication Data
A catalogue record for this book is available from the British Library

Library of Congress Cataloging in Publication Data
A catalog record for this book has been requested

ISBN10: 0–415–37069–8 (pbk)
ISBN10: 0–415–37068–X (hbk)
ISBN10: 0–203–03051–6 (ebk)

ISBN13: 978–0–415–37069–1 (pbk)
ISBN13: 978–0–415–37068–4 (hbk)
ISBN13: 978–0–203–03051–6 (ebk)

CONTENTS

PREFACE

The intention of this book is to provide students (and tutors) with an interdisciplinary approach to explaining criminal behaviour. It describes, reflects on and attempts to evaluate a range of theoretical approaches that have offered explanations for crime, in particular the contributions of sociology, psychology and biology. The central aim of the book is to encourage students to develop a deeper understanding of classic and contemporary theorizing about crime.

CONTENT

Theories of Crime starts by considering the history of criminal behaviour and how it has been punished in Chapter 1. It considers the relative nature of crime and how changing definitions and perceptions impact on studying the history of crime. Chapters 2, 3 and 4 examine the ways in which the different disciplines of biology, psychology and sociology have tried to explain criminal behaviour. In Chapter 2 the focus is on biological explanations. Written by Keith Morgan, with help from Sue Aitken, this chapter considers the controversy over attempting to explain criminal behaviour in biological terms. It starts by debating the value of biology in this context and after looking at the history of biological theorizing it considers in some depth the importance of evolution, genes, physical characteristics of offenders and brain structures in affecting behaviour and, particularly, criminal behaviour. Chapter 3, written by Gareth Norris and Zoe Walkington, looks at the range of different explanations for crime that psychologists have offered. It considers these theories in terms of criminality as being an element of personality, and then examines the precursors, or reasons, why a person may become involved in criminal behaviour. It also highlights how psychological and social factors interact and need to be considered together in offering a full explanation for crime. Chapter 4 turns to explanations offered from sociological perspectives. Although the differences between the different disciplines of biology, psychology and sociology are not absolute or rigid, the emphasis in sociological theorizing is on the social context in which crime takes place – crime and criminal behaviour can be fully understood only in relation to the social structure, to specific social conditions and processes. The chapter starts by looking at classical criminology that emerged in the late eighteenth century, then considers the major early founding writers in sociology (including Durkheim and Marx) and how the theoretical approaches they developed have helped to explain crime. It looks at examples of theorizing within the sociology of crime and deviance that have developed from these major theoretical positions, including interactionism and labelling theory, feminist criminology, the postmodern influence and cultural criminology. The final two chapters apply the different theoretical approaches and perspectives to explaining the patterns of criminal behaviour of women and of ethnic minority groups. Chapter 5, written by Gaynor Melville, looks at how theorizing from the major disciplines has helped provide an understanding of the criminal behaviour of women. After looking at the history of women and crime and the changing patterns and trends in female criminality it discusses a range of theoretical explanations, including naturalistic, biological, psychological, sociological and feminist explanations. Chapter 6, by Ian Marsh and Gaynor Melville, offers a similar approach to considering the criminal behaviour of ethnic-minority groups. After reviewing the patterns and trends in ethnic-minority criminality, it looks at explanations of two main kinds – firstly, ethnic-minority, and especially black, crime is a social reality and the reasons for the greater criminality amongst such groups needs to be examined; secondly, that the criminal justice system is biased against certain ethnic-minority groups and this can explain the higher rate of crime amongst such groups.

FEATURES

Theories of Crime adopts an interactive approach that actively encourages the student to engage with and react to the text and think for herself or himself. There are question breaks throughout the book that provide opportunities for reflection. Some of the question breaks include stimulus material from original studies or contemporary media accounts and ask students to respond to questions on the material; others are just short stop-and-think-type questions. These reflective breaks enable tutors to use the material being examined as exercises for their students to engage with. At the end of each chapter there are suggestions for further reading, including key texts on the subject matter of the chapter and relevant websites.

This book, along with the recently published *Criminal Justice: An Introduction to Philosophies, Theories and Practice* (2004), has been a collaborative venture, and the authors would like to thank Gerhard Boomgarden, Constance Sutherland and the rest of the production team at Routledge for their involvement with the development of the text; and the various anonymous reviewers who have commented on the material.

CHAPTER 1

Crime: The Historical Context

▌ INTRODUCTION

Crime, criminals and how they are dealt with by society are topics of endless fascination. Look at any newspaper or glance at what's on television or at the cinema and it is immediately clear that there is a vast and seemingly insatiable interest in crime and criminals. We are interested both in 'real-life' crime and criminals and in fictional accounts. We could ask why there is so much interest in this area – even if many people break the law from time to time, most people are not involved in spectacular criminality, yet we seem to love to watch and read about it. Maybe such an interest demonstrates a sense of moral outrage and the enjoyment of seeing the wrongdoer punished and justice being done – given that in most fictional crime stories the criminals tend to come off worse eventually. Or perhaps it reflects a sympathy with the underdog and a degree of admiration for those who try to beat the system – with yesterday's public enemies and villains having a habit of becoming present-day cult figures. Or maybe this interest just demonstrates the excitement and enjoyment gained from reading about and watching that which we ourselves would not engage in – a sort of substituted excitement or vicarious pleasure. Whatever the reasons, murder, robbery, fraud, drug smuggling, gang warfare, rape, football hooliganism and so on make good subjects of conversation and exciting and profitable films. Indeed a visitor from another culture might assume crime was a basic and ever present feature of everyone's everyday lives – yet, apart from minor law breaking, very few people go on to become professional criminals.

QUESTION BREAK: CRIMINALS AS CELEBRITIES

'Mad Frankie Fraser', a notorious (ex-)gangster, is now a popular speaker at social functions. The following extracts are taken from his own website.

Frank has been a contract strong-arm, club owner, club minder, company director, Broadmoor inmate, firebomber, prison rioter but – first and last – a thief. 26 convictions. 42 years inside. In the 60s Ron and Reggie Kray sought his services but Frank chose to pitch in with Charlie and Eddie Richardson and their South London alleged 'Torture Gang'.

GUEST APPEARANCES

Frank is available for guest appearances at weddings, birthdays and all special occasions.

Make it a night to remember!

For more info please telephone:

Also available for After Dinner Speeches, Functions and Boxing Tournaments

---

- List other criminals that have become celebrities.
- Why do you think people admire such criminals?

This interest in criminality has existed throughout history. The briefest scan of the history of literature reveals the central role played by crime and criminals – from the Greek tragedies to Shakespeare's Hamlet, to Bill Sykes in Charles Dickens's *Oliver Twist*, to George Orwell's *Nineteen Eighty-four*. Dostoyevsky's *Crime and Punishment* is a classic work of criminal psychology, while the New Testament story of Jesus tells of wrongful accusation, arrest, trial, conviction and execution.

However crime is not a clear-cut or static phenomenon. What was viewed as criminal in the past was often quite different to current notions, just as many contemporary criminal acts would not have been viewed so in earlier times. Indeed in studying crime and punishment over time the most obvious 'finding' is the relative nature of crime. What is seen as and defined as criminal varies according to the particular social context in which it occurs, as the extracts and questions below illustrate.

QUESTION BREAK: THE CULTURAL AND HISTORICAL RELATIVITY OF CRIME

It is easy to think of examples of behaviour which one society sees as criminal and another as quite acceptable and normal; and there are behaviours which are seen as criminal now but which were perfectly acceptable in previous times. Consider the extracts below and the questions that follow them.

It is easily observable that different groups judge different things to be deviant. This should alert us to the possibility that the person making the judgement of deviance, the process by which the judgement is arrived at, and the situation in which it is made will all be intimately involved in the phenomenon of deviance . . .

Deviance is the product of a transaction that takes place between a social group and one who is viewed by that group as a rule breaker. Whether an act is deviant, then, depends on how people react to it . . . The degree to which other people will respond to a given act as deviant varies greatly. Several kinds of variations are worth noting. First of all, there is variation over time. A person believed to have committed a given 'deviant' act may at one time be responded to much more leniently than he would at some other time. The occurrence of 'drives' against various kinds of deviance illustrates this clearly.

(Becker 1963, 4–12)

Burning and hanging women as witches was commonplace in Europe in the 16th and 17th centuries. Witches were believed to have made pacts with the Devil which gave them supernatural powers. They were blamed for all sorts of personal and social misfortunes – illnesses, bad weather, loss of and damage to property.

Although many people associate burning at the stake with witchcraft it was used much less in England than other parts of Europe – particularly France, Switzerland and the Nordic countries. Only a few witches were burnt in England, the majority were hanged, possibly as a cost saving exercise and possibly because the public would not tolerate such a barbaric punishment. Scotland did burn witches and there are at least 38 recorded instances, the last being in 1722.

In the late 19th century cocaine was widely used as a pain killer in the USA – much as aspirin is today – and advertised with pictures of children at play [see poster advert below].

(Johnson 1989, 249)

Alcohol drinking and bigamy illustrate the relative nature of crime and deviance.

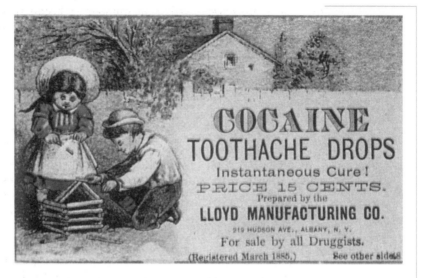

- List other types of behaviour that have been categorized as criminal or deviant in one society but not another.
- Give examples of behaviour that has been criminal or deviant at certain periods of time but not at others.

In looking at responses to crime and deviance Becker refers to 'drives' against certain types of behaviour.

- What types of crime or deviance have been subject to such drives in recent years in the UK?

The fact that crimes, and the ways in which they have been punished, vary from place to place and time to time highlights the importance of social reaction in determining what behaviour is categorized as criminal. There is no particular action that is criminal in itself – an action becomes criminal only if society defines it as such. So even an action such as killing another person, which, in the form of murder, can be the most serious of crimes in modern society, in many contexts can be quite acceptable. Indeed in some situations killing other people can be seen as heroic and people can be punished for not wanting to engage in killing – conscientious objectors were imprisoned in Britain in the First World War as were those who tried to 'dodge the draft' to fight for the US army in Vietnam in the 1960s.

Bearing in mind the relativity of crime and how it is dealt with, it would be useful to consider the history of crime before examining theoretical explanations for it in later chapters. In considering the history of crime we will examine the historical myths and traditions that surround the way in which crime has been and is viewed. Although there is a general awareness that there was horrendous violence and crime in the past, it is a widely held notion that modern, Western societies have become more and more criminal and dangerous places to live in. Given this tendency to think that things are much worse nowadays, we will start our historical overview by considering if there ever was a 'golden age', when 'things were so much better', when violence and criminality were only a marginal part of everyday life.

THE HISTORY OF JUVENILE CRIME

We will start our account by referring to Geoffrey Pearson's study of the history of juvenile crime (1983). Pearson used literary and journalistic accounts of crime to argue that it was important not to view criminality in modern society as a new or unique problem and to make the point that, when examining the history of crime, an appropriate subtitle would be 'there's nothing new under the sun'. Pearson takes issue with the notion of moral degeneracy (of young people in particular), not in an attempt to underplay the problem of violent crime in modern society but to demonstrate that, if anything, it is a continuation of traditions rather than a new phenomenon. He shows that for generations Britain has been plagued by very similar problems and fears but that the myth that Britain has historically been a stable, peaceful, law-abiding nation and that violence is somehow foreign to our national character shows little sign of waning.

The most striking aspect of the history of delinquency is the consistency with which each generation characterizes the youth of the day and the way of life of twenty years previously. In 1829 Edward Irving is quoted as enquiring, 'Is not every juvenile delinquent the evidence of a family in which the family bond is weakened and loosened?' He talks about the 'infinite numbers of unruly and criminal people who now swarm on the surface of this great kingdom'. Thus, while hooliganism and delinquency still make news as alarming and unusual, such behaviour is clearly not new.

QUESTION BREAK: JUVENILE CRIME – THERE'S NOTHING NEW UNDER THE SUN

The following quotations are taken from press, political and literary sources – many are taken from Pearson (1983) although some more recent ones have been added. Place these quotations in historical order – and suggest when they might have been said. (The answers are at the end of the chapter – but see how many you can locate correctly before turning to them.)

1 One of the most marked characteristics of the age is a growing spirit of independence in the children and a corresponding slackening of control in the parents.
2 We have to recognise where crime begins . . . we must do more to teach children the difference between right and wrong. It must start at home. And it must also be taught in our schools.

3 Looked at in his worse light the adolescent can take on an alarming aspect: he has learned no definite moral standards from his parents, is contemptuous of the law, easily bored.

4 The morals of the children are tenfold worse than formerly.

5 (On the increase in juvenile crime). In many cases they (juveniles) find themselves in a large city without friends, without family ties, and belonging to no social circle in which their conduct is either scrutinized or observed.

6 Parents failed to instil respect in their children . . . neighbourliness had broken down in villages, towns and cities. Decades of poor parenting and increasing selfishness has made life a misery for the police.

7 People are bound to ask what is happening to our country . . . having been one of the most law-abiding countries in the world – a byword for stability, order and decency – are we changing into somewhere else?

8 The most characteristic part of their uniform is the substantial leather belt heavily mounted with metal. It is not ornamental, but then it is not intended for ornament.

9 There seems to be a general corruption throughout the kingdom . . . the spirit of luxury and extravagance that seems to have seized on the minds of almost all ranks of men.

10 Any candid judge will acknowledge that manifest superiority of the past century; and in an investigation of the causes which have conspired to produce such an increase of juvenile crime, which is a blot upon the age . . . Is it not (the case that) the working classes have generally deteriorated in moral condition?

Pearson starts his study by looking at contemporary society – and, as the book was published in 1983, at the late 1970s and early 1980s. In introducing his historical account he makes the point that if each generation has a tendency to look back fondly to the recent past, it is sensible to start with present-day society and compare it with the situation twenty or so years previously, and then to compare that generation with its predecessor. Of course, there are bound to be difficulties in comparing different ages and periods – there will be differing definitions of crime and different measuring techniques and, in particular, a lack of adequate records in previous times. None the less, an impression of the style and extent of crime, and of the popular concerns about it, can be gained by looking at contemporary accounts from newspapers and books of the particular period.

As mentioned, Pearson's study starts with present-day attacks on our 'permissive age' by contemporary public figures and 'guardians of morality'. In March 1982 the *Daily Telegraph* suggested that 'we need to consider why the peaceful people of England are changing . . . over the 200 years up to 1945, Britain become so settled in internal peace'. There were warnings of a massive degeneration among the British people which was destroying the nation. Kenneth Oxford, the Chief Constable of Merseyside, prophesied that the 'freedom and way of life we have been accustomed to for so long will vanish'. There are numerous instances of such statements from prominent politicians and public figures alleging that contemporary society was witnessing an unprecedented increase in violence and decline in moral standards. Indeed there was a great consistency in the view of Britain's history as based on stability and decency, and that the moderate 'British way of life' was being undermined by the upsurge in delinquency.

QUESTION BREAK: IMAGES OF CONTEMPORARY YOUTH

- How are youth viewed today?
- What words are commonly associated with contemporary youth? (Consider how many of these words are negative and how many positive.)
- Looking back a generation, how would you characterize British society in the 1960s? What words would you associate with British youth of the 1960s?

Twenty years previously, however, we can find remarkably similar comments. At the Conservative Party conference in 1958 there was discussion of 'this sudden increase in crime and brutality which is so foreign to our nation and our country'. The Teddy Boys were arousing similar apocalyptic warnings of the end of British society. The Teds' style of dress was derived from men's fashion of the reign of Edward VII, which explains the name Teddy Boys. Rock and roll was the musical focus of this youth subculture, and the reaction which the Teddy Boys engendered was one of outrage and panic. The press, in particular, printed sensational reports of the happenings at cinemas and concerts featuring rock and roll films and music. A letter in the *Daily Sketch* (a popular newspaper of the period) in 1956 announced that 'the effect of rock'n'roll on young people is to turn them into devil worshippers; to stimulate self-expression through sex; to provoke carelessness, and destroy the sanctity of marriage'. An article in the *Evening News* of 1954 suggested that 'Teddy Boys . . . are all of unsound mind in the sense that they are all suffering from a form of psychosis. Apart from the birch or the rope, depending on the gravity of their crimes, what they need is rehabilitation in a psychopathic institution.' This reaction was widespread: off-duty soldiers were banned from wearing Teddy Boy suits, and Teddy Boys were viewed by the rest of society as 'folk devils'.

Nowadays when we look back at old photographs and films of the 1950s rock and roll craze and the Teddy Boys we might wonder what all the fuss was about. In comparison to groups who have come since then, they look quite straight. If anything, Teds are remembered with a degree of nostalgia and viewed as something quaint. Quite a contrast with the reaction in the mid-1950s illustrated above.

Pearson asks whether it was pre war Britain that was characterized by a law-abiding youth and a stable society. In fact the Second World War has been seen as a kind of watershed with the postwar period being morally inferior to the 'full rich back street life and culture of pre-war England'. However, when looking more closely at this period familiar declarations and allegations appear. In the 1930s there was a similar bemoaning of the 'passing of parental authority' and the 'absence of restraint'. The targets of criticism have a common ring: football rowdyism and the increasing crime and disorder. In the 1920s there were fierce street battles in North London between Spurs and Arsenal fans, some of whom were armed with iron bars and knives, while a part of Bradford football ground was closed in 1921 after the referee had been pelted with rubbish. It is sometimes implied that such incidents, and delinquencies in general, have become 'more serious' or 'more violent' over time, and since the war. The evidence would not seem to back up such suggestions. Crime in the interwar years was characterized by razor gangs, feuds between armed gangsters, vice rackets and so on.

Moving back to the turn of the century and the pre-First-World-War period Pearson suggests that we seem little nearer to finding the traditional way of life based on a 'healthy respect for law and order'. A wide range of popular culture came under severe criticism in the early twentieth century. The music halls, professional football and the noisy presence of working-class people at seaside resorts on Bank Holidays were all attacked. There was even a good deal of excitement and panic over the 'bicycle craze' of the late 1890s. There are newspaper accounts of youths whizzing about madly on their bikes, dashing along quiet country roads and through peaceful villages with loud shouts, causing pandemonium among the traffic and knocking over pedestrians, with headlines such as 'The Dangers of City Cycling' (*Daily Mail*, 1898) and 'Cyclomania' (*News of the World*, 1898). As ever, youth of the period were compared unfavourably with previous generations. Baden-Powell in his *Scouting for Boys* published in 1908 suggests that professional football is betraying the British traditions of 'fair play' and sportsmanship:

> Thousands of boys and young men, pale, narrow-chested, hunched up, miserable specimens, smoking endless cigarettes, numbers of them betting, all of them learning to be hysterical as they groan and cheer in panic unison with their neighbours – the worst sound of all being the hysterical scream of laughter that greets any little trip or fall of a player. One wonders whether this can be the same nation which had gained for itself the reputation of being a stolid, pipe-sucking manhood, unmoved by panic or excitement, and reliable in the tightest of places.

Neither does nineteenth-century, Victorian Britain provide any comparative baseline of a tranquil, law-abiding society. The first officially named 'Hooligans' of the 1890s and the 'Garrotters' of the 1860s do little to kindle nostalgia for Victorian city life and culture. It was in the late 1890s that the words 'Hooligan' and 'Hooliganism', were used, to describe delinquent youth. There were regular news reports of Hooligan gangs smashing up coffee-stalls and public houses, robbing and assaulting old ladies, attacking foreigners and setting upon policemen in the streets. In line with later youth subcultures and gangs, Hooligans had a distinct style of dress, a recognizable look. As with so many of the later youth subcultures, there was no doubt an over-reaction to Hooligans. Nevertheless, whether correct or not, there was a widely held feeling that hooliganism was a major problem.

Earlier in the Victorian period in the winter of 1862, panic swept through respectable London over a new variety of crime called 'garrotting', a type of violent robbery that involved choking the victim – a Victorian parallel with present-day 'mugging' perhaps. The press reacted in familiar manner, with *The Times* observing that it was 'becoming unsafe for a man to traverse certain parts of London at night'. *Punch* magazine launched an 'anti-garrotte' movement, which invented a variety of somewhat bizarre anti-robbery devices – metal collars with long steel pikes being favoured forms of protection against throttling.

The possibility that it was industrialization that destroyed the stable and peaceful life of pre-industrial Britain does not appear to hold up either. Certainly in the mid nineteenth century it was widely felt that life in the previous century was greatly superior and that the increase in juvenile crime was a blot on this age. However, writing in 1751 Henry Fielding (mayor of London and well-known author) paints a very similar picture with his prediction of an imminent slide into anarchy when the streets of our cities 'will shortly be impassable without the utmost hazard'.

It is difficult to find evidence that there has been a massive deterioration in the morality and behaviour of the common people, in comparison to the pre-industrial world. From the late seventeenth century there have been complaints of increasing wickedness, crime and disorder. The streets of pre-industrial London were extremely dangerous, with no effective system of street-lighting nor a police force.

It is not just societal reaction and fears that echo one another through the ages, and Pearson also examines the recurrent nature of different explanations of the criminal question. Time and again a permissive present is contrasted with the not too distant past. If such accusations are accepted, we would be forced to conclude that with each generation crime and disorder has increased dramatically. The over-representation of youth in the criminal statistics is rediscovered in each wave of concern over crime and delinquency. Looking back over Pearson's historical review, it is hard to believe that Britain's cities are any more perilous today than those of pre-industrial Britain, or when they were frequented by gangs of Garrotters and Hooligans.

STUDYING THE HISTORY OF CRIME

While contemporary sources are important indicators, it is necessary to consider how these sources relate to the findings of historians on crime levels in the past. However, in measuring the history of crime, a statistical approach, while essential, is fraught with difficulties. Sharpe (1995), in examining the different approaches to studying the history of crime, argues that the counting of crime has to go hand in hand with interpreting the meaning of crime to different communities at different times and with considering the changing definitions of crime.

The statistics of crime

Although criminal statistics are usually quoted as 'hard facts', and as such are used by governments and public bodies for making policy decisions with regard to crime and its treatment, they are far from being perfect indicators of the extent or character of crime. There are two major and important deficiencies with them – firstly, the problem of omissions, in that only a proportion of crimes and offenders are included in official figures; and, secondly, the problem of bias, in that those crimes and offenders that are included might not provide a representative picture of all crime and of all offenders. The amount of crime that is not officially known about is termed the 'dark figure' of crime and there are many factors which lead to the non-reporting and non-recording of crime.

QUESTION BREAK: THE DARK FIGURE OF CRIME

There are many reasons why crime statistics might underestimate the amount of criminal activity, including

- Victims being unaware that they are victims of specific crimes
- Victims not wanting to waste time or money in reporting a crime
- Victims feeling that there is no point in informing the police
- Victims dealing with matters informally, outside of the legal system
- Victims' embarrassment
- Victims (or witnesses of a crime) not trusting or liking the police
- Victimless crime – crimes where all parties involved do not wish the police to know about it
- Victims' fears of reprisals.

Consider each of those reasons and suggest how much more (or less) relevant they would be in relation to measuring crimes at different periods of history.

- What other factors might have stopped people from reporting crime in the past?

Sharpe (1999) makes the point that the importance of the dark figure would be reduced if there was a constant relationship between recorded and unrecorded crime. If, for instance, the same proportion of crime, however large or small, was invariably reported, the changes in the crime statistics could be said to indicate changes in the actual level of criminal behaviour. However, there do appear to be substantial variations in the willingness of people to report criminal behaviour – during periods of 'moral panic' the public seem much more ready to report crimes. And the practices and efficiency of the police and other criminal justice agencies will also have an effect on the crime statistics.

Of course, it is highly likely that these problems and deficiencies would be more marked when looking at criminal statistics from hundreds of years ago; and that the 'dark figure' of unrecorded crime would be 'darker' the further back in history we go. Indeed there are no official statistics for crime in England before 1805, and historians of previous periods have to search court records for their data. The further back we go, the fewer official records and sources have survived. However there have been studies that have tried to quantify the extent of crime. For instance, the beginning of the eighteenth century was a low-crime period compared to the previous century, but with increasing urbanization the later 1700s in England were characterized by a significant rise in crime. Later, the growth of an industrialized nation, along with the demobilization of soldiers and sailors after eighteenth-century wars and the defeat of the French in 1815, led to large numbers of the labouring classes living in the growing urbanized areas without adequate incomes; a situation that led, in turn, almost inevitably to a massive rise in property crimes. The relationship between property crime and the growth of an industrial capitalist society was an area of explanation considered by historians of crime. The first half of the 1800s was a period when there were real concerns about rising crime combined with fears of social disintegration; however by the end of the nineteenth century such fears were diminishing, along with the rise of a more prosperous, 'respectable' Victorian working class and a better policed society than ever before. Indeed explanations for the emergence of the modern police in the early to mid nineteenth century highlight this fear of the 'dangerous classes' – the new urban, industrial proletariat.

This notion of the 'dangerous classes' is conflated with that of the 'criminal classes'. Sharpe (1999) indicates that, by the 1850s, the idea of a criminal class was generally accepted. It was seen by Victorian scholars as a product of industrialization and urbanization which concentrated the 'lower orders' in poor, dangerous groups who lived mainly on the proceeds of crime and who were separated from the bourgeoisie but also from the 'respectable poor'. The Victorians saw this new 'criminal class' as essentially the product of rapid and vast economic and social change. However Emsley (1996) suggests that while there may have been groups of habitual criminals such groups did not necessarily form what might be called a 'class', which implies a large and homogeneous group of people. The overwhelming majority of offences in the eighteenth and nineteenth centuries were not organized and large-scale crimes but rather petty thefts and disorderly behaviour. Emsley points to the convenience for 'respectable' society of the idea of a criminal class who act as a sort of alien group committing crime against law-abiding citizens. And it is important to emphasize that, even if the existence of such a class is dubious, the idea that there was one was certainly widely believed by the Victorian population.

COMMUNITIES AND THE CONTROL OF CRIME

Studying how the law was enforced in different communities also helps to fill out the picture of the history of crime and criminals. Certainly informal sanctions played an important role before the emergence of the modern police and will have played a part in the under-recording of criminal activity. Community action against nuisance offenders was commonplace and the widespread opposition from working-class communities to the new police ensured that informal controls existed long after the emergence of a professional police force (as they still do of course – criminals and gangsters throughout history have rarely been willing to involve formal bodies in sorting out their affairs).

In providing an overview of the 'early modern criminal' of the sixteenth and seventeenth centuries, Sharpe (1999) argues that there was little organized or professional crime at this time, 'the pathetic, small-time whore and the opportunistic pilferer were more typical, if more elusive, figures than the high-class madame or the criminal entrepreneur' (171). While there were some people regularly on the wrong side of the law, criminal associations were casual and ad hoc in manner; gangs of highwaymen and horse thieves might have existed but, outside of London, organized crime was 'rarely very sophisticated or permanent'. Sharpe suggests that there was little evidence of anything approaching a criminal subculture or class; and he makes the point that if there was a 'dangerous class' then those in it were far more of a danger to one another than to anybody else – as always, the poor stole from the poor, and assaulted and killed each other rather than those from different backgrounds.

CHANGING DEFINITIONS OF CRIME

As we suggested above, while there are some actions which virtually all societies will define as criminal and sanction accordingly, there are many more activities which are seen as criminal or not depending on the time or place in which they occur. In broad terms, Sharpe (1995) suggests that historians of crime have pointed to a transition from notions of crime based on sin to notions of crime based on concern over ownership of property. In the period up to the mid seventeenth century there was little attempt to separate out the different categories of sin and crime (male homosexuality, for instance, was a made a capital offence in 1563). This is not to say that the link between religion and crime disappeared in the 1700s; the connection between law enforcement and Christian morality remained strong through the next two centuries; and arguably still plays a role in British criminal justice processes.

So while it is clear that crime is a problem in contemporary society, and that we are experiencing serious law and order problems, our predecessors have from time to time felt similar concerns. Sharpe (1995) points to the periods around 1580–1650 and 1800–60 as ones of severe economic dislocation but also as times when the fears about crime eventually proved groundless; and these periods were soon followed by periods of relative stability and harmony. The history of crime shows us how little attitudes have shifted between different 'thens' and now. The panics about Victorian garrotters and Elizabethan vagrants can be seen as examples of the criminal stereotyping that is still prevalent in modern society. The garotters were commented on earlier (p. 8), while Sharpe (1999) refers to the increase in vagrancy in the later sixteenth century being seen as a threat to the social order of the day. Vagrants were not solely criminals and included, as Sharpe puts it, 'the pathetic and the bizarre'. The crimes that were committed by vagrants tended to be opportunistic and small-scale thefts.

Although property crime has always been the most common form of offence, it has always been violent crime that has frightened people and made the most news-worthy stories. In concluding his study of crime between 1750 and 1900, Emsley (1996) suggests that while periods of economic slump and hardship might have increased the temptation towards property crime, the 'steepest overall increase in the criminal statistics during the period 1750 to 1900 coincided with fear for the social order, fear of "the mob", fear of revolution and . . . anxiety about "the dangerous classes"'.

This chapter has briefly looked at the history of criminal behaviour; the rest of the book considers the major theoretical explanations for such behaviour. In particular the next three chapters look (respectively) at biological, psychological and sociological approaches to examining crime – they review early examples of these different theoretical approaches through to current theorizing about crime in each discipline. Chapters 5 and 6 then apply these varied theoretical approaches to explaining the criminal behaviour of women and of ethnic minorities.

FURTHER READING

Emsley, C. (1996), *Crime and Society in England 1750–1900*, second edition. Harlow: Longman. An analysis of the period that highlights the scale of crime in the first part and then explores changes in the courts, police and systems of punishment in the second part.

Pearson, G. (1983), *Hooligan: A History of Respectable Fears*. London: Macmillan. This is a journey back through the history of youthful delinquency and responses to it. Making use of contemporary accounts, including newspapers and pamphlets, it shows that for generations Britain has been plagued by the same problems and fear that today we see as unique to our own society.

Sharpe, J. A. (1999), *Crime in Early Modern England 1550–1750*, second edition. Harlow: Longman. A wide-ranging analysis of crime, criminality and punishment in the early modern period. The book explores the extent, the causes and the control of crime and its impact on society.

WEBSITES

Two easy to navigate websites that provide contemporary accounts to illustrate different periods and enable users to look for coverage of criminal behaviour during those times are www.eyewitnesstohistory.com and www.bbc.co.uk/history/society.

SOURCES OF QUOTATIONS ON pp. 5–6

1 M. Barrett, *Young Delinquents*, 1913
2 M. Howard, Home Secretary, 1993
3 British Medical Association, *The Adolescent*, 1961
4 Lord Ashley, House of Commons, 1843

5   W. Morrison, *Juvenile Offenders*, 1896
6   D. Blunkett, Home Secretary, 2004
7   *Daily Express*, 1981
8   *Daily Graphic*, 1900
9   Daniel Defoe, *The Complete English Tradesman*, 1738
10 H. Worsley, *Juvenile Depravity*, 1849

CHAPTER 2

Biological Explanations for Criminal Behaviour

▌ INTRODUCTION

In this chapter we examine the controversy over attempting to explain criminal behaviour in biological terms. We consider the main types of biological explanation for human behaviour that are used within the subject of criminology and the evidence that underpins them. Typical biological theories are that some people are more likely to commit violent crimes because of the genes that they have inherited; or that there is more chance of acting in an impulsive way that breaks the law if you have attention deficit hyperactivity disorder (ADHD), because it involves a reduction in activity in a part of the brain that helps us both to control our own actions and to see their consequences.

It will be clearer if, before we engage with the criticisms of a biological perspective on criminal behaviour, we set out a very brief outline of why biology must be relevant.

Human beings are surely just one species out of the millions of living creatures on the earth.

Criminal behaviour is still behaviour even if what is regarded as 'criminal' changes over time and place.

All our behaviour, thoughts, feelings, etc. are rooted in our biology.

Given these points, it must be possible to learn about criminal behaviour by taking a biological perspective.

THE DEBATE OVER THE VALUE OF BIOLOGY

When the contents of this textbook were first proposed, several criminologists considered the outline. Some thought that a chapter on biology was valuable, but some said that a chapter about biological explanations of criminal behaviour did not belong in a criminology book. This reflects a lively controversy within criminology (Wright and Miller 1998).

We have sympathy for those who oppose the use of biology within criminology because of two interrelated strands of the history of the social sciences.

Firstly, for the majority of the twentieth century social scientists rejected biological explanations for human behaviours (Tooby and Cosmides 1992), especially social behaviours, of which criminal behaviour is an example (Walsh 2002).

Secondly, biological explanations of human behaviour were used by politicians to legitimize inhumane and invalid policies. This was seen in major countries with diametrically opposed political systems from the first to the last decade of the twentieth century. For example, 'Social Darwinism' refers to a group of theories that claim that Darwinism could be applied to social institutions as well as to organisms. It is best known in the version proposed by the philosopher Herbert Spencer (1820–1903), who wrote on psychology, sociology, evolution and philosophy and influenced Charles Darwin (1809–1882). Darwin published *The Origin of the Species* in 1859, in which he first set out his theory of evolution by natural selection.

Spencer and Darwin were both heavily influenced by Thomas Malthus (1766–1834). In 1798 Malthus published his 'demographic theory' proposing that famine and conflict were inevitable because population grows exponentially (i.e. 2, 4, 8, 16, 32) while resources increase only arithmetically (i.e. 1, 2, 3, 4). He argued that the poor, but not the wealthier members of society, should show moral restraint by having fewer children. His arguments were used to justify laws that made life harder for the most vulnerable.

This type of Social Darwinism was popular from late Victorian times until the Second World War. The results were used to justify the inequalities of wealth found in capitalist society as the natural consequence of the survival of the fittest – a term coined by Spencer – as well as the exclusion of would-be immigrants from Eastern Europe to the USA. They were rejected on the grounds that they were poor because they lacked the biological potential to succeed. Therefore, if they were allowed to enter the USA they would interbreed with, or outbreed, the established American population from largely Western European backgrounds and bring down the country by degrading its biological, genetic, quality.

This position, which now seems clearly to reflect the prejudice of those who supported such policies rather than being an objective consequence of biological theory, was taken by other governments, including the UK, and was a factor in trapping so many Jews in Nazi Europe where they were the target of genocide (Rose 1997).

Another consequence of this crude application of biological principles to political and social issues was the widespread acceptance of eugenics by both left-wing and right-wing political thinkers. Eugenics is selective breeding, whereby people with 'good biological stock' were encouraged to reproduce and those with 'poor biological stock' were discouraged, in the extreme by sterilization and abortion. The Nazis appealed to 'science' to justify their campaign to exterminate the Jews, Slavs, Gypsies, gays and the mentally handicapped – all of whom were said to have inferior biological make-ups. This was used to demand their destruction for the good of humanity. Because the Nazis so enthusiastically embraced eugenics it was publicly rejected by most societies after the Second World War, though even then it was used covertly in several Western countries.

Two American controversies since the 1950s show how biological explanations are still being used to justify discriminatory policy.

Firstly, the claim that black children do badly at school (and, indeed, in life – including their higher rates of criminal conviction) because they are inherently less intelligent than other racial groups for biological reasons (see the discussion of Murray and Herrenstein's book *The Bell Curve* in Chapter 5, p. 170).

Secondly, and directly concerning criminal behaviour, were two American projects to apply biology to criminal behaviour in the inner cities. In 1966 three Harvard professors, Frank Ervin, Vernon Mark and William Sweet, were involved in a federally sponsored, low-profile research programme set up in response to serious inner city riots. They proposed using brain surgery for the ringleaders and other treatments for those who took part. The argument was that the causes could not be poverty, racial discrimination and social breakdown, because then all the people in the area subject to the same factors would have rioted. Fortunately the public became aware of what was going on and the government abruptly changed its policy and removed all funding for research into brain surgery; unfortunately some individuals had already been experimented on and left permanently damaged (Breggin 1995).

Things then went quiet until President George Bush announced the Federal Violence Initiative in 1992 with the goal of identifying biological factors in, and interventions for, criminal behaviour. Once again, as soon as people began to talk about what was going to be done in detail it looked as if it was based on the idea that Black American young males were obviously biologically different. This difference explained their higher levels of violent crime, rather than social, economic and political factors. The respected researcher, Frederick Goodwin, chosen to head the programme, compared unusually aggressive and sexually active monkeys seen in natural populations to inner-city youths (Breggin 1995). After a period of media and political debate Goodwin resigned; later the funding for the overall programme was withdrawn but several of the individual projects are still going on.

The problem here is the implicit assumption that the reason that some groups are poorer, more anti-social and have shorter life-spans etc. is a result of their different biological make-up. The solution is to 'fix' their biology with surgery, electrodes or drugs rather than considering the environmental disadvantages that are much more likely to be relevant.

QUESTION BREAK

- Can you think of any other examples of how biological explanations could be used to justify social policies?
- As some policies based on biology have had terrible consequences, do you think biological explanations should be ignored? Give reasons for your answers.

The historical factors (as shown in these examples) of the political misuse of biological explanations to justify extreme discrimination and of the dominance of non-biological theories within the social sciences make the distrust of biological explanations by criminologists very understandable. However, there is growing support for the recognition of the key role of biology in understanding human behaviour. This chapter argues for the Biosocial Interaction (BSI) model (e.g. Raine 2002b) which recognizes the critical contribution of other factors such as family environment, the peer group and the opportunities to behave in particular ways. BSI is consistent with the vertical integration approach to understanding.

Vertical integration recognizes that we can validly examine something like anti-social or criminal behaviour at many distinct levels of explanation, and that these are arranged in a ladder going from the lowest levels, like physics, through increasingly higher levels such as chemistry to biology to psychology to sociology (Rose 2003a).

Mayr (1982) sets out how explanations of the way that something is caused (for example, rape) need to match both the level of the perspective being used and the question being asked. Explaining rape in terms of physics seems pointless; using a biological perspective may treat rape as being just heterosexual sex against the female's wishes (see the section below on evolution, p. 26); while a sociological approach can include factors such as political change, shifting gender roles and sexual politics. However, a sociological approach is blind to biological factors such as brain systems. One crucial element of this model of understanding is that the rules, relationships and laws at a particular level cannot be predicted simply by knowing all about the lower rungs of the ladder. Even if one could understand all the biology of human development through adolescence it would be difficult to see patterns crucial to the psychology of adolescent development (Steinberg and Morris 2001) such as the experience of first love, or relationships like that between skin colour and chance of being imprisoned. The world as seen from a higher rung is said to 'emerge' from the world as seen from those rungs below it. Consciousness, a key psychological phenomenon, is often held to be an emergent property that is based on biology and yet cannot be explained from a biological perspective.

This example may help: everything that a computer does is based on physics, because a computer is a physical, material thing. If you sit down at your keyboard and compose a love poem it would be possible to give an explanation of this at the level of physics (e.g. how the 'L' of 'Love' was created on the screen by directing electrons using structures and processes within the computer, and even in terms of quantum mechanical interactions within some of the essential components). This could be accurate and correct; however it can never be complete because the world of physics does not have concepts like 'love' – something essential for a full understanding and totally unpredictable from a knowledge of physics alone.

No level is absolutely best: the levels that you use need to reflect the question you want to answer and provide information suitable for the task at hand.

Today's biological researchers largely accept three propositions.

- The brain is the cause of the mind (whatever goes on in your mind is the result of physical processes in your brain).
- The mind is modular (made of many specialized parts, each largely independent of the rest but taking their input from other modules and sending their output to yet others).
- The brain is also made of largely separate, interacting systems.

This suggests certain research questions: for example, which systems are involved in aggression? Are they different in those convicted of violent crimes? How are they different, and can we change this or compensate for it? Are particular brain systems important in impulsive aggression?

Most current biological researchers also accept that the way to understand subjects as complex as human beings is to reduce the complexity by breaking them down into simpler parts: this is termed reductionism. Reductionism suggests that the way to understand, say, road rage attacks is to look for the parts of the brain involved; the organization and activity of neurons that make up those critical parts; the functioning of the chemical messengers that mediate communication between those neurons; the involvement of genes in that functioning and communication; and the effect of all of these on road rage behaviour.

The reductionist approach has been incredibly successful across science and seems rational, but it has limits. For example, suicide bombings are an extreme behaviour so one might expect to find evidence that suicide bombers are different in some biological way. Or if not, that there are clear differences between their experiences and those of other people.

It is important to realize that biologists have no problem with the idea that our biology may predispose us to behave in particular ways in response to outside forces. In this case things like having seen your family maltreated, or how extreme your religious or political education has been, appear plausible suggestions.

However, researchers have looked hard for signs of differences between suicide bombers and others without much success. This is true at the level of personality (an aspect of ourselves clearly connected to our biology (Davidson 2001)) and of experience. Some researchers think they have found slight differences in both areas but they are not enough to suggest that suicide bombers are basically different from the rest of the world. Instead it seems to be largely social pressures that lead to their actions (Bond 2004).

Stanley Milgram's studies, inspired by the savage behaviours of concentration camp guards and other staff during the Second World War, had a very similar outcome. To the amazement of experts and lay people it turned out that almost all normal people can be made to give an innocent stranger apparently lethal electric shocks simply by being told to (Milgram 1983; Blass 2000).

From these two examples of the most extreme anti-social behaviour we can see that biological differences are not necessarily present just because the perpetrators do what most people agree is wrong. In this chapter the emphasis on the interaction of biology with other factors at higher levels is an admission that reductionism cannot explain criminal behaviour.

Biological researchers are also predominantly materialists. This means that they see the real world as being made of physical 'stuff' – matter and energy. If you believe this then you are likely to ask questions about material things such as genes, chemicals and brain structures.

Finally, the majority of modern biologists are determinists. This means that they believe that everything that happens is caused by something else. For example, if someone sexually abuses a child we can assume that the behaviour followed some facilitating thoughts and was motivated by some strong feelings. These in turn will have been caused by other factors such as genetic predispositions or low activity in brain systems involved in self-control.

Our approach is to argue for a 'weak' determinism which suggests that criminal behaviour is determined not solely by the person's biology but rather by the inter-action of various factors including biological ones. The complexity of the interplay between different elements cannot be resolved. This is why we cannot say that one cause is more important than others for criminal behaviour; instead we must look at what seems to increase a person's chance of displaying criminal behaviour and in which environments this is the case.

As they tend to be reductionists, materialists and determinists, biological researchers give more importance to the simpler, biological processes. This easily slips into treating biological factors as causing the psychological, behavioural and sociological phenomena that are relevant to criminal behaviour. BSI explicitly takes biological and non-biological factors as equally important, this reduces the risk of invalidly assuming that our 'biological essence' is the real cause of criminal behaviour.

Critics attack the very assumptions upon which most biological criminology rests (Poole 1994), but the biological perspective on humans is becoming more dominant. Politically and economically the biological paradigm fits with the spirit of the age (American Psychiatric Association 1997; Herbert 1997), and the simple stories it tells are convincing even when the evidence and argument are not really sound (Rose 1997). Indeed the history of biological approaches to human nature demonstrates how easily popular prejudices can be transformed into apparently 'scientific' truths (Sennett 1977).

However, non-biological researchers are just as likely to make these errors: the last century saw the blaming of mothers for every sort of social problem from 'refrigerator mothers' producing schizophrenia in their children to poor mothering creating criminals (Ladd-Taylor and Umansky 1998). It is important to remember that whichever approach we use carries the risk of ignoring factors from other levels of explanation. The BSI model supported here is an example of a non-additive interaction model because the effect of two different factors cannot be predicted reliably by simply adding the effect that the first would have by itself to the effect the second factor would have by itself. Think of a recipe: a cake does not taste like raw flour plus raw eggs and the other ingredients.

QUESTION BREAK

When researching rape, what questions do you think that biological criminologists might ask?

- What might they hypothesize leads to rape?
- What questions and hypotheses do you think psychological or sociological criminologists might use instead?
- Do you think that a biological approach to understanding rape is likely to be a good thing? Why?

Before we briefly consider the history of biological theories of criminal behaviour, there is one simple biological factor that is associated with a big increase in risk of criminal behaviour. Stop here and try to think what this might be before reading the next paragraph.

The factor can be seen from several biological perspectives:

- Possession of a Y chromosome
- Having a penis and testes rather than a vagina and ovaries
- Having higher levels of testosterone
- Behaving more aggressively
- Being a male.

Why should this be so unless the biological differences between males and females are also connected to the very different levels of crime they commit?

Unfortunately it is plausible that such differences could arise from social and cultural factors, together with incidental consequences of the differences in strength and in time spent looking after children, for example. In summary, then, we believe that the differences in criminal activity are due both to biological and to other factors.

THE HISTORY OF BIOLOGICAL THEORIES OF CRIMINAL BEHAVIOUR

Now you have thought about some of the wider issues concerning the value of biological explanations of criminal behaviour we will consider the history of this type of theory.

Since the time of the earliest surviving records, ugliness, disability and deformity have been taken as reflections of evil and criminality. Egyptian papyri, the Bible and Homer's *Iliad* all take the link as valid and this belief has survived to the present day. Physiognomy (assessing personality from facial features) traces its roots to ancient

Greece where the concept that mind, morality and body were intimately interrelated was widely accepted, even by Aristotle (perhaps the most scientific of the ancient Greeks). Socrates was condemned to death partly on the evidence of a physiognomist that his face showed him to be a cruel drunk.

In medieval Europe physical imperfections, such as warts, moles and third nipples, were taken as proof of demonic possession (Einstadter and Henry 1995) and in ordinary, secular, law if two people were under equal suspicion then the uglier was to be found guilty (Wilson and Herrnstein 1985).

The pre-existing belief that appearance reflected inner worth was first woven into a more scientific version of physiognomy by Della Porte (1535–1615). Della Porte studied dead bodies and claimed he had found a connection between facial features such as small ears and large lips with criminal behaviour. Later physiognomists such as Beccaria ('On Crimes and Punishments', 1764) and Lavater ('Physiognomical Fragments', 1775) extended Della Porte's theory.

Many of their claims are still heard in everyday conversation, for example 'weak chins' and 'shifty eyes' are still remarked upon as if they were true indicators of moral weaknesses.

The increasing status of scientific methods encouraged the search for physical signs of moral degeneracy. Phrenology was a theory adopted and publicized by Gall (1758–1828). It proposed that the surface of the skull was raised where it lay over parts of the brain that were more active than average. In many ways it prefigured our present view of the brain as made of many largely independent modules each with a specific task. Indeed, Gall correctly predicted the location of a part of the brain concerned with producing spoken language.

Some of the 'bumps' that phrenologists linked with criminal behaviour actually have some empirical support. The 'destructiveness centre' behind and above the left ear really is prominent in about 17 per cent of criminals, and there are others at the back of the skull that seem to reflect abnormalities of two parts of the brain, the hippocampus and amygdala. You will see that these are thought to be important in violent anti-social or criminal behaviour (see the section below on brain structures, p. 44). It may be that things that distort the development of our brains can also disturb the growth of the neighbouring bone, or vice versa. Injuries later in life certainly can damage the skull and the underlying brain tissue.

The methods, and philosophical understanding, to test Gall's theory did not exist in his lifetime and his attempts to get around these problems ended by invalidating the project. Indeed, the popular success of phrenology (it became quite fashionable to 'have one's bumps felt') led to a counter-movement that focused not only on the problems of testing its claims but also on the idea that our brain was built of largely independent systems.

QUESTION BREAK

Phrenology is a well-known enough fashion for it to have appeared in *The Simpsons*. When Homer's mother comes back and Mr Burns spots her likeness to an ancient 'Wanted' poster the Springfield officers interview him. Officer Friday asks 'Are you sure this is the woman you saw in the post office?' Burns replies 'Absolutely! Who could forget such a monstrous visage? She has the sloping brow and cranial bumpage of the career criminal.' When Smithers objects to Mr Burns's use of phrenology by saying 'Uh, Sir, phrenology was dismissed as quackery 160 years ago', he is met with the unanswerable riposte 'Of course you'd say that: you have the brainpan of a stagecoach tilter' (Appel 1995).

- Have these old ways of thinking about humans disappeared?
- If not, where can you see their influence?

The next major step on the road to current biological theories comes with Lombroso, one of the people who founded modern criminology. As Garland (1997) points out, the founders of criminology as we now understand it were very open to the idea of biological factors leading to criminal behaviour. Lombroso (1876) used Darwin's theory of evolution by natural selection to argue that criminals were biological throwbacks (i.e. their looks, morality and behaviour were atavistic – or like their primitive ancestors). Criminals were physically and morally degenerate.

Biological positivism is the term for theories that claim that criminal behaviour is caused by biological factors: most current criminologists regard it as either false or simplistic. When the claims of physiognomy, phrenology and other similar 'sciences' were disproved by empirical data, biological theorizing in general was brought into disrepute.

However, even if the specific claims were wrong there could still be other biological bases for criminal behaviour. If you are not convinced by Lombroso's claim that prostitutes' feet showed the same prehensile (or gripping) form as our primate relatives (e.g. apes and monkeys), the link between looks and criminal behaviour could still be true. After all, why would an idea have such a long history if it had no basis in reality or was completely invalid? Indeed these ideas are so attractive that they appear in the wider popular culture. For example, in his novel *Crime and Punishment* Dostoyevsky makes a point of the central character's good looks. He does not want readers to assume that his evil acts are a consequence of an innate weakness that would show itself as both a physical and a moral deficiency. Dostoyevsky knew that at that time, 1866, people believed that the two went together in most criminals. Charles Dickens often makes the connection between physical appearance and morality in his novels. Think of *Oliver Twist*, where Oliver, even though he does not know it, is from a 'good family' and thus carries 'good genes' (although that term did not exist then). Oliver turns out to be good because of his biological inheritance while the Artful Dodger, from a classic deprived background, is destined to go to the bad because of his (Dickens 1897).

Lombroso himself studied 383 criminals looking for a set of signs (stigmata) that he argued showed atavism. These included such things as excess digits and an asymmetrical face. He found that about one in five had one sign and over two in five had at least five. On this evidence he argued that five or more stigmata indicated that someone was born biologically destined to be a criminal.

In a later study he found that about one in three anarchists (people who believed that violence was justified to gain their political aims) showed the stigmata compared to about one in eight members of other extreme political factions. He did compare his criminals to a control group of soldiers and used simple statistics but he did not control for variables such as mental illness and ethnic origin. The criminal groups showed more mental illness and had more Sicilian people: both of these would accentuate any differences between criminals and controls. As the methods were not adequate for the task his data cannot be relied upon and should be treated as of historical interest.

The problems with Lombroso's work illustrate the importance of methodology and statistics. Lombroso and Gall both struggled to get around the relatively primitive methodology of their times.

An English scientist responded to Lombroso's claims with one of the earliest convincing tests of the atavism hypothesis. Goring (1913) compared over three thousand habitual criminals with large, varied control groups over a decade: he used objective measures for 37 possible signs of atavism and found no differences other than that the criminals were, on average, two inches shorter and about five pounds lighter. Goring took this as support for his own theory that criminals had inherited a poorer set of genes but it is also consistent with the hypothesis that if people grow up in impoverished environments then they are likely to be physically less developed and more likely to turn to crime.

Interestingly, 26 years after Goring's book, Hooten (1939) published the results of a study of nearly fourteen thousand prisoners compared to 3,200 controls using 33 measures, many of which could have come from Lombroso, including malformed ears and sloping foreheads. Hooten found the criminals to be 'inferior' on all the body-part measures. Unfortunately Hooten's study had serious flaws, such as unsuitable controls and the same plausibility of environmental explanations for the physical differences as for Goring's results. He also claimed differences between types of criminal although many had been previously convicted for different offences. However as mentioned earlier, one would expect people to engage in behaviours for which they are physically suited, so big people are more likely to be able to use force effectively. In addition Hooten's theory and style of writing embody racist assumptions of the time. Indeed, Hooten's work was dismissed with contempt (e.g. Merton 1938) particularly for the circular reasoning that criminals were biologically inferior and therefore whatever physical differences they showed must indicate biological inferiority that must explain their criminality . . . and so on.

QUESTION BREAK

- Do you think it is reasonable to think that there may be a link between looks and criminality?

- What biological explanation(s) might explain any connection?
- What non-biological explanations can you think of?
- How could you test whether looks themselves caused criminal behaviour?

The idea that looks and crime are somehow connected via biology continued to develop, and after the Second World War Sheldon (1949) published a book that proposed a theory that body type was linked to personality. There have been ideas like this for hundreds of years – think of Shakespeare having Caesar say that he did not want lean men like Cassius around him as they were dangerous: 'Yond Cassius has a lean and hungry look, He thinks too much; such men are dangerous' (*Julius Caesar*, I.ii.194), but Sheldon used scientific methods to support his hypotheses. There were three extremes: the round, chubby endomorph who is tolerant, extrovert and likes food and people; the ectomorph who is slender and artistic, sensitive and introverted; and the mesomorph who is muscular, shaped like a triangle pointing down, and aggressive, competitive, fearless and risk-taking. If you imagine a triangle with each extreme at one point we all fall somewhere within it – few people are 'pure' mesomorphs, endomorphs or ectomorphs – but the more a person approached the mesomorphic point then the more likely Sheldon thought they were to be criminal. He produced data to show that convicted offenders are more mesomorphic on average than the rest of the population.

Other researchers have confirmed this: in one study by Eleanor and Sheldon Glueck 60 per cent of delinquents compared to only 30 per cent of non-delinquents had mesomorphic body characteristics (Glueck and Glueck 1950). But the Gluecks' theory is vulnerable to the criticism that of course muscular people are more likely to commit crimes involving aggression and violence. However, you will see later in this chapter that there is some biological support linking testosterone levels with both mesomorphic bodies and aggressive criminal acts.

Whatever the reason there does seem to be a connection between looks and the risk of conviction: Cavior and Howard (1973) took 159 photographs of male juvenile delinquents and 134 of male high-school seniors. University psychology students rated them for attractiveness: the high-school seniors were significantly more likely to be judged attractive.

Even more convincingly Kurtzberg et al. (1978) took one hundred 'ugly' convicts from one of the USA's toughest prisons, Rikers Island, New York, at their release and gave them plastic surgery. They were compared against a control group of equally ugly convicts who did not receive surgery. After 12 months those who had had plastic surgery were significantly less likely to have been rearrested. Finally, Saladin, Saper and Breen (1988) showed that there is a bias to believe that uglier people are more likely to be criminal by showing two psychology classes a set of photographs. The first class rated them for attractiveness and the other rated them on the chance they would commit murder or robbery: those rated less attractive tended to be judged more likely to commit serious crime. All of these studies of attractiveness should remind you of the claims of the physiognomists and the historical beliefs that physical beauty reflects goodness.

This takes us into the 'modern' period of biological thought on which the rest of this chapter concentrates. As you will see, studies of the possible genetic basis of factors related to criminality had already been going on for decades. An important study by Cloninger et al. in 1982 can now be seen as a milestone in the development of methods which highlighted the interaction between biological and social factors: the biosocial interaction model that is the most promising in this area. Also Wilson's revolutionary book (1975) argued that human social behaviour had biological roots and was evolved.

The rest of the discussion is divided into five sections:

- Evolutionary perspectives, to give you a framework within which to interpret the other viewpoints.
- Genes, as the bridge between evolution and our working bodies and brains – this subsection also covers the transmitters that carry signals within the brain.
- Physical characteristics, as some are related to your risk of criminal behaviour.
- Brain structures, as the organ with which we sense, process and respond to the world.
- Development of the brain, as this process ties together the other biological perspectives.

EVOLUTION

The most useful way to begin looking at particular approaches within biology is to consider criminal behaviour from an evolutionary perspective. As the geneticist Dobzhansky (1973) wrote: 'Nothing in biology makes sense except in the light of evolution.' To give you an idea of how this may help understand criminal behaviour, after introducing the concept of evolution below, we will look at three applications: firstly, one of the most convincing, which explains the age–crime curve for males (Kanazawa 2003); secondly, one of the most interesting but contested claims – that step-parents are much more of a danger to children than biological parents (Daly and Wilson 1988, 2002); thirdly, one highly controversial and not very convincing hypothesis – that rape is a behaviour that has evolved to increase men's chance of leaving the greatest number of offspring (Thornhill and Palmer 2000).

Introducing evolution

Evolution applies to populations of animals (including humans) not to individual animals. You *are* the product of many generations of evolution, but the pattern of change that evolution produces can be seen only by looking at the whole population that you are a member of.

Individuals differ in their genes and so in their characteristics. Different characteristics give you differing chances of surviving and leaving successful offspring. Those offspring will carry their parents' genes into the next generation. The more successful descendants a person leaves, the more successful they are in evolutionary terms. (See Dawkins (1976) for an explanation of how it is really genes that are 'successful' or not.)

Thus, if you look at the population as a whole over time you will see evolution: an increase in the proportion of the population carrying versions of genes that fit them well to the environment.

The production of different combinations of genes is ruled by chance. The success of the combinations is tested by the particular environment: evolution is shooting at a moving target: the best combinations of genes now, in Latvia, is not likely to be the same as the best in a thousand years' time in Surinam. The environment 'selects' those genes that lead to more offspring. However, evolution does not produce 'progress'; we are no 'better' than our ancestors; what is good now was not, and will not be, good in other environments.

Humans are as highly evolved as every other living organism, no more, no less. Owing to our shared evolution we share genes with other living things: the more closely related we are (i.e. the more recently that we shared a common ancestor with another species) the more of our genes are shared with them. We share about half of our genes with the banana (Begley 2002), even though that is obviously only distantly related to humans, but chimpanzees and humans have over 96 per cent of their genes in common (Holmes 2005).

Recently researchers have found clear evidence that we are still evolving quickly. Two genes that control development of the brain have versions, or alleles, that are being selected by the environment – this means that people who have the preferred versions are leaving more successful offspring. This seems to be an extension of the differences between humans and chimps and has lead to the selected alleles becoming much more common over the last six thousand to thirty thousand years, broadly speaking up to the period that city life first appeared (Inman 2005). Evidence showing substantial human evolution over the last fifteen thousand years across at least seven hundred of our 25,000 genes has been published with the expectation that many more will be recognized (Douglas 2006).

Evolution will tend to make a really useful adaptation spread throughout the population for example the impulsivity, competitiveness and high sex-drive of 15–30-year-old males are typical of males in general (just as antlers are typical of sexually mature male red deer). This is thought to be due in part to sexual selection where members of one sex prefer mates with certain traits, as when female deer prefer bucks with larger antlers. Then, even if those traits have other disadvantages, the genes that underlie them will become more common. This will go on until the disadvantages (of say huge antlers or extreme competitiveness) outweigh the advantages, always in terms of how many successful offspring you leave. As a general rule in humans females prefer high-status males while males prefer young, sexually mature females (Miller 2001).

There is more than one successful strategy possible. For example one view of psychopaths is that they are a relatively small group within the population who carry genes selected by evolution that suit them for a life of preying on the rest of us (Mealey 1995). Humans are highly adapted for co-operation (Ridley 1996) and are a social animal that relies on working with the group. This often means that we assist someone now and trust them to help us if we need it in the future (reciprocal altruism);

however, this creates a niche for cheats who take the help now but never repay it (Katz 2000). Thus psychopaths are seen not to feel guilt or remorse, to be impulsive and egocentric, and not to be deterred by negative consequences. They understand how others' emotions work but do not care if they hurt someone else, this combination helps them to manipulate others (Hare 1996).

While psychopaths make up about 1 per cent of the general population, because of their persistent and varied offending from an early age, about 20 per cent of prisoners are psychopaths. They commit an even larger fraction of the most extreme offences: in 1992 the FBI found that about half the law enforcement officers killed at work were victims of psychopaths (Hare 1996).

Ellis (2005) uses this style of explanation to cover criminal behaviour in general. Testosterone and related male hormones lead to more competitive or victimizing behaviour while higher intelligence results in this behaviour being less violent and less criminal.

Animals have evolved flexibility and will change their behaviour as the social and physical environment changes. Humans do the same. The Hadza society (a hunter-gatherer people from Tanzania) was regarded as the hardest-hearted he had ever come across by an anthropologist who just happened to have studied them during a severe famine. Evolution produces a range of possible strategies: we are evolved to use unconsciously the one that is most appropriate for the circumstances.

The idea that we do not think out what is best to do, but our behaviour is unconscious, wired into our brains, is crucial. For example, women appear to present themselves in a more sexual way when they are at their most fertile point in the menstrual cycle, but women are not consciously aware of when this is (Miller 2001).

Modern humans and evolution

Presumably something that we would recognize as criminal behaviour must have existed as long as humans have lived in cities. At the moment the oldest city that we have good evidence for is Tell Brak, from about six thousand years ago, although it is thought that in Iraq cities may have been established from eight thousand years ago (Lawton 2004). Some of our earliest written records, for example Hindu texts, the Old Testament, ancient Greek philosophy, discuss issues concerning anti-social behaviour and practical moral issues. Over this time the social and physical environment must have changed drastically, many times, yet – as far as we can make out – crime has always been there and at roughly comparable levels.

Evolution can produce rapid change in biologically determined characters: for example the specialized beaks of the finches that Darwin collected in the Galapagos Islands change in response to the sharp changes in the type of food available (Weiner 1995). However, most biologists believe that humans now are biologically very similar to those from ten thousand years ago.

Biology does not only affect physical things such as hair colour, height, risk of heart disease etc.; it also underlies how we behave. There is good evidence that biology underpins our emotions (Damasio 2003) and thoughts (McGinn 2000) – two factors that motivate and guide our behaviour. Later you will see evidence that the behaviour patterns of attention deficit with hyperactivity disorder (ADHD), a condition that gives an increased risk of criminal convictions and delinquent acts, are due to biological factors. These seem to be often inherited from the person's parents and these behaviours may have been an advantage to their carriers in the past.

When E.O. Wilson published *Sociobiology: A New Synthesis*, in 1975, he argued that, just as in other animals, human social behaviours such as altruism and courtship were based on biology. Although most biologists agreed that there were some human behaviours largely under genetic control there was a powerful negative response to extending this to what were felt to be behaviours shaped by our education, society and moral beliefs, and for which we held people responsible. Wilson's view was attacked from one side for being a right-wing attack on the liberal-left consensus, and from the other as excusing bad behaviour and undermining responsibility (Segerstråle 2000).

Since 1975 Wilson's ideas have been implemented and extended by many researchers. Most evolutionary biologists believe that the genes we carry now evolved to suit our modern human ancestors' way of life. This is typically argued to be on the African grasslands about sixty thousand years ago (Barrett et al. 2006).

For our purposes evolutionary researchers who work in the areas of evolutionary psychology, sociobiology and human behavioural ecology are the most important. They argue that criminal and delinquent behaviour has been shaped by evolution because it has an impact on reproductive success. These approaches will be referred to collectively as human evolutionary psychology (HEP), as Daly and Wilson (1999) suggest.

Three examples of evolutionary explanations of criminal behaviour

The male age–crime curve

The male age–crime curve (MACC) shows how the number of male offenders per thousand males changes as their age increases. There are very few offenders up until about 11 years of age. The curve increases steeply until the proportion who are convicted offenders reaches a peak at about 18 years. From there it drops – steeply at first, but reducing more gently after about 25 years of age. The MACC has been called 'the best accepted fact in criminology' (Gottfredson and Hirschi 1990), although there is disagreement over how universal it actually is, and there have been many attempts to explain it in sociological terms. However the evolutionary explanation is both interesting and useful.

Kanazawa (2003a; 2003b) presents a readable account of his hypothesis that the bulk of offenders are just young men displaying behaviour that evolved to increase their chances of finding a mate and having children. Remember that producing successful children is what drives evolution: we might suspect that the MACC relates to this. We might also guess that the ways in which young males differ from young females are more likely to be linked to reproduction (think of the different mature sexual organs such as the vagina versus the penis, ovaries versus testes, breasts versus chests). We know that young men are more aggressive, impulsive, novelty-seeking and sexually driven than young women and also less empathic. We also know that there are biological changes through puberty and beyond that underlie these differences. One example is the male surge in testosterone levels that begins at about 11 years of age and does not decline until about 30 years of age. Women find men who show the physical changes associated with higher levels of testosterone more sexually attractive (Miller 2001).

QUESTION BREAK

- What is happening to males from about 11 years until about 18 years old?
- What might tend to be happening in men's lives between about 18 and 27 years of age?
- Why do you think young men show off so much to their peers?

Puberty in males begins at about 11 to 13 years of age and usually continues into the late teens. The biological purpose of puberty is to create a sexually mature person who can find a good mate and have children; males are interested in sex and capable of fertilizing a woman from early puberty.

Kanazawa argues that the initial rise in the MACC is set off by puberty; he thinks that the increase in criminal behaviour reflects young males' increased drive to behave aggressively and/or impulsively. Therefore he proposes that these changes are concerned with finding a good mate. Recently it has been claimed that although young women do not prefer risk-taking men, men get higher status among their male peers by taking risks and women prefer men with higher status. Similarly you could argue that aggression and competition between young males are to do with establishing their status in their peer group.

If this is so then one might expect criminal behaviour to be only one type of behaviour that young men will adopt to compete with their fellow males. Kanazawa says that this is exactly what you find with sport, art, music and scientific achievement, and he shows that the curves for each of these for different ages have very similar shapes and characteristics to the MACC.

QUESTION BREAK

- Why do you think that evolutionary psychologists expect young women to have evolved different behaviour patterns than young men?
- What differences do you think there are in what a woman compared to a man looks for in a sexual partner?

The differences between male and female behaviour we see are expected by human evolutionary psychologists. We will use Miller's (2001) account as the basis for our discussion.

Sex has different cost and benefits for males and females. When men have sex they produce millions of sperm each time: sperm are tiny and cheap to produce. Women, once a month, release one (sometimes two) of the eggs that they have stored in their ovaries from birth. Eggs are much more substantial than sperm and women have only a limited number.

If one of the man's sperm fertilizes a woman's egg then he can leave her to bring up his child while he fertilizes more women, leading to lots of potential offspring for him – think of the harem system where powerful men had sexual access to many women who bore them many children. If a woman is pregnant then she is stuck with nine months of pregnancy, using large quantities of energy and exposing her to health risks and making her less able to look after and defend herself. Human birth is a dangerous event: in rich countries we forget that women used to face, and still do in poorer states, a serious chance of dying around the time of giving birth.

Because of this difference women are less keen on promiscuity than men (although contraception has changed behaviour, remember that these tendencies evolved over long periods and act below the level of consciousness) and more selective in whom they choose to have sex with. In particular women want someone who is healthy and carries successful genes *and* who has significant resources and is reliable. Most males do not combine both types of qualities.

HEP can explain the differences in criminal behaviour between males and females naturally. In many species males compete amongst themselves, with the winners having the best chance of being chosen as a mate by the females. Attributes increasing a male's chance of impressing potential mates are then selected by evolution.

The HEP hypothesis that criminal behaviour is often just a way of impressing possible mates by out-competing your peers suggests that schemes that offer alternative ways for young males to compete in public should reduce both crime and anti-social acts. For example, there are projects for young men convicted of joyriding that teach them to repair old cars and then to race them. It also implies that there needs to be an element of genuine danger and that competition itself is necessary for adolescents. Another lesson is that we should expect youths from more disadvantaged homes to be more likely to show anti-social or criminal behaviour because they tend to have poorer educations and fewer opportunities to engage in other competition that satisfies their evolved drives. We should not think that males from less supportive environments are more 'naturally criminal' even if they are more likely to display behaviour for which they could be convicted.

QUESTION BREAK

- Has this view helped you to understand young male anti-social or criminal behaviour?
- Can you see any practical lessons or implications for policy from it?

'The Cinderella hypothesis'

The hypothesis being proposed here is that step-parents are much more dangerous to children than biological parents, and that this is because the step-parents do not share genes with the children. Therefore they have less interest in the children's survival and may even benefit from their death. (This section is based on Daly and Wilson 1998 and 2002.)

This is what we see in numerous animal species, the best known example being the African lion. Lions live in groups of closely related females called prides. Each pride has one or two sexually mature males who are closely related, often brothers, and who fight off others to keep their right to have sole access to mate with the females. Eventually another pair of males will come along and defeat them. When the new lions take over one of their first acts is to search out any young cubs and kill them. There are two reproductive benefits: they do not want to waste any of the resources they could use to bring up cubs of their own on unrelated cubs that will compete with their children; and the lionesses will not come back to peak fertility until they stop breast-feeding.

QUESTION BREAK

- Suggest some reasons why step-parents might look after their stepchildren less carefully than their biological offspring.
- What evidence can you think of that suggests that step-parents might be unhappy to support their stepchildren?
- What sorts of conflict might exist?

In human culture we have worldwide stereotypes of stepmothers (e.g. in 'Cinderella', 'Snow White' or 'Hansel and Gretel') and stepfathers (e.g. King Claudius in *Hamlet*) as being cruel to the children from previous relationships. Although there are many more wicked stepmothers in fiction, in real life it is often stepfathers who are more dangerous. Sociologists looking at how stepfathers actually behave find high levels of conflict in Western stepfamilies. Anthropologists have described the accepted practice in the Pacific island of Tikopia by which new stepfathers publicly state that they are not willing to bring up unrelated children and insist that they are either fostered or killed.

Daly and Wilson analysed evidence on crimes against children within the family. For abuse the USA data showed that in 1976 under-three-year-olds were almost seven times as likely to be recorded as abused if they lived with a stepfather rather than two biological parents. To check that this was not due to cultural bias against stepfathers they looked at more serious cases, ending up with 279 fatalities from nearly 88,000 cases. These records are likely to be accurate because of the seriousness of the crime. When they did this they found that stepchildren were at one hundred times more risk than children living with both biological parents.

There have been criticisms of this work, but most of them do not convincingly undermine the hypothesis.

A sociological perspective would suggest that stepfamilies are under greater stress than first families: there are the effects of whatever led to the break-up of the previous relationship, tensions between step-parent and children due to loyalty to the missing parent, psychological issues such as anger and jealousy, the strain of managing on less income (thinking of the average stepfamily) with the consequential impact on education, housing, diet or recreational opportunity. And all these factors can increase the risk of criminal behaviour via mediating variables like substance misuse, bad peer group, while reducing the protective elements of a happy family life.

The factors in the previous paragraph are clearly relevant and there is great variety of quality within both different stepfamilies and different biological families. After all humans adopt unrelated children (although there is a preference for relatives in adoptions) and invest heavily in them. This may reflect the fact that many adopting parents cannot have children of their own.

A natural history of rape?

The final hypothesis examined is based on a book by Thornhill and Palmer (2000) with the same title as this section. The point they are trying to establish is that human rape is sexually, or reproductively, driven rather than being an act of violence reflecting unbalanced power relations between men and women as Brownmiller (1975) proposed. Brownmiller's position has been dominant for the last 30 years and she does not accept a sexual, reproductive explanation for rape.

Thornhill and Palmer use evidence from animals, including the scorpion fly – an insect whose mating behaviour Thornhill has studied. The normal way for a male scorpion fly to get sexual access to a female is for him to bring her a piece of food. Similarly human females prefer mates with resources. Some males cannot manage this but they have an alternate strategy – the males have a notch in their wing with which they can hold an unwilling female in the correct position for sex. They propose that this is a model of human rape.

To make this argument work, Thornhill and Palmer have to define rape very tightly: it must involve vaginal sex as this is the only way that rape could produce a child. This seems to miss out a sizeable proportion of human rape, for example rape with objects, anal rape, rape followed by murder – especially in conflicts where rape is widely practised, sometimes as a deliberate weapon of terror – or rape of women past reproductive age or of pre-pubertal girls. This is necessary because they want to argue that men show adaptations that help them rape women which are encoded in the genes and so can be selected by the environment, but this can happen only if they leave more children because they rape women. They do not suggest that men have physical adaptations like the scorpion fly but Thornhill thinks that men show psychological adaptations inclining them to rape.

It is certainly true that rape is common, especially when you include date rape and coercion that falls short of legal rape. Rape is found in all cultures and has been so throughout recorded history. It also seems that males try to push for sex more often than women do. Together this is consistent with some biological factor being important. Palmer's position is more plausible: he argues that rape is a side-effect of male traits that do tend to result in more offspring, such as aggression and high sex-drive.

Virtually every aspect of their project has been attacked, from their definition of rape to their interpretation of the statistics, to their suggested advice based on their work, for example that young women should not wear provocative clothing. While their hypothesis may be flawed, the idea that there is a biological side to rape is reasonable, even though it does not yet seem to have produced any useful interpretations. We would not argue that human rape is the same as forced sex in other species because rape has other dimensions and meanings that do not exist in other animals. Human culture and intelligence are likely to be relevant to this, but evolutionary factors such as men's vulnerability to bringing up another man's child and the importance to a woman of choosing her own mate may help us understand the horror that rape arouses.

Summarizing evolution

We have considered the evolutionary perspective at some length to encourage you to see this as the view that unifies and makes sense of the other biological approaches. It has the advantage that it reunites us with the rest of the living world and evolution is being applied to many new areas with impressive results. You will see that the later biological approaches to understanding crime make more sense if you have an evolutionary framework in which to interpret them. The sociological and psycho-logical theories looked at in the next two chapters can also be integrated with this perspective. The evolutionary perspective sees the way that we behave as depending partly on our genes but also on the environment: this is an example of biosocial interaction.

GENES

We have seen how evolution can provide a framework for understanding human behaviour: now we will take a brief look at how genes provide the link between evolution and the biological factors that more directly underlie criminal behaviour. The evidence supports the biosocial interaction model.

The debate over the importance of genes in behaviour has always been intense, from the eugenics movement at the start of the twentieth century right through to the present (e.g. Lewontin, Rose and Kamin 1984). Critics, some from within biology, have attacked the implication that genes largely determine our behaviour as well as the interpretation of the data from some of the methods that form the cornerstone of the genetic approach. For most of the twentieth century the 'nature versus nurture' debate, in which one side argued that biology, especially genes, determined our behaviour and the other that the environment determined how we behaved, was how disagreements were presented. More recently it has become clear that the evidence makes sense only if the biosocial interaction model is used (e.g. Raine 2002b).

No serious biologists think that there is 'a criminal gene': they are looking for genes that make criminal behaviour more probable. If genes can influence our impulsivity, and we know impulsivity makes you more likely to become an offender, then those genes increase the probability that you will perform criminal acts.

We now have compelling evidence that genes are important in establishing the likelihood that we will display particular anti-social and criminal behaviour. For example Brunner et al. (1991) showed that one defective version of a gene that makes an enzyme crucial in how some of our neurons work leads to a massively increased risk of very violent behaviour.

The combination of sustained criticism and improved understanding has resulted in the recognition that the impact of genes depends on the social and physical environment that the person lives in. Investigating the contribution genes make to a behaviour also reveals the importance of the environment. Parens (2004) gives a clear account of our present understanding of the role of each and of the difficulties in interpreting the results from such studies.

As with evolution there are several distinct approaches within genetic research. We will consider two: behavioural genetics and molecular biology.

Behavioural genetics

Behavioural genetics tries to identify how important genes are in particular behaviours using methods that rely on comparing how similar different relatives are on that behaviour. Different relatives share different, predictable proportions of their genes. Humans share about 99 per cent of their genes because most are for crucial biological systems such as your heart, liver etc. Humans all need genes to do the same tasks, so we may all seem to have the same set of genes. However, remember that there will be a variety of versions of the same gene so we will end up with different genotypes. Almost all the genes we have do not appear to be relevant to how likely we are to be anti-social or criminal; that leaves a much smaller number where variations in the versions, or alleles that we inherit may alter our predisposition to criminality. If you share half of your alleles in general with a relative then you will also be likely to share half of those alleles relevant to criminal behaviour.

Identical twins share all their genes; non-identical twins and other brothers and sisters share half their genes; parents share half their genes with each child; an aunt or uncle shares 25 per cent of their nieces' or nephews' genes, and so on. This means that by studying families we can compare how similar they are on, say, having a criminal record and see whether those who share more genes are also more alike on criminality.

- If a study finds that children with criminal parents are more likely to be criminals than those parents' nephews, does this show that being a criminal has genetic roots?
- Why do you think researchers often use twins to study the role of genes in criminal behaviour?
- Studies of twins separated at birth are regarded as especially powerful. Why do you think this is?
- Studies comparing adopted children's behaviour with their biological versus adoptive parents' behaviour are also useful. Why?

Twin studies have shown that genes are relevant to anti-social and criminal behaviour. If we ignore those with small sample sizes (as a rule the larger the sample the more valid the results) there are two early projects that stand out: Dalgaard and Kringlen (1976) and Christiansen (1977). They both compared identical twins with non-identical twins on how alike each type of twin was on adult criminal behaviour (not adolescence-limited anti-social and criminal behaviour). This similarity is called concordance, and can range from 0 per cent (meaning no similarity) up to 100 per cent (meaning if one twin was a criminal the other always was too).

If we combine their results, the concordance for identical twins was 31 per cent and for non-identical 12.9 per cent. As both types of twins share much of their environment this is interpreted as showing that genes are important because sharing all your genes makes you much more alike in adult criminal behaviour than if you share half your genes.

Cloninger and Gottesman (1987) added more subjects to Christiansen's set and reanalysed the data. Now the concordance for identical twins was 74 per cent against 47 per cent for non-identical. This was then used to calculate the importance of genes in adult crime, also called its heritability. They found that 54 per cent of the differences between adults in criminal behaviour were due to genetic differences.

Genes were more important in males than females. Perhaps this is because some of the genes are on the Y sex chromosome that only the male inherits. Or maybe there is less reproductive advantage to females in carrying these genes and therefore female adult criminals are more likely to behave like that either because of biological damage or because of their past or present environment.

More recently Taylor, Iacono and McGue (2000) tested about 140 male twins and found evidence that genes are involved in early-onset delinquency. This is known to be a good predictor of a persistent criminal lifestyle lasting through adulthood.

At this point you need to be aware of some of the criticisms of twin studies. For example, identical twins may be treated more similarly than non-identical twins because of their appearance (identical twins are often dressed identically by their parents): this would make them more alike for non-genetic reasons (see Allen 1976). Also, there is evidence that we seek out environments that suit our genes (Rowe 1990) so identical twins tend to choose similar friends and activities – including anti-social and criminal ones. This is an example of the complexity of environment–gene interactions: similar genes lead people to choose similar environments that amplify the effect of those genes.

Adoption studies are another way of looking for genetic effects. These look at people adopted at an early age and see whether, in later life, they are more like their biological parents (which would suggest that genes are important) or their adoptive parents (which would suggest that the environment dominates).

Mednick, Gabrielli and Hutchings (1984) looked at all adoptions in Denmark from 1924 to 1947, an unbiased set of over fourteen thousand cases. They found strong evidence of genetic influence, with about half of the sons convicted of crimes having criminal biological parents compared to about a third of the sons without criminal convictions. Genes were more important in persistent offending, as in the twin studies.

These results are consistent with other studies, including Bohman et al. (1982) who looked at over 1,750 Swedish cases. This study also found that genes were more important in the daughters. Presumably this difference from the Cloninger and Gottesman (1987) results is because the majority of female offending is also adolescence-limited and Bohman et al. looked at all crime, not just adult crime. Also females differ much more in their tendency toward criminal behaviour in their adolescence than males, and therefore we expect there to be genetic differences underlying the behavioural ones.

As with twin studies there are criticisms of adoption studies. Some studies have included children adopted by relatives, or adopted by an aunt living in the same street as the biological parents with whom they spent a lot of time (Lewontin et al. 1984). Also adoption agencies tend to place children with families similar to their biological one, which will make it more difficult to separate out environmental from biological effects (Jones 2006).

The different methods do seem to find compatible results even though there are differences in the precise figures they produce. Rhee and Waldman (2002) combined the data from 51 twin and adoption studies in a meta-analysis: their conclusion was that genes and environment are both important factors in explaining anti-social behaviour for both males and females. Similarly, Raine (1993) combined results from twin studies and, separately, from adoption studies and made a convincing case for the importance of genes in criminal behaviour across cultures. There is also evidence that this genetic influence is relevant to non-violent property crime but not to violent crime. In the sections on the brain and development we will see how biologists explain violent criminal behaviour.

There are many studies showing evidence that factors we know to be strong predictors of persistent criminal behaviour, such as early bullying, certain personality traits and conduct disorder have genetic components. For example Slutske et al. (1997) used over 2,500 twins to show that genes are a strong risk factor for conduct disorder, while Eley et al. (1999) tested over 1,500 twins and found a genetic factor underlying early onset aggressive bullying. Krueger et al. (1994) directly measured the link between the personality traits of rejection of conventional values, sensation seeking and recklessness and anti-social behaviour in over eight hundred participants and found evidence of a significant genetic influence.

In summary, the genes you inherit do put you at more or less risk of anti-social and criminal behaviour but their impact depends on the environment you grow up in. One final study illustrates the dominance of this non-additive interaction. Cloninger et al. (1982) carried out an adoption study and found that the risk of becoming a criminal if the adoptee had criminal biological parents was 12 per cent, if they had criminal adoptive parents their risk was 7 per cent, but if they had both then the risk shot up to 40 per cent. This shows that we must consider both biology and other factors together if we want to understand crime.

Molecular genetics

Molecular genetics involves the use of sophisticated laboratory-based methods to identify precisely which genes, and which alleles, are linked to particular traits and behaviours. This connects the findings of behavioural genetics to the functioning of brain systems and structures. We will give a flavour of this work because it will suggest how the transmitters and related structures and processes that carry signals within the brain relate to anti-social and criminal behaviour.

Most of this work has focused on the molecules involved in communications between the brain cells (or neurons). To be even more precise, the clearest evidence implicates elements of the communication systems concerned with the neuro-transmitters serotonin and dopamine.

Genes connecting criminal behaviour to serotonin systems

Low serotonin activity has repeatedly been associated with criminality, for example conduct disorder (Coccaro et al. 1997), anti-social personality disorder (Dolan et al. 2002) and young adult offending (Moffitt et al. 1998). Therefore it is not surprising to find that genes involved in different aspects of serotonin function have been linked with various types of anti-social and criminal behaviour.

Brunner et al. (1991) reported a Dutch family with at least six generations of males showing extreme violence and learning disability. One was convicted of raping his sister at 23 years old. In the institution he was sent to he repeatedly got into fights with the other criminally insane inmates; at 35 he drove a pitchfork into the chest of a prison officer. Another relative made his sisters strip at knifepoint, another drove at his sheltered workshop manager when he was criticized. No females showed these behaviours, which made Brunner's team suspect the genetic flaw was on the female sex chromosome (the X). This is because the X is larger than the male Y chromosome and holds more genes. If one of the 'extra' genes is faulty males do not have a matching gene to cover the flaw: this is why genetic developmental disorders are so much more common in males.

The 'Brunner version' cannot be common in violent criminals because it produces learning disabilities and extreme behaviour that are rarely seen in offenders. Offenders like the Dutch family members above are held in special hospitals as they are both very dangerous and felt to be not legally responsible for their violence.

Considering the process by which signals are received by serotonin-using neurons, Quist et al. (2000) found that one version of a gene (the HTR2A gene) that builds one of the serotonin receptors makes a child significantly more likely to have ADHD. ADHD is a substantial risk factor for later criminal behaviour.

QUESTION BREAK

- From what you have read, if serotonin activity and the genes that influence it are likely to be relevant to a person's chance of committing criminal offences, what offences are they more likely to carry out?
- What sort of biological interventions to deal with such behaviour do you guess people might suggest?

There are always problems in carrying out and interpreting these types of studies – for example serotonin activity is almost always measured indirectly because of problems in accessing the brain safely and comfortably. The overall picture suggests that genes that influence serotonin function will affect their holder's tendency to be involved in impulsive and aggressive behaviour.

Because of these links, researchers have tried using drugs that increase serotonin activity in offenders. The SSRIs (Selective Serotonin Reuptake Inhibitors) increase the activity of serotonin-using neurons by preventing neurons re-absorbing serotonin so that it is able to continue stimulating receptors. Prozac and Seroxat are two common brand names in Britain. A small number of male sex offenders who, despite hating their behaviour so much that some had considered suicide, were almost totally unable to resist their urges have been treated with SSRIs with some apparent success (see Rowe 2002 chapter 7). Similarly other researchers have suggested using the same drugs to reduce crime levels in the inner cities (Breggin 1995). Although some are sceptical of the benefits of using such measures widely there is a case for testing them on offenders who seem to be desperate to stop impulsive violent or sexual behaviour and who show signs of low serotonin activity. MDMA (better known by the street name Ecstasy) is known for its enhancement of empathy and positive feelings towards others and it acts primarily by boosting serotonin activity for several hours.

Lawyers have already tried to use molecular genetics research into serotonin systems to excuse or mitigate their clients' criminal acts. For example, Stephen Mobley ('the Domino's Pizza Killer') robbed a pizzeria at gunpoint in Georgia, USA, in 1991 and then for no apparent reason chose to shoot the manager in the back of the neck. At his murder trial his defence tried to have his death sentence commuted to life imprisonment on the basis of a family tree (like that Brunner constructed) showing several relatives with violent and criminal records. The court ruled that this was not relevant, and did not allow him to undergo biological tests of levels of the enzyme (MAO) that was malfunctioning in the Dutch family Brunner studied, or of the relevant transmitter, serotonin (Deno 1996). Mobley was executed on 1 March 2005. You may be interested to know that one of Mobley's brothers, sharing half his genes, became a self-made millionaire. This should make you distrust simplistic genetic determinism as an explanation of anti-social or criminal behaviour.

Genes affecting dopamine function

The other transmitter system that has been researched with encouraging results is the dopamine system. One part of the brain's dopamine system is known to be involved in experiencing reward, or perhaps in the motivation to get a reward. Cocaine and amphetamine act directly on these neurons and other drugs like heroin act on it indirectly (Julien 2004).

One type of transmitter will be used in several systems in the brain, each carrying out a distinct function. There are also several different receptor types for each transmitter, and we assume that these create different results in the neurons that carry them. The Dopamine 4 receptor (D4) has been implicated in characteristics relevant to criminal behaviour, with different versions creating different tendencies to act in particular ways. This type of research is relatively recent. Ebstein et al. (1996) found that Israeli students showed greater novelty-seeking if they carried the '7 repeat' version of the D4 gene. Although this has been retested by several groups with mixed results, it did trigger a burst of research into the gene itself.

The '7 repeat' version of the D4 gene has often been associated with ADHD, a risk factor for anti-social or criminal behaviour. Faraone et al. (2001) reviewed all the studies that could be found (including unpublished data) and concluded that there is clear evidence for a significant link between the '7 repeat' version and ADHD. Interestingly Rowe et al. (2001) found that adults who said that they had been more involved in teenage delinquency were also more likely to have the '7 repeat' allele, but only in males.

There is an evolutionary perspective that regards the characteristics of ADHD as having been useful, and leading to more offspring. Now we make children sit in busy classrooms and judge their progress by how well they can ignore distractions, sit still, be quiet and concentrate on often dull material (Jensen et al. 1997). Indeed many famous people showed traits that we now interpret as elements of ADHD, for example Edison, Mozart, Churchill, Einstein, John Lennon and many sportspeople.

Practical implications

How then might we use the information from genetics? There is already a genuine debate about using genetic information to show that an offender has a predisposition towards anti-social or criminal behaviour, and on that basis altering the sentence they receive (Evansburg 2001). In at least one case in the USA a death sentence has been reduced to life in prison on grounds including genetic vulnerability (see the case study of John Eastlack at the end of the chapter, p. 52).

We could intervene biologically by altering the diets of children with low levels of a transmitter and increasing the amount of the 'building blocks' of that transmitter, or the chemicals involved in making it. For example tryptophan is part of a normal diet and is essential for constructing dopamine; it is easy to eat more foods that contain it. Vitamins, minerals, omega-3 and related essential fatty acids (found in oily fish, cod-liver oil and some plants, such as flax seeds) are essential for effective functioning of our brains. Well-designed studies have clearly and repeatedly shown that simple, cheap supplements in tablets decrease the amount of criminal behaviour. In a series of studies over more than 14 years involving all the relevant children in Mauritius, there was much less anti-social and criminal behaviour in the teenage years if supplements were given in childhood. Poor diets at three years old were linked to criminal behaviour.

There has even been a study in England (Gesch et al. 2002) where males detained in a young offenders' institution were randomly assigned to two groups. One was given a simple supplement, the other was given identical-looking tablets without the supplements. At the end of the trial the records of the supplemented group showed 25 per cent fewer disciplinary offences than those of the unsupplemented group, with the greatest difference for the most serious offences such as hostage-taking and assault (Lawson 2003). These findings raise the question as to why such cheap, effective measures are not applied in prisons, in schools and in schemes for the under-fives – perhaps because there are no great profits to be made?

Genetics is not destiny: to use a metaphor, it is more like playing a long session of poker where each card is a version of one of the genes we inherited from our parents. We need to play until we have been dealt about 25,000 cards (one per gene) so luck is unlikely to be a major factor. Also your hand can be judged only in the context of the other players' cards, and your success depends partly on with whom you are playing. So a child with genes associated with a higher risk of anti-social or criminal behaviour who is brought up in a supportive environment is much more likely to have a happy and successful life than one who has high-risk genes and a poor social and physical environment.

Biosocial interaction is once more the best model. Evolution works because some combinations and versions of genes, in a particular environment, result on average in the person that inherited them leaving more offspring. Those offspring then carry those genes into the next generation.

We have seen how the next step of the process – when the genes produce different characteristics in their holders – works with respect to communication between the neurons that we think are the key brain cells underlying emotions, thoughts, our physical responses and motivations etc. Note that most of the findings we discussed apply to the sort of traits – for example impulsivity, novelty-seeking, aggression – that we saw evolution has selected in young men in general. However we also saw that 'faults' can also help to explain some criminal behaviour, as in Brunner's team's work with the Dutch family.

Systems using serotonin and dopamine are important in the prefrontal cortex and temporal lobe. In the brain structures section (pp. 44–8) you will find that these parts of the brain are implicated in criminal behaviour, and this helps to tie together the different biological perspectives. Firstly, we will look at how those who seem predisposed to criminal behaviour differ from the majority of the population in various physical factors.

PHYSICAL CHARACTERISTICS OF OFFENDERS

In this section we will consider ways in which offenders differ physically from non-offenders. Bear in mind the proposed differences in attractiveness and physical characteristics that you read about in the introduction to this chapter.

QUESTION BREAK

- In what ways do you think offenders differ physically from non-offenders?
- Which ideas mentioned in the introduction to this chapter does this remind you of?
- If we could find differences between offenders and non-offenders what actions or policies do you think would be suggested?

Mesomorphy and testosterone

We looked earlier at Sheldon's theory that males fell into three general body types. Of these the mesomorph, having a muscular body, little body fat and adventurous, fearless, competitive, low empathy, risk-taking personality, is the most likely to become a criminal. It makes sense that physically strong and aggressive people are better equipped for crimes involving force and intimidation. Mike Tyson and Bernard Hopkins are both world champion professional boxers who have committed serious crimes of violence.

Sheldon's work is now seen as simplistic and also as perhaps confusing cause and effect (for example skinny, anxious people are unlikely to be successful armed robbers even if they really want to be); however that is not to say that he was totally mistaken. Even if you cannot tell that someone is a criminal just because they are mesomorphic there is evidence that the physique and personality do often go together, and that they are more common in offenders. Eight studies have tested this relationship and all have found that mesomorphs are more often offenders than the other body types; one study has also found this for males with anti-social personality disorder (Ellis 2005).

In considering why this might be, Ellis convincingly argues that the underlying biological factor that leads to the personality and physical characteristics of the mesomorph that in turn make them more likely to become criminals is the hormone testosterone. Testosterone shapes the brain before we are even born and sets it up to respond in a particular way when puberty sets off the massive increase in testosterone levels many years later. This time delay explains why we do not see large correlations between adult testosterone levels and criminal behaviour, although there are consistent associations between them. There is also evidence that testosterone is especially important in violent offences including domestic violence and other aggressive crimes.

This theory might help to explain why females are so much less likely to be involved in such crimes. Baby girls are not set up in the womb to respond to testosterone in the same way as baby boys, and later levels of testosterone are much lower in females.

Fight or flight

Our response to danger depends on a web of systems that predispose us either to flee from the threat or to fight. There are significant and well-established links between criminal behaviour and different aspects of these systems.

Fearlessness is a trait with biological underpinnings that is linked to offending and anti-social acts. This is associated with the heart rate – which Raine (2002a) has called 'the best-replicated biological correlate of antisocial and aggressive behavior in children' (417). Low resting heart rate has been linked to conduct disorder but not to other psychiatric conditions (i.e. it is specific to a condition diagnosed by extreme anti-social and criminal acts). Five studies that measured resting heart rate at a young age – one at three years old, all before any criminal behaviour – have found that low rates predict aggressive and delinquent behaviour later in life. Moreover, low resting heart rate, by itself, is a predictor of later violence, more so than having a criminal parent!

Males as a group have lower heart rates than females, but among females those with low rates are at greater risk of criminal behaviour. This indicator is particularly good at predicting the small group of anti-social young people who go on to become lifelong offenders. In addition to these reasons to take it seriously, heart rate is also known to be heritable (it is genetically determined to a substantial extent). A high rate protects against other risk factors and it interacts with other, non-biological risk factors (see Raine 2002a).

It could be argued that this factor is so important because of a link with fear-lessness; indeed decorated bomb disposal operatives have very low resting heart rates and low reactivity to threat (Cox et al. 1983), as do decorated British paratroopers (McMillan and Rachman 1987). A more general explanation is that it is part of a general low level of arousal in the several systems underlying fight or flight responses. This is supported by recent research by several groups showing that other measures of arousal are associated with anti-social and delinquent behaviour in children. It also fits with the higher levels of sensation-seeking seen in anti-social, delinquent and criminal populations. The connection is thought to exist because we all have a level of arousal that we find preferable. If we are biologically highly aroused then we do not want to be more stimulated because that takes us past the optimal level; if we are biologically under-aroused then we will seek out stimulation to bring us up to that preferred arousal level (Eysenck 1987).

Joy riding, burglary, street fighting and many other criminal acts are clearly very exciting and arousing and so would be expected to be seen more often in those with low biological arousal than in other people. As there are many other ways to be excited we can also see how this fits with sociological theories linking criminal behaviour with lack of opportunity and with exclusion as this in turn limits access to legal ways of experiencing risk and excitement.

There are other factors that are thought to reflect low arousal and reactivity such as low pulse rate, low levels of sweating when emotionally challenged (galvanic skin response or GSR) and low levels of hormones released in response to stress, especially cortisol (see Raine 2002a and Ellis 2005).

Overall the evidence for lower than normal activity in the body's arousal systems of anti-social, delinquent and criminal persons seems convincing and plausible; it also relates to psychological and sociological theories. It makes sense in the evolutionary framework within which we are considering biological factors. However, it should be obvious that having a low arousal level cannot, by itself, cause crime any more than any other biological factor can. After all besides bomb disposal officers, it is likely that risk-taking sportsmen and women, such as racing drivers or mountaineers, and entrepreneurs would also have low resting arousal levels and responsivity to stress; indeed it is another example of the critical role of interaction between biology and other types of factors.

The final biological factor we will consider concerns those brain structures and functions that seem to be particularly relevant to understanding criminal behaviour.

BRAIN STRUCTURES

This section focuses on research into the frontal lobes of the brain (especially the prefrontal cortex) and the temporal lobes (especially the amygdala and hippocampus). It also considers differences between the two halves of the brain. The reason for looking in some detail at the brain is that a significant proportion of the most extreme, life-course persistent, offenders show clear signs of significant brain damage in exactly the parts of the brain where we would predict their leading to immoral, impulsive, violent, anti-social and unpredictable behaviour.

The prefrontal cortex

In 1848 Phineas Gage, a respected, diligent railway worker, survived a one-metre-long, six-kilogram, iron rod being blasted through the frontal lobe of his brain, landing about ten metres behind him. The destruction was mostly on the left, mainly impacting the prefrontal area, and showed us that traumatic damage to the prefrontal cortex can change a person's character and behaviour dramatically for the worse (Macmillan 1999/2005). Phineas was not allowed to return to his job because his employers said that he had changed from their most capable, reliable, efficient and businesslike foreman into an unreliable, disrespectful, offensive man who could not deal with his fellow workers and showed impulsivity, obstinacy and an inability to decide on and follow any plan. He was said to 'no longer be Phineas Gage', abandoned his family, showed no respect to his fellows, swore, gambled, drank and ended up as a freak exhibit for the Barnum museum in New York and working in stables in Chile (Macmillan 2000). Notice that the way Phineas was after damaging his prefrontal cortex is similar to the collection of characteristics that are seen in many of those who have been convicted of crimes.

Less sudden damage to the frontal and/or temporal cortex can also produce anti-social behaviour in people with frontal-temporal dementia (FTD). Miller et al. (1997) compared 22 patients with FTD against 22 with Alzheimer's dementia (which damages structures further back in the brain). Their families said that the FTD group had been responsible, competent, reliable citizens before their dementia began; therefore it is unlikely that the FTD 'unmasked' pre-existing anti-social characteristics. The diagnoses were made before the dementia was severe enough to explain their anti-social actions as due to cognitive difficulties.

There was a large difference between the groups: ten out of the 22 with FTD had records of socially disruptive behaviours including theft, assault, inappropriate sexual behaviour, unethical behaviour at work and even one hit-and-run. Three had been arrested and two others had avoided arrest only because their families persuaded the police that they were ill. The Alzheimer's group had only one patient with a socially disruptive record. Once again we can see the same types of behaviours that are seen in criminals, especially those with anti-social personality disorder and those who belong in the life-course-persistent subgroup of offenders.

Many children thought to have conditions predisposing them to criminal behaviour (especially the disruptive behaviour disorders that include conduct disorder, oppositional-defiant disorder (ODD) and the attention deficit disorders (ADHD)) show differences in brain function (and even structure) when compared to children who do not have these conditions.

There are also cases of brain injury in children. It is generally agreed that conduct disorder and other behaviour problems commonly appear after such damage (Raine 2002a). The frontal lobes and the tip of the temporal lobe (where the amygdala and hippocampus lie) are particularly vulnerable to head injury. More specifically, children can have damage limited to the prefrontal cortex. For example, Anderson et al. (1999) studied two young adults whose prefrontal cortex had been damaged before 16 months. One was a 20-year-old woman who was intelligent but stole, abused others verbally and physically, lied, was sexually promiscuous, never expressed guilt and had no empathy for her illegitimate child. The other was a 23-year-old man who was apathetic, slovenly, financially reckless, lied, physically assaulted others, stole in ways that were easily detected, never showed guilt and also had no empathy for his illegitimate child. Both had good environments but had shown such behaviours consistently since the damage with no apparent effect of punishment; also neither had been able even to learn social and moral conventions, let alone act upon them.

Vargha-Khadem et al. (2000) report on two British teenagers with childhood frontal damage who then developed delinquent behaviour that got worse until they were found guilty of criminal offences. Pennington and Bennetto (1993) discuss nine other children with frontal damage under the age of ten years. All showed behavioural disorders after their injuries, seven of them having conduct disorder, while one showed impulsive, unpredictable behaviour and another uncontrollable behaviour.

This evidence shows that childhood damage to the prefrontal cortex can cause later criminal behaviour, and is consistent with childhood abnormalities of structure or function being strong predictors of adult anti-social or criminal behaviour.

It is important to understand that, although you may be born with this type of brain, it is also easy to produce this pattern of damage by direct physical abuse.

Shaking a baby or infant, falls and other blows can produce damage to the prefrontal cortex. Even more worryingly it is now established that simply growing up in a family where it witnesses domestic abuse is associated with brain changes that make the child more likely to respond violently in future (Margolin and Gordis 2000).

In adults there is much more direct evidence of abnormal function and structure in the prefrontal cortex being linked with criminal behaviour. There have been several reviews of functional brain-imaging studies. These look at studies using diverse methods and testing different types of anti-social or criminal individuals; also the number of subjects tested is often low. Bearing these issues in mind it is impressive to what extent there is agreement that violent offenders show abnormal patterns of activity in their prefrontal cortex (Raine 2002a). Probably the best studies are a series by Raine's team which ended up by comparing 41 murderers to 41 non-offenders matched for age, sex and schizophrenia. They found an underactive prefrontal cortex in the murderers, with the reduction being greater in impulsive, emotion-driven murderers than in predatory murderers who killed to achieve a goal.

Paedophilia has also been associated with prefrontal damage. Langevin reported that paedophiles' brains were structurally different in a series of papers from 1985, but the methods did not allow very fine resolution (Freund 1994). In 2003 Burns and Swerdlow described a 40-year-old married male teacher with conventional sexual behaviour who had begun visiting child pornography websites, using prostitutes and propositioning young children. His wife left him and he was soon convicted of child molestation, then he was expelled from his treatment programme for soliciting sex from the women on the course. Fortunately he went to hospital complaining of headaches and a fear that he would rape his landlady. The doctors spotted other signs of brain dysfunction and scanned his brain, finding a large tumour in his right prefrontal cortex. An operation removed the growth and he returned to his old self. Some time later his sexual deviance returned and they found that the tumour had regrown. On its removal he once again became his original, sexually conventional self. This is strong evidence that his behaviour was caused by the tumour impairing prefrontal functions.

More recently, Tost et al. (2004) used tasks based in the prefrontal cortex to show that four paedophiles were very impaired, while their performance on tasks associated with other brain structures was normal. Together these studies suggest a role for the prefrontal cortex in paedophilia: it may be that moral judgement, or self-control, or some other function, is both important in keeping levels of child abuse down and also based in the prefrontal cortex.

There are also many cases where previously law-abiding adults who have had their prefrontal cortex damaged have then developed anti-social, psychopathic character-istics, including low arousal, thus supporting the research we have discussed.

The temporal lobe

The temporal lobes have a covering of cortex like a tablecloth on a table. Under this is a sizeable space where the amygdala sits: this is known to be critical in strong negative emotions like anger and fear. Along its lower side the sheet of cortex is rolled up like a Swiss roll: the edge that ends up in the centre of the roll is hemmed with the hippocampus, a structure critical in anxiety, memory and controlling anger. Damage to the hippocampus, amygdala and the front half of the temporal cortex on the left side of the brain has been shown to often produce violent behaviour, and the amygdala is part of a system including the prefrontal cortex that controls aggressive behaviour. Damage to the amygdala can result also in an inability to empathize with others, the loss of emotional memory and emotional under-arousal, all factors which we have seen to be linked to criminal behaviour (Martens 2002).

Mendez and colleagues (2000) found that two patients with homosexual paedophilia starting after brain damage showed substantial underactivity in the front half of their right temporal lobe. One was a case of frontotemporal dementia, the other had damage to the hippocampus on both sides of the brain. This is consistent with other evidence that damage to the right temporal lobe can produce an increase in sexual behaviour, especially inappropriate sexual acts.

So how can we make sense of all this? Bufkin and Luttrell (2005) have recently reviewed 17 brain-imaging studies on aggressive, violent offenders. They argue that the prefrontal cortex and the temporal lobe in the amygdala and hippocampus region work together in a system to regulate negative emotions. Kiehl et al. (2001) found that criminal psychopaths showed significantly less emotionally related activity in the temporal cortex and in part of the prefrontal cortex as well as in a connected part of the brain important in producing behaviour (the striatum). At the same time the rest of their prefrontal and temporal cortex was over-active.

This seems to tie together the studies that implicate the frontal cortex with those highlighting the temporal lobe: both are part of a system critically important in emotional processing and controlling impulsive, aggressive and sexual behaviour.

The two sides of the brain

There is evidence that lower than normal right-hemisphere functioning might be important in the lower heart rate clearly linked to higher risk of criminal behaviour. Damage to the right side of the brain in adulthood has been shown to reduce the patient's response to negative emotional stimuli. This supports the idea that the fearlessness and impaired ability to learn from negative consequences known to be risk factors for criminal behaviour might be due to right-hemisphere underactivity (Raine 2002a).

Dysfunction of the left hemisphere has been convincingly associated with violence and criminal behaviour in psychopaths, sex offenders, people with conduct disorder, children showing anti-social behaviour, male violent offenders and others, using several methods (Raine 1993). More recently, Raine et al. (2003b) have measured the size of the corpus callosum (the great band of fibres connecting the two halves of the cortex) in 15 men with anti-social personality disorder and high psychopathy scores and in 25 controls. They found several differences that imply greater connectivity between the two halves in the anti-social group. The greater the volume of the corpus callosum the lower the men's response to stress was and the more they showed the signs of psychopathy.

The type of evidence outlined here, although quite detailed and technical, suggests that the balance of activity between the hemispheres might be abnormal in those predisposed to criminal behaviour, although it is not yet clear how best to interpret it.

QUESTION BREAK

- Do you think that frontal damage, or frontal malfunction from birth, should be taken into account when deciding guilt?
- What about when deciding sentence?
- What should we do with such people after they have served their sentence?

In summary, there is evidence that the brains of some offenders are different in function and structure from those of non-offenders. This is particularly striking for life-course-persistent, impulsive, violent offenders.

DEVELOPMENT OF THE BRAIN

This section brings together many of the ideas from this chapter and will help you to understand how the different biological perspectives interlock. It also emphasizes the biosocial interaction at the heart of human life.

Anti-social behaviour is not unusual, so it is unlikely that much of it is caused by dramatic problems such as tumours, maladaptive genes or injuries. Over the last fifty years researchers have begun to understand the normal processes by which our brain develops in response to our environment (Schore 1997). This development certainly continues into our early twenties (Andersen 2003) and in all likelihood will be found to go on past the age of 30. In this section on early development we look at what happens up to puberty.

Even in the womb the baby is sensitive to the mother's environment. At the end of the Second World War there was a famine in the Netherlands where the population was reduced to eating such things as tulip bulbs, grass and rats (Hart 1993). Women who were in the third trimester of pregnancy at the time gave birth to underweight babies. However, those in the first trimester had overweight babies on average and when the females grew up and went on to have their own children they too were heavier than average (Motluk 2004). This was unexpected and shows the power of the environment to change biology: it is argued that this is a response to adapt the baby to the environment it is going to be living in (Vines 1998) and it may be working by a mechanism called imprinting where genes can be turned off for long periods before being passed on to the next generation or even beyond.

Even more dramatic effects can be seen in many mammals if a pregnant female is stressed during pregnancy: for example rabbits will reabsorb growing embryos and, after birth, stressed guinea pigs will eat their own babies. Both of these behaviours save resources for when they can be better used to bring up offspring successfully. In humans it is suspected that maternal stress can predispose a child to be anxious and in one study to double the chance of hyperactivity in boys (Glover and O'Connor 2002).

In humans, babies exposed to alcohol in the womb can have their development impaired. If the mother drinks heavily the babies may show foetal alcohol syndrome (FAS) which is seen in about one in five hundred births worldwide. FAS is due to brain damage, especially to the prefrontal cortex, which leads to impulsivity, hyperactivity, attention difficulties, learning disabilities and problems with thinking things out – all of which, as we have seen, are risk factors for criminal behaviour. Unsurprisingly when they grow into their teens and beyond such children are at significantly greater risk of being imprisoned (Boland et al. 1998). Recently there has been evidence that even low levels of drinking during pregnancy can lead to less severe forms of these problems (Hall 2005).

Using drugs such as cocaine (powder or crack), heroin or methamphetamine can have severe consequences for the baby's brain, behaviour and likelihood of later criminal behaviour (MedlinePlus 2005). People are often surprised that smoking tobacco during pregnancy has been shown to increase the child's chance of criminal behaviour: in six studies since 1992, four showed clear evidence and two limited support. These are not small effects: one study found twice the risk of a criminal record at 22 years.

Besides drugs, exposure to toxins such as lead, mercury, pesticides, industrial chemicals that mimic hormones (such as pthalates which are used to keep some plastics soft) and many other environmentally widespread poisons can distort brain development and lead to increased chances of criminal behaviour (Galen 2000). If there are medical problems during pregnancy, for example bleeding or infections, there is an increased chance of the baby having minor physical anomalies (MPAs) such as lower ears than average or a furrowed tongue. These are an indicator of disturbed development and mean that is likely that the brain has also been slightly affected. MPAs are associated with aggression, impulsivity and behavioural problems at school in children from the age of three years. They have also been shown to indicate a higher risk of teenage conduct disorder and adult violent offending (Raine 2002a). Note the link to earlier beliefs that to be physically ugly indicated moral weakness.

The next danger is at birth itself where complications such as lack of oxygen, forceps delivery and pre-eclampsia have been linked to conduct disorder, delinquency, impulsive crimes and violence as an adult in a range of studies (Raine 2002a).

In case you are now terrified of having a child, or feeling guilty for having given birth to the next serial killer, here is the good news: there is very strong and convincing evidence that all of these factors can be counteracted by a stable, supportive upbringing (Raine 2002b). As we have repeatedly seen, it is when there are both a biological predisposition and then a bad environment that the most serious problems arise. This is an example of biological research showing the importance of the non-biological environment and gives a very encouraging message to parents as well as suggesting how governments might reduce biologically influenced anti-social or criminal behaviour without doping our children up on the latest pharmaceutical product.

- What type of environment do you think will lead to successful biological development?
- How might a child's upbringing change the impact of early biological disruption?
- How might growing up as a witness to domestic violence or as a subject of abuse disturb normal biological development?

As regards the complex interactions between mother and baby, and identifying some of the key factors leading to successful early maturation, it is now believed that the first two to three years of life are crucial in the development of emotion (or affect). In the aftermath of the Second World War there were a great many orphans and the World Health Organization funded research into their needs. In a famous report Bowlby (1951) showed the dire effects of being brought up with enough food, clothes and other physical staples but without real emotional contact with a carer. Such children grew up to be emotionally damaged. These findings have been replicated many times in group settings (e.g. Groza et al. 2003) and in individual cases of extreme neglect (e.g. Rymer 1993).

The more recent studies do show the possibility of counteracting the damage by providing a supportive, patient family environment through later childhood but also emphasize the long-term consequences in behaviour, emotional sensitivity and expression and mental health if early neglect is not dealt with effectively. These studies emphasize the interplay between biology and the social and physical environment. A person's earliest experiences shape the development of their brain and so change the way they will respond in future. We know that children with the types of behavioural patterns that make them more likely to become criminals are also more likely to have had neglectful or abusive childhoods.

The evidence that genes are important in conduct disorder (AACAP 1997) and that systems using the transmitter serotonin are disturbed (Lahey et al. 1993) highlights the biological-environmental interaction at the heart of human development. This seems to be a common way in which biological systems have evolved: our genes describe a generally useful set-up but the set-up then adapts to the environment we happen to have been born into. This is a powerful way of dealing with the fact that evolution is 'blind' and cannot tell what the world will be like in the future.

One of the psychological constructs most clearly linked to development is that of attachment. Bowlby (1951) and Harlow (1962) set the stage for later work, especially by Ainsworth and her colleagues (Ainsworth et al. 1978). Cicchetti and Barnett (1991) found that a massive 80 per cent of abused or maltreated infants showed signs of attachment disorders.

In addition to attachment researchers have shown that the style of discipline in a family has important long-term consequences (Wade and Kendler 2001). Discipline styles may be summarized as warm-consistent (clear rules, talking not hitting), warm-inconsistent (rules not clear, but talking not hitting), cold-consistent (clear rules, physically enforced) and cold-inconsistent (rules not clear with hitting not talking): these styles interact with attachment styles and together lead to long-term consequences (Kerr et al. 2004; Johnson and Smailes 2004).

It is clear that these psychological differences reflect biological differences and will also make it more or less likely that a person will engage in anti-social and criminal activity – for example an impulsive, uncontrolled person who has grown up without clear rules in an atmosphere of arbitrary violence is more likely to behave anti-socially as an adult (Hirschi 1995; George and West 1999).

Extreme or chronic stressful experiences, such as abuse or witnessing domestic violence, lead to high levels of stress-related hormones that damage the brain, including the hippocampus which is critical in memory, dealing with stress and controlling aggression (McEwen 1999).

Case studies of serial killers often find that their childhood attachments and family discipline seem to be one of the building blocks that lead to their extreme criminal acts. Harvey Carignan, convicted of multiple rape and homicide, was the illegitimate son of a 20-year-old who could not cope. She passed him round numerous temporary carers, thus undermining any proper attachment and exposing him to inconsistent but physical discipline. He grew up to be a very hostile man who hated all women (Berry-Dee 2003).

We are now in a position to see how all the biological threads can be drawn together to suggest a consistent model of the biology underlying criminal behaviour. The evidence also shows how preposterous it is to suggest that biology alone, or even more ridiculously just one biological factor, can explain criminal behaviour – only a biosocial interaction model is consistent with the evidence.

QUESTION BREAK

- Which aspects of early family life might be important in how an infant develops as a person?
- Thinking about yourself, your children or people you know, can you identify behaviours that we have seen are linked to offending?
- Did they always show them or was it more obvious at one period of their lives?
- Do you think people can be anti-social and delinquent in their teens and early twenties but good citizens later in life?

CONCLUSION

In concluding this chapter we will use two case studies to try and draw the various threads and issues together. Read through them and then consider the questions at the end.

John Eastlack

John Eastlack was sentenced to death for brutally beating an elderly Tucson couple, Kathryn and Leicester Sherrill, to death in their home in 1989. At appeal his sentence was reduced to life imprisonment. In her decision the judge said that the biological vulnerabilities caused by his previously undiagnosed foetal alcohol syndrome, together with his genetic vulnerability – deduced from his biological family's history of generations of substantial mental illness and criminality – made him less able to understand what was right and wrong, not able to feel guilt and less able to control his behaviour.

Eastlack was taken from his mother at birth, then went through various foster homes (one of which had handed him back so the foster parents could more easily go on holiday). His father was shot to death soon after John's birth when caught stealing cash from a pinball machine.

By the time he was adopted by a loving, supportive family he was already a habitual liar and thief with learning difficulties. Bringing up a child who was so demanding, and who soon began to get into trouble at school and ended up in an institution for juvenile criminals for theft, was a reason behind the divorce of his adoptive parents.

Eventually he was sentenced to nine years' imprisonment for credit card fraud but he escaped from the Arizona State prison, and was on the run when he broke into the Sherrills' home. At the trial he said that the wife had attacked him with a poker and he had then beaten them both to death and fled in their car. He said that he had felt as if he was watching events unfold rather than as if he was actually committing them himself (Revere 1999).

This is a typical case of biological damage and illustrates the interaction between the biological and environmental factors that make it almost impossible to decide what was the ultimate cause of his actions that night.

Charles Whitman

This case also illustrates the danger that taking the 'obvious' biological view may lead you to miss the environmental factors that are at least as important in understanding an offence.

Whitman was one of the first 'spree' killers to be widely covered in the media. In 1966 he climbed the University of Texas Tower and spent 96 minutes shooting randomly chosen victims before killing himself. At autopsy he was found to have a tumour on the amygdala, an area known to be critical in intense negative emotions. Stimulation of the amygdala in animals, or damage to it in humans, is known to be capable of causing extreme violence. Therefore that may well have been a critical factor behind the murders he committed that day.

However a more detailed examination of his story (MacLeod n.d.) reveals evidence of other possible biological factors. Whitman's father had an extreme temper, leading to his beating his wife and son. This is consistent with a genetic vulnerability in his son, but of course also illustrates a family environment that taught the use of violence. As with John Eastman, the domestic violence he witnessed and experienced are likely to have led to biological changes that increased the likelihood of him offending as well.

If his, relatively small, tumour was important we might expect his violence to be something that began near the time of the murders. Several years previously he had said to a number of people that the tower would be a perfect place from which to shoot passers-by, suggesting that the thought patterns shown in his crime were already present, in part.

He was sponsored by the Marines to attend university, but without clear rules he began to display criminal and violent behaviours. He was arrested for poaching deer, did not pay gambling debts and got poor grades, ending his sponsorship. Back at a Marine camp at the end of 1963 he was court-martialled for gambling, unauthorized possession of firearms and threatening a fellow soldier over a debt of $30. In addition, he had beaten his wife on several occasions: although he made efforts to stop this behaviour with some success, he also had fits of temper; she filed for divorce in 1966.

In early 1966 his wife did report that he had been getting depressed and anxious, which is consistent both with a tumour and with the growing pressures in his life. He went to a doctor, and told him that he had fantasized about shooting people from the tower.

Whitman then began using amphetamines to help him work. Amphetamine use increases the chance of violent behaviour. Drug or alcohol abuse is perhaps the most important risk factor for violent crime in general: it increases a person's risk to others by about fourteen times (in comparison severe schizophrenia increases a person's danger to others by only about four times) (Eisenberg 2005).

In his suicide note he did state that his violent fantasies had been increasing and that his treatment had not helped. He also wrote that he was going to kill his wife and mother because the world was such an awful place that he did not want to leave them to suffer. This is not an unusual theme in cases where depression drives a parent to commit suicide and also kill their own children: depression is influenced by both biological and environmental factors.

He then killed his mother followed by his wife and completed his thorough preparations to enact his fantasy. During his killing spree he murdered 14 passers-by and wounded dozens more.

QUESTION BREAK

The case studies above illustrate some of the difficulties in determining causes of criminal behaviour – and the difficulty of settling on either biology or the environment as *the* cause.

- Do you agree with the appeal court judge's comments concerning John Eastlack? Suggest reasons for and against her decision that Eastlack was not as culpable as someone who had not had the biological vulnerabilities he had thrust upon him.

- On consideration of the second case, do you think the genes Whitman inherited made him more likely to act violently, or that his environment was a more convincing cause? Why might people feel that he was less culpable if his biology had been an obvious cause than if the dominant cause was his family and later environment?

SUMMARY

As we have stressed, modern biologists do not look for 'the crime gene', they look for genes that increase a person's probability of committing particular types of offence in certain environments. The large majority of them do not think that black young men in the USA and Britain are more likely to be imprisoned because of their biology. Even if there were to be biological differences there are clear factors such as poverty that are much more plausible causal factors (Jones 2005).

Evolutionary psychologists do not think that biological explanations will destroy the utility of concepts such as responsibility and morality. If a child shoots a friend dead while playing a game of soldiers with the father's loaded handgun we accept that they are not morally, or legally, responsible owing to their age and consequent immaturity. Surely we can find a way to deal with cases of people who, for other biological reasons, may have reduced culpability?

Violent and other crimes seem to be universally found in human societies: indeed the evidence suggests that levels of violence and murder are considerably higher in pre-state, hunter-gatherer groups than in the type of state we find in Europe and many other parts of the world (Pinker 2005): when the state structure breaks down, as in the former Yugoslavia, crime rates soar. Surely we do have evolved tendencies to behave in certain anti-social and criminal ways in certain circumstances, and part of normal male development is to compete in ways that include criminal behaviour. Although this does not mean that we have to accept behaviours that harm other members of society, 'natural' does not mean 'moral' or 'right'.

As to the role of biological perspectives on anti-social and criminal behaviour in helping to understand and deal with such behaviour, maybe the effective response is not to try to ignore biology but to learn enough so that you can understand it and make an informed contribution to the debate (Stangroom 2005). The greatest dangers have arisen when people without scientific knowledge (including politicians like Stalin or Hitler) have taken up scientific hypotheses with no real understanding and based policies upon their own ignorance.

FURTHER READING

Daly, M. and Wilson, M. (1998) *The Truth About Cinderella*. London: Weidenfeld & Nicolson. A very short and easy read. Clearly sets out their argument that stepfathers are much more dangerous to children than biological fathers. Puts it in an evolutionary psychology framework.

Raine, A. (1994) *The Psychopathology of Crime: Criminal Behavior as a Clinical Disorder*. New York: Academic Press. The most important text in this area. Sets out to address the most common criticisms made of the biological approach to explaining crime. Clearly written but does assume some knowledge.

Rowe, D. (2002) *Biology and Crime*. Los Angeles: Roxbury. A short textbook that is especially good on the genetic and evolutionary explanations. If you are new to this area read it with a 'Dummy's Guide' to genetics and evolution by your side and you should be able to understand it all.

WEBSITE

http://www.crime-times.org/. A website devoted to spreading the word about biological explanations of crime. Very clear and covers the latest research and has archives going back at least ten years.

Psychological Explanations for Criminal Behaviour

INTRODUCTION

For many centuries, we have attempted to find out which people are likely to become criminals and what drives certain individuals to commit a particular type of crime in the first place. Over the years psychologists have considered a range of different explanations in order to answer these difficult questions. Some have argued that there may be a genetic explanation which is at the centre of explaining criminal behaviour; others have suggested that it is the environment in which people live which can influence their chance of becoming criminal.

At different periods in history these ideas have been prominent in the minds of not only psychologists but also other professionals and the public alike. However nobody has seemingly provided a comprehensive and infallible answer to the question of criminality. This chapter will introduce some of the key theories that psychologists have attempted to use to explain criminal behaviour, such as personality, social factors and cognition.

CRIMINALITY AS AN ELEMENT OF PERSONALITY

It is common for us to attach labels to criminals and attempt to explain their behaviour through describing them as possessing a certain character trait. For example, it is common to refer to some criminals as 'psychos' – particularly in films and the newspapers. This type of person is actually called a psychopath and labels such as these have been developed by psychologists to help us understand the different types of personality category that people fit into. Not all of these are criminal, but it is assumed that many criminals possess similar personality characteristics. Clearly there are some important factors to criminality that can be explained by situational and developmental factors, but there is also the psychological element to criminal activity that is relatively unique to that individual. One possible explanation for this desire to uncover the psychological traits of offenders is that it provides a quantifiable difference between 'us' and 'them' and to some extent further defines law-breakers as being almost another 'breed' of person. The following section will describe the different explanations of *criminal personality* and why some people are more prone to criminal behaviour than others.

QUESTION BREAK

- Consider your own personality and list the key characteristics of it.
- Where did these characteristics come from?
- Describe what you think a criminal personality might consist of.

You might find it interesting to refer back to these answers when you have finished this chapter.

Intelligence

One prominent idea surrounding the nature of criminal personality concerns the notion of intelligence. When we talk about intelligence we are generally referring to a person's intellectual ability or IQ (Intelligence Quotient – usually measured by an IQ test, such as the 11+ exam that used to be taken by children at the end of their primary school education). The link between intelligence and crime is regarded as being *negatively correlated* (i.e. as the rate of one rises the prevalence of the other diminishes) and it is thought that people with low IQs are more likely to become criminals. One of the first to propose this was Goddard (1914) in his book called *Feeble-Mindedness: Its Causes and Consequences*. Here Goddard suggested that it was low intelligence that made criminals unable to learn socially acceptable conduct and resist offending behaviour. A later study by Zeleny (1933) postulated that criminals were nearly twice as likely to be low scorers on IQ tests than non-criminals. These studies and many similar ones have suggested that people who have low intelligence are for many reasons (mostly the inability to learn rules) more likely to become criminals. It is probably due to its simplicity that this theory has been popular for many years and indeed still does have a significant research interest in more recent times.

Longitudinal studies have consistently shown that intelligence is a relatively reliable predictor in children of later adolescent and adult offending. One such examination known as the Cambridge Study (Farrington 1992) followed a group of males from birth into adulthood. Farrington reported that over a third of the eight-to-ten year-old boys who scored less than 90 (below average) on a test of non-verbal intelligence were later convicted of a criminal offence. This was twice the conviction rate of the remainder of the sample. It was also discovered that this low level of non-verbal intelligence was particularly characteristic of recidivism in juveniles and of those who were to be convicted of offences when aged ten to 13 years.

There could be a number of explanations as to why intelligence may be related to criminal behaviour in this way. Firstly, there is a possibility that those with low intelligence could be more likely to be actually caught when committing crime. Their evaluation and selection of crimes may not be as successful as those who are more astute. However, West and Farrington (1977) also found that this link remained even when the measurement of offending was not arrest data but individual self-report measures. The second possibility is that the less intelligent could simply be more ready to admit to committing crime. This could be in an interrogation by the police or in self-report evaluations. Quay (1987) believes this could be also as a result of not understanding the charges being presented to them. Such a hypothesis remains largely untested and difficult to quantify. There is support however for the differences between offenders and non-offenders on measures of intelligence reflecting only *verbal* intelligence. Hirschi and Hindelang (1977) found limited support for any real discrepancies between the two groups in *non-verbal* intelligence.

However, despite these early assumptions regarding intelligence and criminal behaviour there are a number of problems in simply accepting this apparent link. Firstly, defining exactly what we mean by 'crime' and similarly 'intelligence' is not as simple as it may first appear. Although the development and use of IQ tests has improved considerably since the days of Goddard and Zelany, there is still debate as to what intelligence actually is. For example, some people may be highly competent mathematicians but have poor social skills and other people may be excellent artists but poor at organizing themselves. Secondly, what makes somebody a criminal is also open to some debate. It cannot be assumed that what makes a person a criminal is the fact that they have been convicted of breaking a law. The majority of people have probably committed a crime of some description – even if it was as seemingly minor as breaking the speed limit whilst driving – so it is inappropriate that just because someone was caught, they should then be seen as different from those who eluded being apprehended. In addition, there are probably big differences between someone convicted of financial fraud and a violent murderer. In short, it is therefore difficult both to define and to measure intelligence and crime so easily.

Despite these limitations in allowing us to explain criminal behaviour in this way, there are many studies that still include intelligence as a variable when assessing offenders. There is now, though, the recognition that low intelligence might not be a personality feature of the individual *per se*, but in fact a result of poverty or other social factors. Instead of low intelligence causing crime, it could equally be possible that coming from a poor neighbourhood influences the educational skills available to a person. There is extensive research to support the idea that people with low incomes and limited access to employment are more likely to be involved in criminal activities. Hence it is too simplistic to assume that a person who does not score high on an IQ test will become a criminal for that reason alone.

There are many other factors that may vary in their influence on unlawful behaviour. For example, if two people with similar IQ scores came from two different localities – one rich, one poor – then their risk of offending is likely to be different. Their behaviour is not purely a function of their intelligence. Hence it is almost impossible to separate the link between intelligence and propensity for criminal behaviour from environmental and even possible hereditary factors. Hirschi and Hindelang (1977) reviewed many studies reporting the link between crime and intelligence, and discovered overall that, when socio-economic factors are statistically controlled for, the pattern remains. Nevertheless, there is a vast amount of research into intelligence and crime and it highlights the difficulties in researching criminal behaviour in general and finding one simple answer to explain this type of activity. It should be remembered that, although there is often a relationship between intelligence and crime, it is seldom proposed that low intelligence actually *causes* crime.

QUESTION BREAK

- How would a researcher go about testing whether criminal behaviour was a result of a poor upbringing or as a result of poor intelligence?
- Suggest the advantages and disadvantages of different research methods.
- What other areas of social research have used similar methods?

CASE STUDY BOX 3.1 TWIN STUDIES

When researchers are interested in finding out if behaviour is a result of genetics or the environment which an individual grows up in, they often try to isolate one variable by using twins as their subjects. Mono-zygotic (MZ) or identical twins have exactly the same DNA, meaning they should have exactly the same physical and mental attributes. Research into intelligence has made significant use of such methods. If intelligence is genetically based, then two identical people (i.e. MZ twins) should have the same IQ score even if they were raised in different environments. Similarly, if crime were genetically based, then two MZ twins would have the same predisposition for crime. Indeed, Blackburn (1999) reports that most MZ twins reared apart show comparable levels of intelligence, and similarities on personality and attitude measures. Twin studies are popular in the social sciences as they allow any genetic influence to be controlled and the behaviours that are observed to be accounted for by other factors. Such research is expensive and, although many twins volunteer to be included in studies, access to samples is difficult.

For more detail on twin studies in relation to studying criminal behaviour, see Chapter 2, pp. 35–6.

Impulsivity

Aside from intelligence, there are other personality traits that have been implicated in the acquisition of criminal tendencies. One such area has been termed *impulsivity*. From a clinical perspective, being impulsive describes behaviours where people are likely to act almost on instinct and seldom weigh up the consequences of their actions. This process of 'acting without thinking' has found a receptive audience amongst criminologists and forensic psychologists in providing another way of explaining why some people commit crime and others don't. Glueck and Glueck (1950) were early pioneers of such thought, and believed that poor self-control mechanisms led to impulsive and often criminal behaviour. The public perception of the rampaging, 'out of control' offender also found harmony with these ideas. The modern-day juvenile is often described as being a 'hooligan' and certainly conjures up images of marauding gangs of youths who are seemingly uncontrollable. Large-scale public unrest and protests also fuel this image of people being out of control.

Early sociologists debated the idea that there were differences in the social classes' ability to *delay gratification* – people from higher social classes were assumed to be able to plan for the future and set a path to reap greater rewards for sacrificing earlier gains. For example, attending higher education courses was seen as delaying the immediate benefits of employment in order to access better-paid jobs in the future. Similarly, criminals have been assumed to act in a way that seeks to maximize their immediate desires without considering the likely future consequences that these actions may have, such as imprisonment. Criminals are therefore assumed to have poor control mechanisms that cause them to seek immediate satisfaction of their needs (see Gottfredson and Hirschi 1990 and Chapter 4 below). Longitudinal studies that follow individuals over a period of time or even their whole lifetime have shown this to be a relatively enduring and stable trait amongst offenders (e.g. Farrington 1992). However, as with intelligence, the link between impulsivity and crime is not so simple. Indeed much criminal behaviour is meticulously planned. Many financial frauds and robberies require very detailed planning and a complete lack of any impulsive behaviour.

Support for the link between impulsivity and crime has been mixed, in that reckless and spontaneous activity of a criminal nature is often observed in conjunction with many other personality and situational variables, e.g. in offenders who are under the influence of drugs and alcohol. Other researchers have elaborated on the nature of impulsivity and seldom describe it as an umbrella term to encompass any behaviour that has shown irresponsible and uncontrolled factors. For example, Dickman (1990) hypothesized that impulsivity was composed of two separate entities: functional and dysfunctional. Impulsive behaviour does not necessarily lead to offending behaviour, and indeed some spontaneity is often applauded in certain situations. Increased activity, adventurousness and enthusiasm were characteristic of the functional type of impulsivity. Hence, dysfunctional impulsivity is more closely linked with offending in that the behaviours generally have negative consequences for the individual. Disorderliness, poor appraisal of facts and lack of concern for the consequences of actions were symptomatic of people experiencing dysfunctional impulsivity. The difference between these two forms has been supported both in adults (Claes,

Vertommen and Braspenning 2000) and in children (Brunas-Wagstaff et al. 1997). Its prevalence in criminal populations has yet to be sufficiently established. But the ineffective thinking styles that are implicated in criminal activity are quite apparent between the two types. Impulsive criminals have also been seen to behave in a generally reckless – not necessarily criminal – way and to seek excitement in many situations.

QUESTION BREAK

Draw a line and write 'impulsivity' at one end of it and 'careful planning' at the other.

Place the following crimes at where you feel to be the appropriate place on this line:

- Shoplifting
- Drug dealing
- Fraud
- Burglary
- Assault

Think of other crimes and add them to the line.

Part of the problem with assessing impulsivity as a correlate of criminal behaviour is the differing theoretical perspectives that underpin the explanation of this personality trait. For example, as with the psychodynamic theory (see p. 67), impulsivity is suggested to be a result of poor ego-control. The drive impulses of the id are not adequately suppressed and the individual seeks to satisfy them in a manner that may infringe on current laws. Conversely, social learning theorists see the suggestion of impulsivity as a lack of self-control as being determined by situational forces as well as the individual's own inner narrative. Regardless of the theoretical paradigm as to where impulsivity is believed to originate from, there is also a practical problem in its measurement and intensity. Blackburn (1999) reports numerous measures of impulsivity that have originated from more general personality inventories. One problem with using these scales is that they have usually not been validated on offender populations. When personality measures are created, they are tested and retested on very large samples to ensure that they are valid and reliable. If it is valid and it measures what the researchers hoped it would (i.e. a personality feature) then they must make sure that it could do this over and over again – its reliability in identifying this trait. This means that a 'normal' score is based upon certain factors and generally applies to the population that they tested during developing these scales. Hence, offenders might score differently only because they interpret the questions differently, not because they are actually unalike. Nevertheless, they do show some marked differences between the control 'non-offender' samples. There is also the question as to whether impulsivity merely predicts the prevalence of offending behaviour rather than its simple occurrence.

CASE STUDY BOX 3.2 ATTENTION DEFICIT AND HYPERACTIVITY DISORDER

Attention deficit and hyperactivity disorder (or ADHD as it is commonly abbreviated) is a personality disorder that was proposed in the American Psychological Society's *Diagnostic and Statistical Manual* (DSM). The DSM lists a number of symptoms that psychologists and psychiatrists have identified as defining a particular abnormal pattern of behaviour. Those for ADHD are:

- Symptoms of inattention: missing important work details, not listening, forgetting instructions, forgetful, always losing things
- Symptoms of hyperactivity: frequent fidgeting, excessive talking, inability to remain seated
- Symptoms of impulsivity: blurting out answers to questions, inability to wait their turn, constant interruption of others.

Researchers have only recently explored the link between ADHD and crime. There is also some debate about the diagnosis of ADHD and about the fact that it is being used to explain any children who have even minor behavioural problems. But the link with impulsivity and crime is a compelling one and the role of the frontal lobes of the brain are implicated in explaining both ADHD and impulsivity (see Chapter 2 for a detailed discussion on the brain and behaviour). Research in this area is relatively new and no firm conclusions can be drawn as yet. What is apparent, though, is that many of the symptoms of ADHD have been found in longitudinal studies of juveniles and their likelihood of committing crime (see Farrington 1992). Moffitt (1990) and many other researchers also believe that ADHD sufferers are at increased risk of becoming chronic alcohol and drug users. Coupled with the interpersonal effects of impulsivity, there are then the added dangers that the well-documented links with drugs and crime pose.

Locus of control

A factor related to impulsivity and another prominent feature that has been hypothesized as being related to personality and a tendency for criminal behaviour is the idea of *locus of control* (Rotter 1975). Whereas impulsivity was concerned with the way in which offenders might not anticipate the consequences of their actions adequately, the idea of having a locus of control describes the way in which people accept there being different explanations for things that happen. People with an *internal* locus of control perceive events as being largely under their own command. Those with an *external* locus of control see occurrences as resulting from forces beyond their influence. With regard to criminal behaviour, offenders are generally assumed to have a distinct external bias in their personality. Hence offenders generally put the consequences of their actions, for example being arrested or injured, down to other forces such as luck. Foglia (2000) believes that children who are repeatedly exposed to situations where they only have minimal influence – in particular absent or mentally ill parents – are more likely to develop an external orientation to their being. What results is often an increased risk of delinquency. As with impulsivity, offenders with an external locus of control are unlikely to adequately appreciate the consequences of their actions, but for very different reasons.

Rotter's (1975) theory has a widely accepted audience both from criminal researchers and from wider social science users, but the research is inconclusive with regard to providing an adequate explanation of criminal behaviour. Although some studies have indicated that some offenders have a high external locus of control, others have not. Indeed some have shown that certain offender populations have a higher internal locus of control than non-offender samples. As with many of the discussions on the criminal personality, the inconsistencies in research findings are possibly attributable to the difficulty of adequately defining both the concept in question and what exactly constitutes a criminal. For example, internal and external controls have been shown to deviate depending upon the subject under examination, e.g. a job interview versus a political event (Mirels 1970). Despite these contradictions, locus of control has been argued to be an important predictor of people who are at *risk* of becoming involved in criminal behaviour (Werner 1989). In addition, many cognitive-behavioural rehabilitation programmes delivered in prisons attempt to address offenders' behaviour by questioning such belief systems.

Cognitive behavioural theories (the work of Hans Eysenck)

Intelligence, impulsivity and locus of control are just some of the more prominent theories that have emerged in an attempt to explain criminal personalities. It can be seen that there are many shortcomings in trying to assign this to any one cause. Subsequently, many researchers believe that offending is multi-faceted – it has more than one cause and more than one explanation. For example, the fact that someone has a low IQ does not necessarily mean that they will commit crime. Similarly, some offenders might have high levels of impulse control, but choose to offend for entirely different reasons. Owing to this, there have been a number of 'complete' theories that try to show how the interplays between these and many other variables interact and result in criminal behaviour. Two in particular will be discussed in more detail – those of Hans Eysenck and his *Theory of Crime* (see below) and Yochelson and Samenow's idea of a *Criminal Personality* (later in this chapter, see p. 75).

Hans Eysenck is perhaps one of the most well-known and widely published psychologists in recent times, and his research interests span many areas from general personality to intelligence and also criminal behaviour. Eysenck's (1974) theory of crime is a combination theory in that it includes elements of biological antecedents and environmental influences, along with specific personality traits that are assumed to underpin criminal behaviour. For Eysenck, it was impossible to ignore hereditary and social causes of offending. Instead he believed that poor cognitive or 'thinking' skills were passed down through generations, which then affected the person's ability to effectively deal with external situations and in particular unlawful ones that presented themselves. The interplay between poor social conditioning and inability to comprehend such conditioning subsequently created the criminal personality. Eysenck believed that there were many similarities in the way that a mental illness is acquired and how criminality developed. For example, schizophrenia often runs in families and can therefore be regarded as having a genetic component. However, not everybody will inherit this disorder if they have schizophrenic parents and likewise it is also possible to acquire this disease without any hereditary component. Both genetic factors (having schizophrenic parents) *and* social factors (such as drug taking) can lead to schizophrenia. Hence, in the same way, certain types of personality were more inclined to act in a criminal manner in light of environmental stimuli.

Eysenck's theory of crime essentially explained the criminal personality as resulting from the interaction between three major psychological traits: *neuroticism* (N), *extraversion* (E) and *psychoticism* (P). To begin with, a neurotic can be loosely defined as a person who is suffering from anxiety and appear 'nervous' and 'moody'. However, the manner in which neurotics are defined in Eysenck's theory is not the strict clinical meaning and many 'neurotic criminals' would not be seen as suffering from a mental disorder. The second and perhaps most integral part of this explanation of criminal personality is the dimension known as Introvert–Extrovert. Generally introverts are described as being quiet, withdrawn people and conversely extroverts as being outgoing and impulsive. Explanations for this vary, but from within this current theory it is the level of cortical (or brain) stimulation that is important. Extroverts have low cortical arousal and seek excitement to maintain levels of stimulation; Introverts are over-stimulated and avoid stirring situations to avoid becoming over-aroused. Finally psychoticism – which is similar to the more modern term of psychopathy (see Hare 1980) – describes people whose personality is characterized by poor emotion, sensation-seeking and general lack of empathy for others. This final variable was added later to the theory, as it was not initially characteristic of all offenders. Later testing did indicate a certain prevalence of this trait amongst many offender groups.

The relationship between these three personality dimensions is for Eysenck the essence of the criminal personality. Specifically, the interplay between these variables is assumed to limit severely the ability of an individual to be conditioned or socialized into a non-criminal way of thinking and behaving. People who were highly neurotic, highly psychotic and were also extraverts epitomized the criminal being. Alternatively, those who were introverts with low scores on neuroticism and psychoticism were seen to be ideal candidates for social conditioning and less likely therefore to become involved in criminal activity. Interestingly, psychoticism is regarded as being particularly prominent in offenders who display hostility towards others (Hollin 1989). Individual differences relating to the speed and intensity of conditioned responses would therefore explain the correlations between personality dimensions and levels of criminality. An evolution of the separate N, E and P scales was the amalgamation of the highest scoring items to create the *criminality* (C) scale (Eysenck and Eysenck,

1971). These are the actual statements that best identified the criminals from the non-criminals, which were then combined to make this separate scale. This has been reported to be an even greater discriminator in identifying offenders – both adult and juvenile. Interestingly, Eysenck (1987) reports that little in the way of gender differences have been reported, but that high levels of neuroticism are associated with adult offending, and extraversion is more prominent in younger offenders. Possible reasons for this included the potential difficulty for adult offenders who had been incarcerated in accurately reflecting social activity important for assessing extraversion.

CASE STUDY BOX 3.3 CRIMINAL PERSONALITY PROFILING

Criminal personality profiling, or offender profiling, is an investigative technique used by the police to help catch criminals. Many profilers believe that the personality of a criminal is reflected in the way they commit their crimes. One of the first major studies into offender profiling was conducted in the USA by the FBI (Ressler, Burgess and Douglas 1988). They conducted interviews with 36 incarcerated sexual murderers and ascertained a number of significant variables that were features of these offenders. In particular, they were to propose that these offenders could be separated into two main types: the organized and the disorganized. By examining the crime scene it was possible to determine which sort of offender had committed the crime. This then gave an indication of the 'type' of person they were looking for. For example, an organized offender was likely to be employed in semi-skilled labour, be married and have access to a vehicle. By contrast, a disorganized offender would be unemployed, live alone and have poor personal hygiene. This information could then be used to prioritize suspects during an investigation. Critics have suggested that this depiction of offenders is too simplistic and further research has produced alternative models. Holmes and Holmes (1996) for example propose a more varied taxonomy, which includes up to six different types of murderer.

Profiling is a useful tool for the police to help identify a suspect from a list of likely offenders, but is not always successful. One of the first cases where a profiler was used in Britain was in the case of the 'Railway Rapist' John Duffy who raped and murdered a number of women in the south of England in the 1980s. A psychologist called David Canter helped the police to identify a number of characteristics of the offender, which led the police to suspect Duffy (Canter 1994). In particular, Canter provided a geographic profile that showed that the likely offender would live in a certain area. This was done by analysing the criminal's spatial behaviour and the fact that he had a good knowledge of the railway system – Duffy worked as a carpenter for British Rail and usually offended near stations; hence the name given to him by the media. Other cases that have not been so successful include the murder of Rachel Nickell, who was stabbed as she walked with her young son on Wimbledon Common in 1991. Paul Britton, who was a well-known forensic psychologist, assisted the police and led them to suspect a man named Colin Stagg. When the police set up a trap using an undercover policewoman to try and get him to confess to the crime, Britton guided the operation by telling the police the way in which he believed Stagg would act (Britton 1997). He never confessed to the crime and when they brought him to court the judge refused to hear the case as they had inappropriately used profiling to try to trap a suspect. Nobody has ever been caught for the crime. Profiling can be useful to the police during difficult investigations but doesn't always lead to a suspect and must be used very carefully.

Although Eysenck and his colleagues have continually developed and refined their ideas on the nature of crime and personality, empirical support for its validity has also reported many discrepancies. McGurk and McDougall (1981) found high levels of neuroticism, extraversion and psychoticism amongst a cohort of juvenile offenders. Whilst there were mixtures of the three personality traits amongst these individuals and a control group of non-offenders, only these three variables were *all* present in the offenders. The converse – low-N, low-E and low-P – was discovered only in the non-offending sample. So whilst a mixture of these (e.g. low-N, high-E and high-P) might be present in both offenders and non-offenders, it was the extremes of each variable in combination that predicted criminal behaviour. Others disagree with these relationships and have reported differing levels of all three variables amongst criminal and non-criminal groups.

Eysenck's theory of crime has been widely reported in criminal research and indeed forms the basis of many discussions on the nature of criminal personality. Given the inconsistent findings of the high-E, high-N and high-P combinations amongst offender populations, it is generally regarded as too simplistic to define all criminal behaviour in these terms. Further to this there is a wider debate as to whether crime can be explained with reference to psychological factors at all and suggesting that the causes of crime are much further-reaching. Although Eysenck believed that biological and environmental factors essentially created these personality types, the issue of 'cause and effect' remained largely unanswered. But what did emerge was that criminal behaviour did have a cognitive element, in that it was an individual's thinking style and subsequent behaviour that led to criminal activity. It was a similar notion that drove Yochelson and Samenow (1976) to develop their theory of *The Criminal Personality* which will be explained in the section on cognitive theories of crime (p. 75).

QUESTION BREAK: USING SELF-REPORT INVENTORIES FOR ASSESSING PERSONALITY

When researchers attempt to explain and measure criminal personalities, they often use what are called 'self-report' inventories. Generally these are questionnaires that have a number of statements with which people respond to. For example, if we were trying to measure impulsivity, we might ask people a number of questions like: *Do you act without thinking about the consequences?* It is usual to give people a Likert-style response option, such as strongly agree, agree, don't know, disagree, strongly disagree. Each choice is then given a score and then all the responses are added up to give a total. Somebody who marks 'strongly agree' to the questions on the extraversion scale from Eysenck's Personality Inventory would therefore be judged to be an extravert. Psychologists then make judgements about the person on the strength of these scores and for instance, whether they are likely to commit crime. These types of test are widely used in all fields of psychology to measure different types of personality traits and attitudes, such as depression or self-esteem. However, although they can be used to explain why people differ on these personality traits, it is less clear as to why people with different characteristics behave in the way that they do. There is also the question of how they acquire these dispositions.

- Can you think of any problems associated with this method for identifying features of people's personality?
- What other ways might we use for assessing the psychological traits people show?

PRECURSORS OF CRIMINAL BEHAVIOUR

Other psychological explanations have not tried to explain crime in terms of a particular personality type. Such theories have typically looked for 'precursors', or reasons why a person may become involved in criminal behaviour, reasons which lie outside that individual's personality.

Psychodynamic theories – the influence of Sigmund Freud

A major early theory which attempted to explain criminal behaviour is the psychodynamic theory. The psychodynamic approach is based closely around the ideas of perhaps the most widely known psychologist, Sigmund Freud (1856–1939). Freud's ideas have been developed and modified by other psychologists over the years; however the work of Freud and his followers is still generically referred to as psychodynamic theory.

Psychodynamic ideas are extremely complex but a key notion is that of the 'unconscious mind'. Freud believed that much of our conscious behaviour is determined by unconscious influences of which we are unaware. The mind has a complicated structure which is built up through various stages of development. Freud thought there to be three key elements to the mind. Firstly there is the id, which Freud saw as the basic instincts that drive our behaviour. Secondly, the ego controls these basic urges by operating according to the reality principle. Thirdly, the superego is a form of internalization of the standards of society. At each stage of development the instincts of the id (within the unconscious mind) are expressed. You may have heard of, for example, the 'oral stage' where babies have an instinct to explore objects with their mouths. During this stage, if you give an infant a new toy, it is very likely that the infant will put the toy in its mouth. Freud thought that later psychological problems arose when there were problems in the expression of these basic instincts at different stages of development.

One psychologist who was strongly influenced by these ideas of Freud was John Bowlby. Bowlby took particular interest in the close relationship formed between a parent and a child, which he termed attachment. Attachment refers to the strong social and emotional bond between an infant and its carer. He argued that the bond works both ways; carer and child provide comfort and warm feelings for one another. He argued that the attachment bond is critical in shaping the future behaviour of the infant. Bowlby (1946) examined a sample of 44 juveniles who had all stolen and were referred to a child guidance clinic. He found that, compared to a non-delinquent control group (who also attended the guidance clinic), a much higher proportion of the delinquents (almost 40 per cent compared to 5 per cent in the control group) had been separated from their mothers for more than six months in the first five years of their lives. This evidence does seem to be consistent with the idea that early relationships with the mother are important for a child's psychological development. Despite this finding, other researchers such as Rutter (1971) have pointed out that the research of Bowlby in this area has not been substantially replicated. Rutter argued that separation from the mother in itself is not the problem, but found that failure to form a bond with a carer (not necessarily the mother) was critical in future delinquency.

CASE STUDY BOX 3.4 FREUD AND RESEARCH

Freud conducted his research not by conducting experiments but by in-depth observations of individual patients. The image of a patient on the psychologist's 'couch' stems from Freud's work in understanding behaviour. Freud drew inferences about the human mind from the detailed cases which he observed. He was deeply impressed by work on the phenomenon of hysteria. His psychodynamic theory is complex and capable of almost infinite variation, meaning that it can be adapted to explain almost any occurrence. However this is all on the basis of inference (i.e. Freud inventing his own possible explanation predicated by his own hypotheses) and not experimentation.

The problem with psychodynamic theories is that because they rely on unconscious processes they are hard to test empirically and this has been one of the major criticisms of this approach. Because they focus on internal conflicts and unconscious processes (which are things we cannot see or measure), it is impossible to prove or disprove them. It is worth noting that in the present day many theorists (although not all) feel that the role of explaining criminality in psychodynamic theory is limited.

QUESTION BREAK: THE KRAY TWINS

Ronald and Reginald Kray were two highly feared notorious London gangsters. They were both sentenced to life imprisonment for murder, and both twins have since died in prison. Yet both of the twins were famously very close to their mother Violet and valued their family identity very highly. Read the following extract from Pearson's account of their lives and consider the questions below.

The Krays were an old-fashioned East End family – tight, self-sufficient and devoted to each other . . . The centre of their world was to remain the tiny terrace house at 178 Vallance Road where they grew up and where their Aunt May and their maternal grandparents still lived . . . For Violet none of this mattered. Her parents were just around the corner: so was her sister, Rose. Her other sister, May, was next door but one, and her brother, John Lee, kept the café across the street.

And old grandfather Lee . . . would sit with the twins for hours in his special chair by the fire . . . And sometimes the old man would talk about the other heroes of the old East End, its criminals.

(Adapted from Pearson 1972 12–27)

- What does this say about maternal deprivation as an influence on criminal behaviour?
- More generally, do you think the behaviour of children can be blamed on their parents? (List the arguments for and against.)

Behaviourist theories

Whilst Freud proposed that our behaviour is the result of tension and conflict between psychodynamic forces that cannot be seen, other theorists have proposed an alternative approach which focuses much more on observable behaviour.

Behaviourism relies on the fact that any behaviour can be learned. The behaviourists would posit that there is no such distinction as 'us' (non-criminals) and 'them' (criminals). Rather, they would argue that as we develop and interact with other people we learn, through trial and error, how to behave in different ways. Depending on how and what we learn, we either may or may not learn to behave in either criminal or non-criminal ways.

These underpinnings of behaviourism began at the beginning of the twentieth century with the work of Ivan Pavlov (1849–1936) whose ideas of 'classical conditioning' or 'learning by association' had a huge impact on the development of psychology and criminology in the twentieth century. Pavlov's first significant discovery came about by chance when he was studying the digestive systems of dogs. Whilst it is quite normal for dogs to start to salivate at the sight of food, he noted that the dogs would start to salivate at cues associated with the presence of food, such as the sound of food being prepared. He explained this behaviour by noting that stimuli (i.e. environmental events such as the sound of the dog bowl scraping as the food is prepared) can be associated with a natural reflex response (i.e. salivation). This response can become conditional on the stimuli. So by ringing a bell before the dogs were fed, he noted that they would begin to salivate even if he didn't actually feed them. For this reason, learning by association is called 'classical conditioning'. The main tenet of this new approach was that people's behaviour could be explained not by forces inside a person (as in psychodynamic theory) but by the interaction between the person and their environment. Behaviour could be learned through interacting with the world.

This new approach to psychology was termed behaviourism and many researchers expanded upon the approach since Pavlov. For example John B. Watson (1878–1958) argued that humans are born with various innate stimulus response reflexes, in the same way that some animals are. He argued that through 'learning by association' humans could develop increasingly complex chains of behaviour. Pavlov and Watson, like Freud, had started a new way of thinking about the world and upon these behaviourist ideas were based some important criminological theories.

The Chicago school and criminology

In the USA, at around the same time as Watson was developing the behaviourist approach, a group of researchers were dissatisfied with the biological and Lombrosian approach of 'the criminal man' (as outlined in Chapter 2, pp. 23–4). During the 1920s and 1930s this Chicago University-based research group developed the idea that crime was not the result of biological or psychological factors associated with individuals, but was instead the product of social forces. They noted that people who lived in areas of community disorganization, with poorer social conditions, had an increased risk of being delinquent. They hypothesized that, once a delinquent culture became established in a particular neighbourhood, other youths would be drawn into this subculture by associating with the delinquent group.

Edwin Sutherland (1883–1950) was one of what was named the 'Chicago school' of researchers, and had an interest both in the social creation of crime and in the role of the individual. He was interested in establishing how criminal behaviour was transmitted through the generations and why some people would be drawn into crime when others would not. He was particularly interested in how criminal behaviour can be learned. Sutherland argued that crime is defined socially. Those with power within society decide what is considered a criminal act and what is not. Therefore crime as a concept has both a social and a political dimension. So why, asked Sutherland, do some people obey these socially and politically created laws when others do not? Sutherland argued that this depended on the person's 'definitions' i.e. their attitudes towards breaking the law. A definition, according to Sutherland, is the way a person views crime, depending on the social forces in their life. Some individuals will hold definitions that are favourable to crime and others will not. Therefore to understand a person's criminal behaviour we need to understand their history of individual learning experiences. Sutherland argued that learning took place through association with other people, and that the learning might be about specific criminal techniques as well as about attitudes towards committing crimes. The important point is that each person's learning experience is different, depending on whom they are exposed to, and so the theory was termed differential association theory. Sutherland believed that learning criminal behaviour was no different from any other sort of learning. Sutherland's theory was highly influential, but it left many questions unanswered. For example what social conditions are likely to lead to learning criminal attitudes? How does the learning actually happen?

QUESTION BREAK: GIRL GANGS

Rates of girls joining gang culture have increased rapidly over the years. Gangs first emerged in the 1930s, and were predominantly male gangs. However even in such gangs women could often be seen on the periphery of gang activity. Women would often hide weapons for the men and get involved at the fringes of fights. In the present day female gang membership has risen sharply, particularly in the USA. Read the following extract and consider the questions below it.

Two teenage girls who led a violent gang in Surrey were jailed for life at the Old Bailey yesterday for kicking and beating a man to death at a drunken party. The court heard how the teenagers from Walton on Thames, Surrey, spent their time with a 'violent peer group' drinking heavily and taking drugs. The group aged between 14 and 19 were notorious in the area according to police. Detective Chief Inspector Graham Hill, who led the murder inquiry, said the girls were part of a group of teenagers who hung around the local area causing criminal damage and generally making a nuisance of themselves. 'They existed in a culture in which there was a hierarchy within the group and these two were in it' he said. 'They spent their time engaged in anti-social behaviour and causing chaos. They felt they could get away with anything.'
(Sandra Laville, *The Guardian*, 9 February 2005)

- What are the social conditions which you could identify which may account for such a rise?
- How could you explain why women may join gangs by using learning-based theories?

Skinner and behaviour analysis

From 1930 to 1935 a researcher at Harvard University laid the foundations for a new way of understanding behaviour. His name was Burrhus Skinner, and the new approach he championed was behaviour analysis. Skinner formulated, through experimental research, the principles by which we can understand the relationships between behaviour, the consequences of behaviour and the learning of new patterns of behaviour. Skinner's early work was conducted with animals (much like the researchers who had gone before him) but rather than focus on classical conditioning he looked at what is known as operant behaviour. Operant behaviour is the sort of behaviour which operates on the environment to produce consequences – for example if a rat in a cage pushes a lever to receive a food treat as a reward. The rat operates on the lever, which produces a consequence (the food). The relationship between a behaviour and its consequences he termed a contingency, and he identified two types of contingency: reinforcement and punishment.

These types of reinforcement were subsequently used to develop differential association theory to give an explanation for both acquiring and maintaining criminal behaviour. To understand why someone commits crime it is necessary to understand their individual learning history and what has reinforced their behaviour. Differential association theorists suggest that there are two types of conditions likely to make a crime happen. The first being the background factors of individuals which might make them more likely to be involved in crime (for example low IQ, poor parenting techniques or peer groups – to name just a few). Secondly, the setting events at the time of the criminal act are of importance – in other words the environmental cues, which indicate to the offender whether or not their behaviour is likely to be rewarding. For example, if an empty house appears easy to access because it has a window left open, it is more likely to be burgled.

Crimes can be rewarding in many ways: they can be materially rewarding in terms of financial gain, but they can also be rewarding in terms of peer status. Yet, on the flip side, they can also have aversive effects such as imprisonment and the subsequent disruption of family relationships. Each individual will have a unique learning history so that their individual history of reinforcement and punishment will determine their risk of criminal behaviour when the opportunity arises. Therefore the precise circumstances that lead an individual to commit crime will be unique to that person, depending on the context they are within.

CASE STUDY BOX 3.5 BEHAVIOURISM AND RESEARCH

The behaviourist school discovered their 'facts' by using rigorous experimentation in a laboratory. Their participants were usually animals, rather than humans. This allowed their researchers a great deal of control over their experiments. For example, because of being able to control an animal's environment totally, the researchers

continued

are able to isolate the one variable of interest, and make sure that, apart from that variable, absolutely everything else is the same about the groups of animals being tested. This is at the heart of experimental psychology. Unless we can be sure that there is only one variable that is different we cannot be sure that our results are due to that variable. This is very hard to achieve outside a laboratory setting and is particularly hard to control when we are working with humans.

One obvious problem of this approach is that real life does not work like a laboratory. In real life several forces may operate at once, rather than there being tight control. Additionally some theorists have been critical of the concept of studies which have at their basis animals as participants – they argue that because humans are so much more complex than animals it is hard to draw conclusions from observing animal behaviour. Another drawback is that behaviourists are interested only in observable behaviour – they are not interested in a person's innermost thoughts – yet a lot of people believe that our inner thoughts are what set us apart from animals, and are at the heart of what being human is about. When trying to use such theories to explain criminal activity it is obviously very hard to find out about a person's unique learning history, owing to the complexity of human life. This therefore makes some of the theories based in behaviourism hard to apply to our lives.

QUESTION BREAK: LEARNING HISTORIES

Think about your own life to date. Think about the situation you are now in. For example you may be working full-time and studying at night school, or you may have just enrolled in an undergraduate degree.

- What learning experiences have contributed to your current situation?
- What experiences do you think reinforced you along the way? For example did you have particularly encouraging parents or did a particular teacher put you off education?
- Do you think it is possible to try and view your current situation as a result of many individual learning experiences?
- How might 'learning history' relate to involvement (or not) in criminal behaviour?

Media aggression theories

An alternative theory that has been suggested is the idea that, although criminal behaviour may be learned, this isn't necessarily from a person with whom the individual physically interacts. This is the central tenet of the media aggression hypothesis. There have been concerns for several years that exposure to violence, via television or video games, may cause an increase in aggression. Much of the research has looked at short-term increases in small acts of aggression in children, which may have only limited application to criminologists. However, some research has looked also at longer-term effects on criminal violence. From those who believe that media can cause aggression the current view is that filmed violence has a small significant effect on viewers (e.g. Passer and Smith 2001). However, various factors can interact with the effect of the media on aggression. For example research suggests that if the violence is depicted as being justified it has a greater effect, and there are individual differences in the extent to which people are affected by media violence. In addition, certain individual factors such as unpopularity and low educational attainment are also involved in the interaction (Blackburn 1999).

Despite this research many criminologists and psychologists adopt a critical stance on the studies conducted in this area (e.g. Fowles 1999). This is largely due to the problem of how media aggression has been studied. Much of the research has looked at short-term influences on minor acts of aggression, and has been based in laboratories. However it is hard to extrapolate from such lab-based research whether or not viewing violent material would be likely to make someone be physically violent in the real world. Other research has attempted to take real violent criminals and find out about the level of violence in the television programmes they used to watch. This is very difficult – for example, how do you rate and compare cartoon violence to violence in an 18-rated film? And how likely is it that a 'true figure' can be established on how much violence someone has actually been exposed to? These are just a few of the reasons that the research in this area remains controversial.

QUESTION BREAK: MEDIA AGGRESSION RESEARCH

Think of possible reasons why the media aggression research may have been problematic to carry out. Imagine you are a media aggression researcher wanting to establish whether or not violent video games cause violence in adulthood.

- How would you design such a study?
- What problems are there with this design and with implementing it?

One of the main problems with the research into media and aggression is that the relationship is likely to be bi-directional in that the aggressive person is more likely to choose to want to watch violent television or play violent video games, which then influences further the level of aggression. Most of the research in this area comes from laboratory-based studies and it could be asked whether this is appropriate when we are trying to use media aggression hypothesis as an explanation for serious crimes such as murder. When using field-based retrospective studies (i.e. taking a sample of violent adults and asking them if they were exposed to media violence as they grew up) there will be huge problems with remembering what was watched many years ago.

In the discussion above we provided a few of the reasons why researchers are often sceptical about the research conducted into media aggression.

- Can you think of any other arguments against the view that violence in the media leads to violent and aggressive behaviour?
- Can you think of arguments to support the notion of a link between media violence and aggressive behaviour?

Cognitive theories

One area of psychology that has not been particularly linked with criminal behaviour is known as cognitive psychology. The majority of research conducted by cognitive psychologists concerns internal mental processes, such as attention and memory and is generally studied in a laboratory setting. Although it is perhaps easier to understand how people can acquire criminal tendencies by learning them from other criminals, identifying how 'thinking' in a criminal way leads to offending is more difficult.

Using the data retrieved from a series of interviews with acute offenders from a Washington secure unit, Yochelson and Samenow (1976) believed that the 'choices' an individual made led to criminal behaviour. These preferences for action were under the person's rational control. What made these people criminal was that they had learned poor and ineffective thinking styles that were at odds with prevailing societal conventions and laws. In particular, criminals' thinking patterns were characterized by a lack of empathy, poor perspective of time, perception of themselves as victims and general concreteness in their beliefs (Hollin 1989). They identified over fifty of these different 'thinking errors' and these were further separated into three main categories. The first category comprised simple character traits that related to overriding needs for power and control (Blackburn 1999). Second were the generalized thinking styles of poor decision-making, lack of trust and failure to honour obligations. The third and final category relates to the judgements directly related to criminal acts. These can take the form of anti-social fantasies, removal or ignorance of deterrents and an elevated sense of optimism. Hence, criminals see nothing wrong with the way they behave and often fail to understand the consequences of their actions. Blackburn (1999) reiterates that Yochelson and Samenow didn't see criminal acts as opportunist but that they were premeditated; if not by actual planning then through general anti-social values and beliefs that instigated offending patterns. From a cognitive perspective, criminals have internalized different ways of thinking about the world and also fail to understand why they must not behave as they do.

The origins of these 'cognition errors' were believed to be in childhood, and, as with Eysenck, the relationships with parents – both genetic and environmental – were important antecedents to acquiring these flawed thinking styles. As with most criminological research, there were mixed results to support this theory of a general criminal personality, i.e. as a definitive definition of criminality. Many of the cognition errors identified in the interviews have been found to be present in various criminal populations. But their attempt to produce an all-encompassing theory was flawed in a number of important ways. Firstly, their assumptions were based on a small number of incarcerated offenders (240 in total) with no control group for comparison. This sample is both small and also curiously flawed in that all the subjects were incarcerated for being 'guilty by reason of insanity'. Hence to make assertions on the nature of human criminality from these few individuals who quite likely had mental health problems was inappropriate. Hollin (1989) also raises the point that Yochelson and Samenow were labelled as being 'neo-Lombrosian' (see pp. 23–4) owing to the way that they define these different types of criminal as being a different 'breed' from other people and without sufficient explanation as to why this should be so.

Despite the inherent problems in the theories of Eysenck (see pp. 63–6 above) and Yochelson and Samenow, explaining criminal behaviour by way of cognition or flawed thinking styles became a renewed area of research. Where intelligence and locus of control had failed to provide adequate explanations of why individuals committed crime, cognitively based theories had less basis in social class or poverty. Two prominent names in the development of this theory have been Ross and Fabiano (1985). They have provided some lucid accounts of how poor upbringing – whether due to general poverty or to parental neglect – can hamper the formation of cognitive skills that are appropriate for pro-social behaviour. Ross and Fabiano believe that the way in which people make decisions – their cognitive or 'brain ' functioning – will influence future criminality. In contrast to the 'grand' theories which provided elaborate answers to the influence of various factors involved in criminality, the idea that poor thinking patterns could be largely responsible for such behaviour was enduring. The emphasis for the responsibility for committing unlawful acts was also placed firmly with the offender.

Although we talk about flawed cognition in the execution of criminal behaviour, the main emphasis is on social cognition. Social cognition refers to the way in which we think in social situations. For example, if you are in a pub then you are likely to behave differently from how you would behave in a church. Similarly, if you are talking to a policeman or teacher then there will be different ways in which you behave towards them, and this is part of social cognition. More specifically, this process is important when considering rules and how to behave. Social cognition amongst criminals is assumed to be flawed, in that they have not learnt socially acceptable ways of thinking. For example, taking drugs or stealing may not be seen by some people to be wrong. There are many different theories about these styles of thinking and how they are acquired. One such example of this is *moral development* (see box below).

QUESTION BREAK: THE STAGES OF MORAL DEVELOPMENT

Psychologist Jean Piaget and later Lawrence Kohlberg were to develop theories of moral development that consisted of a number of stages that individuals passed through. Whilst it was Piaget who provided the basis of this theory, it would be Kohlberg who developed this into a consistent and detailed account. As children develop, they begin to learn different ways of behaving. Children begin at Level 1 and then progress through the stages as they grow older. Each person advances somewhat at their own pace and doesn't necessarily reach the higher levels even when they are adults. Essentially, he proposed there to be three levels of moral judgement, each with two separate stages:

Level 1: Pre-conventional morality (age nine and below) – At this level, rules are essentially external and self-serving. They are obeyed so as either to avoid punishment or to gain rewards. Young children often see an act as wrong only if they are told off or may persist in misbehaving because the rewards are great. A child who eats somebody else's sweets may do so because the consequences may be outweighed by the benefits!

Level 2: Conventional morality (most adolescents and adults) – The approval of others now plays an important role in moral behaviour in the second level and the perceptions of others are first recognized before embarking on any course of action. Hence, a person may have the opportunity to commit a crime, but desist from doing so as they know that it may have dire consequences for the victim. In particular, they may not want others to think that they are a bad person.

Level 3: Post-conventional or principled morality (only 10–15 per cent of adults before age 30) – The two highest levels of moral reasoning are characterized by the broader principles of justice, and the idea that they may be surpassed by other obligations. Legally right and morally right become two separate components of behaviour orientation – so although stealing is *legally* wrong, stealing medicine to save someone's life may be seen as *morally* right.

- Have you ever considered others when deciding what to do – for example, returning a wallet or purse even though you might have wanted to keep the money?
- Have you ever seen or heard about something that made you think that it was unfair and that the law was wrong?
- If you think back, do you see a change in the way you behave now as compared with how you behaved when younger?

There is some debate from within the wider psychological literature as to the way in which people pass through the stages and also some gender and cultural biases in the overall theory (Gilligan 1993). For example, the theory was mostly developed during interviews with Western males, and hence may not apply to the way that females and non-Western people debate moral issues. Nevertheless, the links with crime and social cognition are clearly observable. Kohlberg (1978) believed that criminal behaviour was a direct result of a setback in moral development whereby the individual is 'stuck' reasoning at the lower *pre-morality* levels. These stages are characterized by seeking fulfilment of one's needs, lack of concern for others and avoiding punishment. The parallels with many descriptions of offenders' behaviour and personality traits are glaringly apparent. The earlier (Level 1) stages are concerned with maximizing rewards whilst avoiding or minimizing punishment. Higher stages (Level 3) are linked with values of morality and less to do with being punished. Criminals are often regarded as thinking within the lower stages of moral reasoning, where they will commit crime so long as the rewards outweigh the potential penalty if they are caught. People who reason at the higher stages may desist from crime as it is at odds with their values of right and wrong; being caught has little significance. Farrington (1992) interviewed many delinquents in his longitudinal studies and revealed that the way offenders thought about crime was quite simple. For some, they cared only about being caught or not, and many didn't care about the victims of their actions. Studies have shown clear differences in the judged acceptability of various offences and behaviour and level of moral reasoning. Some people may regard certain behaviours as reasonable and care only about the chances of getting caught. Others have provided an inclination that lower levels of moral reasoning are symptomatic of individuals nominated as being psychopathic (Hare 1980). Psychopaths generally have little sympathy for their victims and think only about themselves. If they think that they can get away with a crime they generally won't consider the wider implications of their actions (e.g. their victims) and this is similar to people who reason at the first stage of moral reasoning.

Criticisms of this simple explanation of criminal behaviour are significant, and are not related solely to the hypothesized relationship. In particular, there are concerns over whether the actual stages proposed by Kohlberg are somewhat arbitrary in that they need not necessarily be passed through in sequential order. Including the gender and cultural biases mentioned by Gilligan (1993), Kohlberg himself was to remove the final stage (universal ethical principles) as being largely unattainable and suggested that people could be 'coached' to record higher scores than they probably should. With regards to crime, research has been accused of putting much much emphasis on the *content* of the moral judgements than on the *processes* involved in attaining these decisions. In a similar way to which culture in the non-criminal sense has been found to influence moral reasoning, the 'subcultural' environment that has been argued as a characteristic of criminal fraternities may operate in a similar fashion. By imposing our own moral 'code' on which we judge offenders, we may simply be missing their own values and attitudes that represent different societies. Other theories of morality and its influence on crime have been proposed to confront this anomaly. Bandura (1990) proposed that people could actually become detached from their own moral principles in certain situations. The *theory of moral disengagement* highlights how people can separate themselves from generally accepted morally contemptible decisions by utilizing various psychological 'techniques'. The most common form of disengagement found amongst a cohort of young offenders was to dehumanize the victim. Hence it is not always the offenders' own actual moral code that is adhered to, and indeed they can devise justifications as to why they offend. For example, people may join gangs to save becoming the actual victim of these groups.

The idea of cognition and crime is closely related to the classical theory of criminology, in that offenders are seen as being responsible for their own behaviour.

Psychological explanations of crime see the personality of the offender as having a major influence on their actions; criminal behaviour is regarded as being an almost rational choice that is made by the individual. Although genetic and environmental factors can never be discounted, psychological traits that lead to an offender making decisions to offend can be identified. Cook (1980) believed that offenders conduct a rudimentary cost-benefit analysis when deciding to commit a criminal act. Subsequently if the rewards outweighed the potential negative consequences, it was likely that a crime would be committed. This is generally referred to as the *deterrence hypothesis*. These ideas were refined and developed by Cornish and Clarke (1987) into the *rational choice theory* of crime.

The basic premise of this theory is related to the rewards that potential offenders seek from their crimes. This is done by certain decision-making processes that are unique to the individual (e.g. skill) and to the dynamics of the actual situation (e.g. time available). Rational choice theory clearly believes that certain crimes are selected by offenders and committed for specific reasons.

QUESTION BREAK

Think of three particular types of crimes.

- What are the rewards gained from committing these crimes?
- What are the main 'dangers' and difficulties involved in committing such crimes?
- What generally held moral values have to be 'controlled' to encourage people to commit those crimes?

Cornish and Clarke (1987) developed a list of such choice properties, which included technical know-how, resources needed, confrontation with victim and moral evaluation. Although these related primarily to property offences and offences committed for financial gain, the authors believe that they are easily transferable to violent and sexual crimes. However, despite there being over fifteen different reasoning patterns, research has shown that it is the amount of punishment that exerted the biggest influence on whether to offend or not. Hence the relative 'cost' of offending greatly outweighs the 'benefits' of committing the act. In particular, Bridges and Stone (1986) have shown that prior experience of punishment – in the form of prison or other punishment – vastly influenced this equation. So offenders who have been caught and punished for their crimes were able to evaluate the potential costs more accurately and effectively.

factors such as family size. Such factors could also add further confounds to the study. An additional weakness is that cross-sectional studies do not allow researchers to look at development of individual, over time, as they are just a one-off picture of a group.

Longitudinal designs

Longitudinal designs differ from cross-sectional designs, in that, rather than taking a one-off measure of individuals, they actually look at changes over time within the same person. For example in a longitudinal study the same 'cohort' of participants may be tested once a year for ten years, to see the changes which take place in the group over time. The advantages of longitudinal studies are that they allow researchers to predict later outcomes from information they have when the group members are first selected. They also look at the development of the person and can see if any particular developmental sequences are critical in the person becoming criminal in later life (Loeber and Farrington 1994). There are two different kinds of longitudinal study: *retrospective* and *prospective*.

Retrospective designs

In retrospective designs researchers might identify a group of people whom they wish to study, for example murderers. They would then analyse existing information on that group, focusing on information from their past (for example their childhood upbringing). Whilst this approach is very useful if you want to study a particular group of people (e.g. people who have already committed a murder) it does have some disadvantages.

One problem is that information may well have been lost over time as the people studied will not have known that in the future they would be asked to be a participant in such a research project. A lot of the information gleaned will be dependent on people's remembered experience and this in itself relies upon the human memory processes, which we know can be unreliable. This method is most useful when researchers are interested in a rare phenomenon such as murder, or arson.

Prospective designs

Prospective designs identify a large sample of people and regularly, over time, test them on various criteria. This overcomes many of the problems with retrospective designs as the measures are taken at various points in time throughout the person's life and so rely less on memory. The researchers can then follow their cohort through their lives and look at who goes on to become criminal, and who does not, and make comparisons between the two groups. An example of a successful longitudinal prospective study would be the Cambridge study of delinquency by Farrington (1995) which looked at the development of 411 boys starting in 1961 and is still in progress today.

The weakness of this type of research is that it is very expensive (because of the amount of testing required), and is often dependent on the same researchers sticking with the project throughout to give continuity to the research project.

In spite of the weaknesses, these types of study have helped psychologists to identify several social factors which to some degree can be used to predict criminal behaviour. We would like you to start to think about some of these research findings in light of the theories we have already discussed in this chapter.

One of the things you have probably already noticed is that psychologists have come up with several different types of theories which rely on totally different factors as an explanation, ranging from unconscious processes to different learning experiences to how we think. And yet all of these theories are attempting to explain exactly the same thing – why certain people engage in criminal behaviour. What you can see therefore is the crucial point in psychology and criminology – that psychologists and criminologists will come up with quite different theories which can be based on exactly the same evidence. Understanding this fact is a crucial point in developing what are called 'critical evaluation' skills. Critical evaluation skills refer to the ability to look at either theories or research methods and provide critical comments. A good example in this chapter is the section above on longitudinal and cross-sectional research designs. If you had read some research which had been carried out utilizing a cross-sectional research design, you could critically analyse this research by commenting on the weaknesses of such designs, and could comment on whether or not you felt this was the most appropriate design to deal with the participant group who were being studied.

To test your evaluation skills, the rest of this section asks you to consider some of the key research findings in the area of social factors and how they may predict criminality, and to attempt to apply the different theories we have covered to these findings. These social factors are major areas of enquiry: here we will introduce them only very briefly and highlight some of the issues they raise in relation to criminal behaviour.

Family characteristics

There is a common belief that offenders are more likely to have been raised in homes where one or more parents are not present as a result of separation, divorce or death. Indeed early research seemed to find evidence to support this view.

Wells and Rankin (1991) conducted a meta-analysis of fifty studies published between 1926 and 1988 that investigated the relationship between delinquency and broken homes. A meta-analysis is a type of research project where instead of gathering data first-hand the researchers re-analyse the data collected by previous researchers but include the data from lots of different studies on the same topic. This allows the researchers to draw some broad-based findings on a specific topic area. In their meta-analysis Wells and Rankin found that the prevalence of delinquency in broken homes was 10–15 per cent greater than in intact homes.

The relationship was stronger for less serious *status* offences (a status offence is an offence dependent only on the age of the offender, e.g. drinking under the age of 18) than for more serious *index* offences (e.g. burglary and assault). Interestingly, it would seem that simply having one parent absent does not lead to such high levels of delinquency. For example in families where one parent had died compared to families where there had been a divorce the children were not as likely to become delinquent (Wadsworth 1979). So the common belief that offenders are more likely to come from homes where both parents are not present seems to be a little misleading.

As a possible explanation for such a finding McCord (1982) looked at the prevalence of offending behaviour among groups of boys who were raised in intact and broken homes, but also took into consideration the presence of a loving mother and the amount of parental conflict. McCord found that the prevalence of offending was:

- broken home, without a loving mother – 62 per cent
- intact home, with parental conflict – 52 per cent
- intact home, no parental conflict – 26 per cent
- broken home with a loving mother – 22 per cent

That is to say offending was highest in the broken home without a loving mother. However with a loving mother present, even in a broken home, the prevalence of offending was lower than in intact homes with no parental conflict at all.

QUESTION BREAK: LOVING MOTHERS – DIFFERENT EXPLANATIONS

- As we have discussed previously it is common for psychologists to come up with alternative theories to explain the same phenomenon. How do you think the different theories we have covered would explain this finding?
- What would personality theory say is a possible explanation?
- What would psychodynamic theory argue?
- Can we apply differential association theory to this research, if so how?
- Try and put yourself in the position of Eysenck, Freud and Sutherland. How do you think they would evaluate McCord's findings?

Child-rearing practices

There is little doubt that the family is a highly influential social institution. Most of us look to our family upbringing to explain our own behaviour as an adult. References to this in popular culture are common. The baddie of many a film was 'turned bad' by some sort of bad experience as a child. This common conception is at least in some way supported by research which shows that family functioning plays a large role in how children adjust and develop (for reviews see Farrington et al. 1996). Early work on the relationship between how a family functions and delinquency led to the formulation of 'typologies' of parenting style (e.g. Baumrind 1978). A typology attempts to put different types of behaviour into categories of some. For example Baumrind evaluated parental behaviour through interviews with parents and teachers and through direct observation of parents with their children. From this she devised four different types of parenting style:

- Authoritarian – parents place value on obedience and favour punitive punishment in order to exert control over children.
- Permissive – parents nurture their children, but prefer to allow them freedom of expression.
- Indulgent and neglectful – parents neglect their children.
- Authoritative – parents fall between the extremes of the authoritarian and permissive styles, and use an inductive (see below) style of discipline.

(Baumrind 1978)

Baumrind found that, of these types of parenting style, the authoritative style was found to be least associated with producing delinquent children, and was indeed considered the most effective parenting style.

It is perhaps unsurprising (considering our discussion of behavioural theory earlier on in this chapter) that psychologists agree that for discipline to work effectively it needs to be applied consistently, and needs to depend on the child's behaviour. However further research by Hoffman (1977) identified that there are differing styles of delivering discipline, which have different associations with the development of delinquency. Hoffman identified three types of disciplinary practices:

- power assertion – includes the use of physical punishment, criticism of the child and threats of maternal deprivation (e.g. saying to the child 'you are a bad little boy, mummy won't love you any more if you do that')
- love withdrawal – involves expressing disapproval, but not in a physical way, and the witholding of affection (e.g. saying to the child 'That's a bad thing to do' and not cuddling the child)
- induction – involves reasoning with the child, and talking through the consequences of the child's behaviour on others (e.g. saying to the child 'It makes Jonny upset if you steal his toy rabbit and it hurts his feelings, if someone did that to you you would be upset too, wouldn't you?').

Of these three types of discipline power assertion was the technique most used by the parents of delinquent offspring.

QUESTION BREAK: DISCIPLINING CHILDREN

Power assertion was the technique most used by the parents of delinquent offspring. How do you think these different theories would explain this finding?

- Psychodynamic theory

- Behaviourist theory
- Cognitive theory

Take a sheet of paper and write the three theories as headings: try to think about how each theory might explain this finding (you may need to refer back to each theory in order to help you do this).

Finally, under each explanation which you have created, try to think of some possible criticism of why that theory may not fully explain the finding – when you do this you will be critically analysing that theory.

What must be borne in mind when considering parenting skills is that even parenting which closely meets the ideal may be disrupted by stressful experiences which may have an effect (temporarily or longer-term) on the skills being utilized. External stressors such as unemployment, poverty, illness and parental conflict could all disrupt the most effective parenting techniques. The coping strategy of the parents in dealing with such stressful life events will play an important mediating role in how these factors may affect the children they raise.

Parental criminality

Many common phrases refer to the fact that similarity often seems to be passed down from generation to generation. Phrases such as 'like father, like son' and 'he's a chip off the old block' reflect this common conception. Once again some research seems to support the adage. McCord (1979) noted that criminal fathers tend to have criminal sons. In support of this finding West and Farrington (1977) found in their longitudinal study that having a convicted parent predicted later offending in both adolescence and adulthood.

QUESTION BREAK: LIKE FATHER LIKE SON

There are a number of possible explanations for the finding that criminal fathers tend to have criminal sons.

This time try not only to consider the theories covered in this chapter: consider the explanations offered in other parts of this book. How do you think the finding can best be explained? Choose any two theoretical positions (e.g. biological explanations versus labelling theory, for example).

- Firstly try and work out how each theory you selected might explain the findings.
- Secondly try and work out how each theory would criticize the assumptions of the other.

Peer influences

It is a common saying that a child 'fell in with the wrong crowd'. Children have strong peer attachments and friendships are critical to them. Research has found that friends can play a role in encouraging or inhibiting delinquent behaviour. There are two consistent findings in the literature:

- Adolescents with close friends who are delinquent are more likely to behave delinquently.
- Delinquents are more likely than non-delinquents to have delinquent friends (West and Farrington 1973).

Both of these findings hold true both for self-reported crime and for crime as reported in the official statistics. This is an important point as not all people who commit crime get caught and so do not show up in the official crime statistics. Moffitt (1990) came up with an intriguing theory to explain why many adolescents become involved in offending when they are teenagers, but then desist from offending when they become adults. Moffitt argued that the peak in offending rates, which happens in adolescence, conceals two different types of offender. One type is the 'adolescent limited offender', who will be likely to have a short period of time (during their teenage years) in which they offend, before they 'grow out' of the behaviour. The other type is the 'life-course-persistent offender', who is likely to progress from offending in adolescence to further and more prolific offending in adulthood. Moffitt argued that life-course-persistent offending is very different in its etiology to adolescent limited offending. Indeed it is likely that there may be some element of neuropsychological risk in the life course of persistent offending which can be worsened by problem interactions, and by the individual becoming ensnared as a result of an offending lifestyle. What is interesting though is why the adolescent limited offenders ever become involved in criminal activity. Moffitt argued that in our modern society children in their teenage years are held in a sort of 'maturity gap'. They are not considered adult enough to have jobs, and yet they are no longer children. As a result they can become frustrated and seek ways to break away from their parents' control. Moffitt argued that in this period where adolescents feel that they are in a 'no man's land' they begin to look around them and realize that some people are plunging ahead with an exciting lifestyle – potentially drinking, engaging in criminal activity, maybe even becoming parents themselves. These people are likely to be the life-course-persistant offenders. To the other adolescent offenders these more exciting peers can effectively become role models, and the adolescent limited offenders become involved in offending in an attempt to emulate the life-course-persistant offenders. This then explains the sharp rise in offending around the age of 17. The adolescent limited offenders are able to stop offending – by adapting to changing contingencies, i.e. when it becomes more beneficial to them to stop offending they can do. When they realize they will gain more benefit from getting a job, or continuing with education, they desist from offending. However the life-course-persistent offenders do not (or cannot) adapt to these changing contingencies and continue to offend.

QUESTION BREAK: THE PEAK IN CRIMINAL BEHAVIOUR

Moffitt's theory is of particular interest because it combines elements of several of the theories we have discussed in this chapter.

- Try to work through Moffitt's theory and identify the different elements which may come from the theories we have studied.

Unemployment

Recently a lot of attention has been paid to the idea that if someone is employed they are less likely to be involved in criminal activity. Research indicates that the most important issue is someone's ability to hold down a job to which they are committed (Jeffery 1977). It has been proven that offenders have higher rate of unemployment than non-offenders (Freeman 1983). However there is a complex relationship at play because it can be harder for someone, once they have a criminal record, to obtain employment. Furthermore once released from prison, if the person is able to find employment they are less likely to re-offend (Rossi, Berk and Lenihan 1980).

QUESTION BREAK: EMPLOYING OFFENDERS

We know that if offenders can be released into the community with a job which they are committed to it will reduce their risk of re-offending. Imagine you are working with an ex-offender trying to secure them a job.

- What challenges do you think you will face in convincing employers to give an ex-offender a job?
- How might you go about overcoming these challenges?

Child abuse

Research has shown that children who have been victims of severe physical abuse in the home are around three times more likely than other children to use alchohol and drugs, to deliberately damage property and to get into fights. Additionally they are about four times more likely to be arrested than other children (Gelles 1997). Wisdom (1989) carried out a 20-year follow-up study of children who had been abused or neglected and found they were more likely than the control group to have been arrested as juveniles, as adults and for violent crimes. Two things that must be borne in mind though when considering research into people who have suffered abuse are firstly that it is hard to know exactly who has been abused as many people never report the abuse, and secondly that the research can be problematic as the sample sizes are often small, making the research harder to form generalizations from.

School characteristics

There has been found to be a consistent correlation between academic ability and delinquency. However more important than ability, it has been found that actual performance is the key measure in predicting delinquency (i.e. how the child actually performs at school regardless of how capable they may be academically). The relationship between performance and delinquency is robust and remains when other factors associated with delinquency have been controlled for (Patterson and Dishion 1985). Those who fail academically at school are at increased risk of delinquency regardless of whether the outcome measure of success is self-report or using official criteria (Elliott and Voss 1974).

Interestingly, despite individual variation between pupils, the prevalence of delinquency is not evenly distributed between schools (Farrington 1972). Owing to this finding, some theorists have attempted to explain delinquency in terms of the actual school itself. For example Power et al. (1967) looked at the delinquency rate of 20 inner London schools. They calculated the delinquency rate of each school for six years, using the measure of the number of court appearances of children. They found that rates of delinquency did not relate to the catchment area, and concluded it must be something within the school itself which caused the difference in rates. On the other hand some researchers argue that the individual characteristics of pupils lead to so-called delinquent schools. Farrington (1972) studied boys from six primary schools with similar delinquency rates and found that when the boys moved on at age 11 there were differences in delinquency rates between the schools. Farrington therefore argued that the 'delinquency proneness' of the schools' intake has an effect on its delinquency rates. In summary the relationship between school factors and delinquency is a complex one, with the nature of the association between the school and delinquency being quite unclear. It seems unlikely that the school itself can cause delinquency. However is is possible that the school can act as a catalyst for conduct problems.

This section has covered just a few of the social factors which have been shown to have some link with criminality. However there are many more that we have not had the opportunity to explore in more detail, for example family size and poverty. It must be borne in mind that no one social factor can really be taken out of context and seen as an explanation in isolation. In reality several social, as well as individual, factors will interrelate, to play a role in someone potentially engaging in criminal behaviour.

SUMMARY

This chapter has endeavoured to show that many different psychological theories have all tried to explain the same phenomenon – why people engage in criminal activity.

Through a series of reflective question breaks you have had the opportunity to start to think about these different types of theory, and point out both their strengths and also their weaknesses. In so doing you have started to learn how to analyse different theories critically. In addition, we have introduced some of the different methods which psychologists have used to try to research the question of why people become criminal. In learning these different methods you have had the chance to gain an insight into the ways psychologists study human behaviour, and have learned that sometimes, as in any area of social science, these methods seem less than ideal.

There is no doubt that in trying to predict who becomes criminal a whole range of theories and explanations are likely to be at play and it would be naive to expect a simple explanation. Hopefully this broad review of psychological explanations has allowed you to become a step closer to formulating your own opinions as to the relative importance of different types of factors.

FURTHER READING

Ainsworth, P. B. (1999) *Psychology and Crime: Myths and Reality*. London: Longman. An accessible introduction to the basic concepts that relate to psychological explanations of criminal behaviour. As its name suggests, this book attempts to explore many of the misconceptions people have about psychology and its application to crime.

Blackburn, R. (1995) *The Psychology of Criminal Conduct: Theory, Research and Practice*. London: Wiley. This is probably the most comprehensive book on the market and covers in detail all the major theories and applications of psychology to criminal behaviour. This book is essential reading for all students of forensic psychology and criminology.

Howitt, D. (2006) *Introduction to Forensic and Criminal Psychology* (2nd edition). Harlow: Pearson. The text is excellently laid out and provides the reader with an easy understanding of the major theories and concepts in forensic and criminal psychology.

WEBSITES

http://www.jdi.ucl.ac.uk/. The Jill Dando Institute for Crime Science at the University of London – Specifically aimed at reducing crime, this website provides a wealth of information on various aspects of crime from some of the world's leading academics.

http://scienceandresearch.homeoffice.gov.uk/hosdb/. The Home Office Scientific Development Branch – although this is not exclusively related to psychology and crime, there are many high-quality publications available to read and download.

CHAPTER 4

Sociological Explanations for Criminal Behaviour

INTRODUCTION

When we looked at the historical context for crime (Chapter 1), the extent and range of criminal behaviour were emphasized, along with its massive influence on everyday life. Having looked at theoretical explanations from biological and psychological perspectives in the previous two chapters, here we will turn to explanations from sociological perspectives. And as we will see, the divisions between the different 'subjects' of biology, psychology and sociology are by no means obvious or rigid. However, while not seeing non-sociological theories as necessarily 'wrong', sociologists would consider them to offer only partial explanations at best. The emphasis in sociological theorizing is on the social context in which crime takes place – crime and criminals can be fully understood only in relation to the social structure, to specific social conditions and processes. Of course within this broad argument that criminal behaviour can only be explained by social factors, there is a wide variety of specific theoretical positions.

Explanations for criminal behaviour are as old as the types of behaviour themselves – debate and discussion about why people break rules have excited general and scholarly interest throughout history. Indeed most people have their own views as to what are the most likely causes of such behaviour; and these views are all likely to contain some elements of 'truth' without being complete explanations. Inherited defects, overcrowding, inadequate parental supervision and getting in with the 'wrong crowd', for example, have all been proposed as causes of criminal behaviour.

Moreover in looking at theories we should not expect to find some complete explanation or ultimate cause of criminal behaviour. Indeed this behaviour encompasses so massive a range of activities that such an aim is clearly unrealistic. After all, why should one form of explanation or theory be able to explain why some people in well-paid jobs embezzle money and why other people engage in domestic violence and still others get involved in fighting on a night out? To put it another way, is it likely that the criminal identity of a fraudster would be the same as a burglar or a 'professional' armed robber? Furthermore, even if it could be proved that juvenile delinquency was linked to poor parental supervision, it would be necessary to consider why such delinquency occurred amongst some poorly supervised juveniles but not others. Then it would be important to consider why those parents were unable to provide adequate supervision – was it because of their living conditions and, if so, why were they living in such poor conditions? Was this because of government housing policies or a poor employment record? It is clear that we are moving further and further away from explaining the cause of the criminal behaviour. This is not to say it is not important to look for explanations of criminal behaviour; but we do need to be aware that different theoretical approaches and explanations may help explain certain forms of criminal behaviour but not others and that there is no 'ultimate explanation' waiting to be discovered.

Attempting to categorize the wide range of sociological explanations is fraught with difficulty and here we will use an essentially chronological approach to map our way through the different approaches and traditions.

CLASSICAL CRIMINOLOGY

Sometimes known as classical jurisprudence, classical criminology emerged from the period known as the Enlightenment and was developed by penal reformers in the later eighteenth and early nineteenth centuries who wanted to create a fair and legitimate criminal justice system based on equality. The intention was to develop a rational and efficient means of delivering justice in place of previous arbitrary, corrupt and prejudiced forms of punishment. Based on the Enlightenment emphasis on individual rights, rather than the unquestioning acceptance of traditional forms of authority, the core ideas of classical criminology were that the punishment for a crime should be proportionate to the particular criminal act and that it should be seen as a deterrent. As this introductory comment indicates, the focus of classical criminology is very much on the relationship between crime, justice and punishment, rather than with explaining why certain individuals become offenders. Classical criminology was based on the notion that individuals had free will and made rational choices about the way in which they would behave. People, including those who commit criminal acts, have to be considered as rational, and so an individual's behaviour will be based on a rational calculation of the consequences. The major control over a person exercising their free will is particularly fear of pain. The fear of pain, in the form of punishment, would, then, deter an individual from criminal activities and act as a control on their behaviour. The two Enlightenment philosophers most associated with developing this approach were Cesare Beccaria and Jeremy Bentham.

Beccaria was an Italian university professor who, at the age of only 26, wrote an essay on punishment entitled *Dei deliti e delle pene* (*On Crimes and Punishment*) that was published in 1764. This book, which was written at a time when severe and barbaric punishments were the norm, caused something of an outcry with its rational approach to punishment – although condemned by the Catholic Church it was widely read and translated into 22 languages. Essentially Beccaria advocated a reformed system of criminal justice that provided a more logical and rational approach to the punishment of crime. Among his ideas were the notion that there must be a proper proportion between crimes and punishment, that to be just and useful punishment should be administered promptly and that one of the greatest curbs on crime is the certainty, rather than the cruelty, of punishment. Indeed one section of his text is entitled 'Of the proportion between crimes and punishment'. He starts this section by suggesting the need to classify crimes according to their severity:

A scale of crimes may be formed, of which the first degree should consist of those which immediately tend to the dissolution of society, and the last of the smallest possible injustice done to a private member of that society. Between these extremes will be comprehended all actions contrary to the public good which are called criminal, and which descend by insensible degrees, decreasing from the highest to the lowest. If mathematical calculation could be applied to the obscure and infinite combinations of human actions, there might be a corresponding scale of punishments, descending from the greatest to the least.

In elaborating on this he argues that crimes have to be ranked according to the injury done to society:

Some crimes are immediately destructive of society, or its representative; others attack the private security of the life, property or honour of individuals; and a third class consists of such actions as are contrary to the laws which relate to the general good of the community . . . The first, which are of the highest degree, as they are most destructive to society, are called crimes of leze-majesty (High Treason) . . . To these succeed crimes which are destructive of the security of individuals. This security being the principal end of all society, and to which every citizen have an undoubted right, it becomes indispensably necessary, that to these crimes the greatest of punishments should be assigned.

And in relation to punishment:

> If an equal punishment be ordained for two crimes that injure society in different degrees, there is nothing to deter men from committing the greater as often as it is attended with greater advantage.

QUESTION BREAK

- In our society which crimes are ranked as most and least serious?
- What factors determine this ranking?
- To what extent do you agree with the way crimes are ranked?
- How does the contemporary ranking of crime relate to Beccaria's arguments?

While the language may sound dated, many of Beccaria's ideas have formed the basis of modern criminological theorizing. In discussing the ranking of crimes within society, Beccaria acknowledges and highlights the relative nature of crime and the social reaction to it – a notion central to the work of the interactionist, labelling theorists whose work became very much in vogue in the sociology of the 1960s and 1970s (see pp. 113–18 below):

> Whoever reads, with a philosophic eye, the history of nations, and their laws, will generally find, that the ideas of virtue and vice, of a good or bad citizen, change with the revolution of ages, not in proportion to the alteration of circumstances, and consequently conformability to the common good, but in proportion to the passions and errors by which the different lawgivers were successively influenced. He will frequently observe that the passions and vices of one age are the foundation of the morality of the following . . . Hence the uncertainty of our notions of honour and virtue; an uncertainty which will ever remain, because they change with the revolutions of time . . . they change with the boundaries of states.

In particular, Beccaria is known for his advocating of a utilitarian approach to the law and punishment, arguing that although the laws of a society might affect the liberty of a few they would be acceptable if they resulted in the greater happiness of the majority. He believed that human behaviour was essentially rational and based on the pleasure–pain principle. As regards punishment, the pain of punishment should be greater than the potential pleasure resulting from the criminal act – so the punishment should be proportionate to the harm done to society by the crime. Beccaria hoped that making punishment proportionate to the social harm done would limit the arbitrary punishments meted out by judges. This idea suggests that an offender's characters and circumstances should not be taken into account when determining and delivering punishment – all offenders should be treated equally, as abstract legal subjects. The essence of Beccaria's argument is illustrated by the concluding remarks he makes in his essay:

From what has been demonstrated, one may deduce a theorem of considerable utility . . . In order for punishment not to be, in every instance, an act of violence of one or of many against a private citizen, it must be essentially public, prompt, necessary, the least possible in the given circumstances, proportionate to the crimes, dictated by the laws.

In similar vein, Jeremy Bentham (an English philosopher and follower of Beccaria writing in the 1790s) promoted the utilitarian approach, and argued that punishment should be carefully calculated to inflict pain in proportion to the harm done to the public by the particular crime. This sort of argument was based on the notion that criminals and non-criminals were similar in that criminals were reasoning individuals who had made an error of judgement in committing a crime; and that rational, swift and certain punishment was the best way to stop such behaviour recurring. Influenced by Beccaria, Bentham believed that people behaved rationally and would seek pleasure and aim to avoid pain. So punishment must outweigh any pleasure that might be derived from criminal behaviour. Bentham claimed that all law and punishments should be based on the utilitarian principle of 'the greatest happiness of the greatest number' and on calculating degrees of pain and pleasure – so the pain of punishment could be justified only if it prevented more and greater pain.

Classical criminology certainly seemed to offer a much fairer and more open philosophy and system of punishment than the previous cruel and harsh systems. However, in emphasizing the free will and rationality of individuals, it did not consider issues of social inequality which might encourage certain individuals to commit crime and it assumed there was a generally agreed set of values or goals in society, ignoring the conflicting aims and goals of different groups (as we will see below, this is a criticism that is also made of later theoretical positions).

The influence of classical criminology is evident in our legal system today in the way that sentences for crimes are structured, with more severe punishments for more serious crimes – what is known as the 'tariff' for sentences. And the 'just deserts' approach to punishment, that anyone found guilty of a crime should be punished (irrespective of their background – equality before the law) and that punishment must be commensurate (or proportional) to the seriousness of the offence, clearly reflects the classical approach of Beccaria and Bentham.

EMILE DURKHEIM

Of the founding, 'classic' sociological theorists it was Emile Durkheim who wrote most on crime (and on punishment). As he was the founder of the structural functionalist approach in sociology we will start by briefly setting out his broad theoretical position before examining his application of this to explaining crime.

Durkheim, along with other classic sociological theorists, was interested in explaining how industrial society had come about and how such a complex structure held together – in particular, how social order was maintained in a modern industrial society compared to what he deemed the simpler, pre-industrial society. The 'problem of order' has been seen as key issue in the development of sociological theorizing.

At the time Durkheim was writing (the end of the nineteenth and early twentieth centuries), industrialization and urbanization had led to profound changes in the nature of modern societies and many early social theorists were attempting to understand these changes and their impact on society. Indeed many compared the new modern industrial societies unfavourably with a more communal, pre-industrial form of society. Durkheim, however, interpreted such changes from an evolutionary perspective and considered how societies adapted to the new context.

He argued that social order had to be based on a core of shared values which formed the moral basis for what he termed social solidarity. Durkheim believed that without the regulation of society individuals would simply aim to satisfy their own needs and wishes without regard for others. As mentioned, this regulation would have to be based on shared values which were generally accepted by members of the society. He called these shared, commonly held values the collective conscience of the society, which he defined as 'the totality of beliefs and sentiments common to average citizens of the same society'.

QUESTION BREAK

While phrases such as 'average citizens' and 'common to' raise broad issues of interpretation and definition, the notion of the collective conscience can be clearly related to criminal behaviour and the responses to it.

- Consider a range of different crimes.
- What are the differences in the way that they are responded to?
- Why are there such varied responses to different forms of crime?
- Which values does this suggest are particularly strongly held by the 'collective conscience'?

So the notion of the collective conscience is central to Durkheim's work – indeed social life, based on social order and solidarity, would be impossible without such collective standards and values. However, in line with his evolutionary perspective on social change, the form or style of social solidarity is not fixed and will adapt to the different, changing forms of society. In his first major work, *The Division of Labour in Society* (1893), Durkheim examined the changing form of social solidarity from pre-industrial to modern, industrial societies. In modern societies, the division of labour serves to integrate individuals who fulfil complementary tasks and roles. He uses the terms 'mechanical' and 'organic' to distinguish the different forms of social solidarity that characterize the two different forms of society. Less complex, pre-industrial societies are characterized by mechanical solidarity, where individuals tend to hold very similar beliefs and emotions and where there is relatively little specialization in terms of occupations. In such situations tradition is particularly strong and collective feelings predominate. By contrast organic solidarity characterizes modern societies, with individuals pursuing a much wider range of different tasks.

This leads to a great deal of interdependence – individuals are dependent on others to perform specific tasks and roles. Individuals in such societies pursue different and complementary functions but are still bound together by a strong moral consensus.

Durkheim's theorizing is couched at a very general, abstract level and he did not advocate a simple, straightforward divide between the two forms of social solidarity – for him all societies need a consensus, a collective conscience. However the strength of this collective conscience will vary from one form of society to another. The mechanical form of solidarity dominates the consciences of individuals more strongly than does the organic form – in modern, industrial societies there is greater scope for individuality and for individuals to express their own feelings and preferences.

Within this general approach to theorizing about the nature of society, crime (and how it is dealt with) was a central aspect of Durkheim's sociological analysis. The importance of a collective conscience based on shared values and norms is central to his explanation of crime. Crime is behaviour that breaks or deviates from these shared values and norms. It is also seen by Durkheim as a social fact and must, therefore, perform a social function – along with other institutions in and parts of a society. Given that crime is behaviour that breaks rules it might seem odd to talk about its functions. However Durkheim developed the argument that crime is universal, it exists, albeit to varying extents, in all known societies and must therefore be inevitable. And as well as being inevitable it must also be necessary and useful for society. Put simply, as crime is normal it must also be functional: 'There is no society that is not confronted with the problem of criminality . . . It is a factor in public health, an integral part of all healthy societies' (Durkheim 1895).

Durkheim then explains how crime does have positive functions – firstly, through encouraging social change and evolution and, secondly, through helping to sustain conformity and stability. In terms of encouraging social change, criminal behaviour can introduce new ideas into a society and so allow a society to move on and develop. Tierney (1996) calls this the 'adaptive function' of crime – criminals can be innovators who help society to adapt to changing circumstances. Durkheim gives the example of Socrates who was condemned as a criminal in his own time but whose (criminal) ideas benefited Greek society. As he put it:

> According to Athenian law, Socrates was a criminal. However, his crime, namely the independence of his thought, rendered a service not only to humanity but to his country . . . Nor is the case of Socrates unique; it is reproduced periodically in history. It would never have been possible to establish the freedom of thought we now enjoy if the regulations prohibiting it had not been violated. At that time, however, the violation was a crime.
>
> (Durkheim 1964, 67–71)

As regards its role in promoting social cohesion, Durkheim refers to the way in which the sense of outrage that crime can produce helps to reinforce generally held values and beliefs in the majority of people. Tierney (1996) refers to this as a 'boundary maintenance function', reinforcing the boundary between 'good' and 'bad' behaviour. When someone commits a crime, particularly certain forms of generally despised crimes, people often feel closer together through sharing their collective outrage. Through bringing people together crime can thereby have the effect of contributing to social cohesion. The presence of the criminal allows the rest of society to draw together and reaffirm their values – it strengthens the society or social group, and does this by drawing a boundary between acceptable and unacceptable behaviour.

Of course, it is not the criminal actions themselves which draw people together; it is the publicizing and punishing of crime that does that. It is the reaction to crime, evidenced in the way that it is punished, that is of central importance for Durkheim's argument. The public trial of criminals and the media's obsession with portraying crime and criminal trials help to clarify the boundaries of acceptable and unaccept-able behaviour. While the social reaction to and punishment of crime might not always correspond with the extent of social harm done by that criminal action, it does, according to Durkheim, illustrate and express the strength of generally held values and standards. For instance, the extent of social harm done by a specific violent act on a child may be slight compared to the number of people harmed by a company ignoring industrial safety or pollution laws. However the reaction against the child violator will be far stronger than against the offending company. From this viewpoint, the reaction to crime is seen as essentially emotional rather than rational and the demand for punishment as demonstrating a desire to see the offender suffer pain. This emotional reaction is demonstrated by the angry crowds which gather around courtrooms during particularly horrific murder trials. These sorts of responses are best understood if crime is seen as behaviour that offends against strongly held norms and values. Durkheim argued that, in order for there to be agreement and social cohesion, people had to be able to react against those who break the shared rules and values and that crime provides such an opportunity. It is this sort of approach to theorizing about crime that allows him to argue that:

> From this point of view the fundamental facts of criminality present themselves to us in an entirely new light. Contrary to current ideas, the criminal no longer seems a totally unsociable being, a sort of parasitic element. On the contrary, he plays a definite role in social life.
>
> (Durkheim 1964, 72)

QUESTION BREAK

- What specific types of criminal behaviour might lead to the introduction of new ideas and social change?
- Can you think of any individuals who were punished for their views but who later became widely respected and looked up to?
- What specific types of criminal behaviour might help to draw people together?
- Consider some recent crimes (and the trials of them) which have attracted media and public attention. How have they helped to promote greater 'social cohesion'?

As well as exploring the functions of crime for society, Durkheim argued that the increased individualism of modern industrial societies and the lesser degree of social cohesion and regulation would encourage a greater degree of social disorganization and lead to a variety of different social problems, including crime. He developed this argument in trying to explain the increase in criminal behaviour in modern industrial societies. During periods of rapid social change, when societies are rapidly modernizing and industrializing for instance, there is less control exerted over people's aspirations – as Burke puts it, 'such societies encourage a state of unbridled egoism that is contrary to the maintenance of social solidarity and conformity to the law' (2005, 94). And during such times of rapid change, new forms of control have not developed sufficiently to replace older ones, resulting in societies being in a state of 'anomie' – where there is a breakdown in norms and common values and understandings.

THE CHICAGO SCHOOL

Durkheim's early sociological theorizing on crime has been developed in a number of directions by later social theorists and criminologists. Here we will look at the work of the Chicago school on the relationship between increasing social disorganization and criminal behaviour and, in the next section, at the 'strain' theory developed by Robert Merton and linking anomie with criminal behaviour. The notion that modern, industrializing and urbanizing societies would bring with them greater social disorganization and therefore a growth in social problems, including crime, underpinned the work of sociologists at the University of Chicago in the 1920s and 1930s. The approach and theorizing of these sociologists has become known as the Chicago school – Chicago grew at a phenomenal rate in the early years of the twentieth century into a massive metropolis with a diverse population including European immigrants from Ireland, Germany and Eastern Europe and black Americans from the southern USA. It has been described as a vast social laboratory and it is perhaps no coincidence that the first university sociology department in the USA was established there in 1892.

On the basis of Durkheim's work, the Chicago school saw crime as a social, rather than an individual, phenomenon. They argued that social life in certain areas and neighbourhoods was chaotic and pathological and that in such situations crime was an expected and normal response. This view was coloured with a degree of optimism in that it was felt such a situation was only temporary owing to the rapid social changes brought on by industrialization and urbanization and that in this context a certain amount of crime was inevitable and of no particular threat to the basis of society. A key figure in establishing the reputation of the Chicago school was Robert Park. He believed that in order to study crime sociologists should actually go out into the city and engage in first-hand research – a view that encouraged the development of a number of important and renowned ethnographic research studies by sociologists at the University of Chicago.

Park and colleagues argued that cities should be considered as ecological systems, with different areas and neighbourhoods within them developing at different times and in specific ways. As Tierney puts it:

Thus cities such as Chicago had not developed on a random basis, but rather this development was patterned according to 'natural' social processes. The outcome was that cities evolve their own particular types of neighbourhood, each with their own type of social life. Some of these are stable, well organized neighbourhoods, but others are more socially disorganized, and it is here that social problems, including crime, are concentrated.

(1996, 90)

Ernest Burgess, another leading Chicago school sociologist, developed this 'ecological' approach by mapping out the different 'zones' of Chicago which formed five concentric circles covering the whole city. At the centre there was a business area of banks and offices and outside of this were different residential zones – what was termed the 'zone of transition' just beyond the central business zone, then the zone of workingmen's (*sic*) homes, the residential zone and the commuters' zone. The zone of transition was the area where most crime, as well as other social problems, occurred. Clifford Shaw and Henry McKay, two researchers closely associated with the University of Chicago Sociology Department, developed Burgess's approach to examine patterns of juvenile crime in Chicago. In this zone the housing was typically run down and the inhabitants were often new immigrants and others lacking the means to live elsewhere in the city. They found that in this deprived area with a transient population who were unable to put down roots, the values and norms that led to criminal behaviour were most likely to be found.

The high rates of juvenile crime found in the zone of transition were said to be linked to the social disorganisation in those areas. In the absence of strong normative controls from the family and the community, juveniles were likely to engage in delinquent activities.

(Tierney 1996, 91)

More generally, Shaw and McKay found that the extent of criminal behaviour was inversely related to the affluence of the area of the city, which was reflected in the distance the area was from the central business zone. They showed that crime rates were highest in 'slum' neighbourhoods regardless of who lived in those areas, and used these findings to argue that it was the nature of neighbourhoods, rather than of particular individuals or groups who lived in them, that determined the level of involvement in crime. Hence the description of the Chicago school as an ecological approach to explaining criminal behaviour.

QUESTION BREAK

- Divide the town or city you live in (or one you are familiar with) into different zones and give a brief description of those zones.

- Are there any areas or zones which you know to be particularly prone to crime?
- To what extent do your findings match those of the Chicago school?

ROBERT MERTON

This notion that crime was linked to a breakdown in social control has been a major influence on a number of later sociological writers who developed the structural functional approach of Durkheim to explain the nature of crime in contemporary society. In particular the link between the notion of anomie and crime was explored and developed by Robert Merton.

Merton's work in this area, known as 'strain' theory or 'anomie' theory, attempts to explain a wide range of forms of deviant behaviour, including crime. As with Durkheim, Merton was not a criminology specialist; he was a key figure in the functionalist school of thought that was predominant in American sociology from the 1930s to the 1950s. He started his theorizing on crime and deviance from the basic functionalist position that social stability is based on a strong consensus of values, which the majority of people in a society come to share. His most famous statement in this area was a paper entitled 'Social structure and anomie', originally published in 1938. The title indicates the influence of Durkheim's concept of anomie, while the term 'strain theory' indicates the basic issue Merton examined – what sort of social conditions and situations lead some people to break rules and act in criminal or deviant ways. Merton rejected individualistic explanations for such behaviour, arguing, rather, that it came from individuals or groups of people responding in an expected and normal manner to the social situations they found themselves in. In particular it resulted from a disjuncture between the cultural goals of a society and the legitimate means available to achieve those goals. His argument that criminal and rule-breaking behaviour results from 'differentials in access to the success goals of society by legitimate means' has become a classic sociological explanation and is worth exploring in a little depth.

Although Merton's work has been criticized (see p. 103), his paper, written over sixty years ago, remains a remarkably prescient view of the nature of contemporary society. Indeed the criticisms often seem to fail to appreciate the vitality and radical aspects of this important example of sociological theorizing on crime and deviance. Merton starts by pointing to the tendency in previous theorizing about crime to focus on biological drives – seeing it as 'anchored in original nature'. He criticizes this view of man (*sic*) being set against society in a 'war between biological impulse and social restraint', suggesting that 'the image of man as an untamed bundle of impulses begins to look more like a caricature than a portrait'. The fact that the frequency and type of criminal and deviant behaviour varies within different social structures questions the role of biological impulses.

In developing a systematic approach to studying such behaviour he aimed to discover how 'some social structures exert a definite pressure upon certain persons in the society to engage in nonconformist rather than conformist conduct'. High rates of deviant behaviour amongst certain groups of people would, he argued, be due to those people responding normally to their social situation and the pressures they faced in that situation. Merton highlighted two specific elements of the social structure which were crucial to his sociological explanation. Firstly, there are culturally defined goals which are seen as legitimate objectives for everyone – they are things 'worth striving for'. Secondly there are the acceptable modes of reaching those goals – usually called the 'means' in discussions of Merton's work; he used the term 'institutionalized norms'. These cultural goals and institutional norms are not fixed in a constant relation to one another with the emphasis on one or other varying according to the social context. He describes the two extreme situations between which there will be this variation – on the one hand, a context where 'any and all procedures which promise attainment of the all-important goal would be permitted' and, on the other, a situation where the overall purposes of an activity are forgotten and 'conduct becomes a matter of ritual'. Between these extremes are societies which maintain a balance between emphasis on cultural goals and institutional means; and an effective equilibrium is maintained so long as individuals who conform to the norms achieve the satisfactions and goals they aim for. Merton goes on to argue that 'aberrant (deviant) behaviour may be regarded sociologically as a symptom of dissociation between culturally prescribed aspirations and socially structured avenues for realizing these aspirations'.

Having made these general points, he then considers the particular types of society where the emphasis on goals is especially strong in comparison to the emphasis on institutional procedures. Although all societies have norms that govern behaviour, the pressure to attain goals can become predominant, leading to a situation where 'the technically most effective procedure, whether legitimate or not, becomes typically preferred to institutionally prescribed conduct'. In such situations the society becomes unstable and 'develops what Durkheim termed "anomie" (or normlessness)'. The examples Merton used from the world of sport to illustrate this situation – such as illegally 'nobbling' an opponent or using illicit techniques (or substances) to improve chances of winning – will be easily recognizable to anyone with even only a passing interest in contemporary sport.

QUESTION BREAK

Give examples of behaviour that illustrates the win-at-all-cost attitude from

- different sports
- other areas of life.

As indicated by the questions above, the notion that it is only success, rather than participation, that can provide gratification is not restricted to competitive sports. Indeed Merton suggests that 'contemporary American culture appears to approximate the polar type in which great emphasis upon certain success goals occurs without equivalent emphasis upon institutional means'. In particular, he considers how money has become a value in itself, a 'symbol of prestige', and however it is acquired (legally or not) it can still be used to purchase the same goods and services. It is worth remembering that Merton was writing in the 1930s when he stated that: 'To say that the goal of monetary success is entrenched in American culture is only to say that Americans are bombarded on every side by precepts which affirm the right or, often, the duty of retaining the goal even in the face of repeated frustration.' In highlighting the prestige attached to monetary success, Merton provided examples from American business magazines of 'self-made men' whose ambitions drove them to success against all the odds. Of course the corollary of high ambition is that those who do not aspire to success are admonished as 'quitters'.

Individuals have to adapt to the cultural context described by Merton, and his explanation of different forms of criminal and deviant behaviour is based around the different responses people make if they are faced with a discrepancy between the aspirations or goals that society has 'taught' them and the ways that they have available to realize such aspirations (their 'means'). On the basis of this explanation, Merton suggested five different ways of adapting to this gap – five different 'modes of adaptation' as he put it. Here we will just provide a brief introduction to each of these modes of adaptation.

Firstly, *conformity* involves the individual accepting both the goals and means. This is the usual form of adaptation – indeed if it were not so societies would become extremely unstable. The other four modes of adaptation describe ways of dealing with the strain caused by social inequalities. Merton calls the second category or adaptation *innovation*, which involves the adopting of unconventional methods of chasing the goals. These methods could include criminal ways of achieving successes and it is this category which is most relevant to studying and explaining crime. Third is *ritualism*, where the goals are abandoned but the individual sticks rigidly to the legitimate means of attaining success. Fourth is *retreatism*, which occurs when both the goals and the means are abandoned, with the individual perhaps 'dropping out' of society. Fifth is *rebellion*, with the goals and means given up but replaced with new ones.

QUESTION BREAK

- Give an example of behaviour, or perhaps an occupation, that would fit each of Merton's five cases of adaptation.
- Think of a particular person (either a 'real' person or a fictional character) who would fit each of those categories.

As suggested earlier, Merton's ground-breaking sociological theorizing has been subject to criticism. In this relatively brief overview we cannot go into a detailed critique but will raise some general points. Although providing a clearly sociological explanation for certain forms of nonconformity, Merton's theory does not adequately explain all types of criminal behaviour. It is difficult to point to the material goals that juvenile delinquents, hooligans or rapists, for example, could be seen as chasing. More generally the theory seems to have a middle-class bias: as well as assuming that criminals and rule-breakers accept and cherish middle-class goals, the model tends to focus on working-class crime. This is a problem that faces any theorizing based on a consensus views of society – a view that society is held together by common values which are shared by everyone. This bias might be exaggerated by the reliance of Merton on official crime statistics which arguably underestimate middle-class crime and predict too much working-class crime.

In terms of the different types of adaptation forwarded by Merton, there is no real explanation as to why some individuals who are faced with specific situations, perhaps of anomie, conform while others break the rules. Nor does it explain why one particular form of adaptation rather than another occurs – why innovation rather than retreatism for instance.

Having said that, Merton's theory does have certain strengths. It explains crime in terms of the structure and culture of society, rather than individual characteristics. As such it is a structural theory of crime which laid the basis for later theorizing based on the notion of subcultures – the idea that certain groups are more predisposed to break the rules of society than others. Such approaches are introduced below.

ALBERT COHEN AND SUBCULTURAL THEORIES

In his widely cited study *Delinquent Boys*, published in 1955, Albert Cohen provides a different version of strain theory. The influence of Merton is apparent through his focusing on features of contemporary American society that create strains for individuals which eventually lead to delinquent behaviour – in particular the importance of the values which form the 'American way of life'. However, Cohen questions whether criminal and delinquent behaviour is caused by a desire for material goals. Like Merton, he focuses on the working-class delinquency but argues that a large amount of such behaviour is expressive in character and not centred on acquiring money or goods. Delinquency centred on vandalism or violence is a clear example of such behaviour that is not concerned with material gain.

Cohen's argument is that American society is dominated by middle-class values and norms which are passed on through the education system and mass media. He looks to the education system in particular for his explanation of delinquency. Schools emphasize and embody middle-class values and so working-class boys (he focused on males) are ill-equipped to compete with middle-class boys, or 'college boys', and to gain status through education. Such working-class boys, or 'corner boys' as Cohen called them, suffer status frustration at school and respond by attempting to turn the middle-class value system on its head. Anything the school disapproves of the corner boy will see as good, with delinquency seen as a direct denial of middle-class values. Working-class, corner boys reject the values of the school and form groups which emphasize different, essentially delinquent, values – they form what Cohen defined as a delinquent subculture.

At the start of *Delinquent Boys*, Cohen provides his definition of the term delinquent subculture, before going on to offer a sociological explanation for how this subculture is central to the occurrence of delinquency. Cohen's definition is provided below.

> The expression 'the delinquent subculture', may be new to some readers of this volume. The idea for which it stands, however, is a commonplace of folk – as well as scientific – thinking. When Mrs Jones says: 'My Johnny is really a good boy but got to running around with the wrong bunch and got into trouble', she is making a set of assumptions which, when spelled out explicitly, constitute the foundations of an important school of thought in the scientific study of juvenile delinquency. She is affirming that delinquency is neither an inborn disposition nor something the child has contrived by himself; that children learn to become delinquents by becoming members of groups in which delinquent conduct is already established and the 'thing to do'; and that a child need not be 'different ' from other children, that he need not have any twists or defects of personality or intelligence, in order to become a delinquent.
>
> In the language of contemporary sociology, she is saying that juvenile delinquency is a subculture . . .
>
> When we speak of a delinquent subculture, we speak of a way of life that has somehow become traditional among certain groups in American society. These groups are the boys' gangs that flourish most conspicuously in the 'delinquent neighbourhoods' of our large American cities. The members of these gangs grow up, some to become law-abiding citizens and others to graduate to more professional and adult forms of criminality, but the delinquent tradition is kept alive by the age-groups that succeed them . . .
>
> Delinquency, according to this view, is not an expression or contrivance of a particular kind of personality; it may be imposed upon any kind of personality if circumstances favour intimate association with delinquent models. The process of becoming a delinquent is the same as the process of becoming, let us say, a Boy Scout. The difference lies only in the cultural pattern with which the children associate.
>
> (Cohen 1955, 11–14)

- What specific social factors do you think would predispose certain individuals to join delinquent subcultures?
- What problems can you think of with explaining delinquent behaviour as a collective, subcultural response?

The stress on delinquency as a collective response is a key aspect of Cohen's sociological theorizing. In contrast to Merton's argument, such behaviour is not an individual response to a failure to achieve middle-class goals. However, his approach can be criticized along the same lines as Merton's for its middle-class bias – he assumes that working-class delinquents cherish middle-class status goals such as doing well educationally. Furthermore, the extent to which working-class delinquents do really hold anti-middle-class, oppositional values is certainly debatable. As Tierney puts it:

> Cohen's theory of delinquency is based upon the assumption that the typical working class delinquent to some degree internalizes middle class norms and values prior to the creation of the subculture . . . the assumption is that middle class culture is widely dispersed and accepted throughout all social classes.
>
> (1996, 102–3)

Both Cohen and Merton see criminal behaviour as resulting from the strains that occur as a result of the inequality of opportunity that is inherent to modern (in their case American) society. This implies that equality of opportunity would be desirable and have an impact on the extent of criminal behaviour. Tierney points to a basic contradiction in such an approach in that equality of opportunity to succeed implies an equality of opportunity to fail – 'the concept of equality of opportunity presupposes the existence of social class inequality'. And, as we have seen, the structural and subcultural theories of Merton and Cohen see criminal behaviour as an inevitable response to such inequality.

Other theorists have developed variations of subcultural theorizing about criminal behaviour and we will mention some of this work here. Walter Miller (1958), writing a few years after Cohen, suggested that working-class culture (or 'lower class culture' as he put it) was characterized by certain 'focal concerns' and that these concerns – such as toughness, smartness and excitement – encouraged aggressive and often delinquent and criminal behaviour. So just being working- rather than middle-class would predispose individuals towards criminality, with the delinquent subculture seen as one sort of response to working-class life.

A more detailed analysis of delinquent subcultures was offered by Cloward and Ohlin (1960). They followed Merton's argument in highlighting the anomie that results from the lack of opportunities available to young working-class males. They also borrowed from Sutherland's work on differential association (see p. 111 below) and Cohen's emphasis on the collective, gang response by focusing on how such individuals will find and join up with others facing the same situation as themselves. Cloward and Ohlin then consider different 'illegitimate avenues' for achieving success. They suggest that the potential delinquent may respond to his situation by joining one of three distinct types of subculture – a criminal subculture where delinquency is linked with adult criminality; a conflict subculture which occurs in areas where links between juvenile and adult criminality are not established; and a retreatist or escapist subculture based around illegal drug use and attracting those who have failed to gain access to either legitimate or criminal subcultures.

Again a range of criticisms have been levelled at these early American subcultural theories. The sort of delinquent offenders they portray are seen as somehow different from non-offenders and who have been forced into delinquency by circumstances almost beyond their control. Such an explanation seems to ignore the fact that the majority of young males faced with similar situations do not join delinquent gangs. Also, the very notion of offending in gangs is questionable – a lot of juvenile offending is a solitary activity or involves only a small number of individuals. Subcultural theories focus on young offenders reacting against middle-class society and the norms associated with it; however they offer no explanation as to why such young offenders stop offending as they become older. Most people remain in the same social class after they reach adulthood and are still likely to experience the same lack of 'success'. This raises the question of why their behaviour changes away from delinquency, although, of course, other factors such as increased responsibilities are likely to play a part. Other criticisms include the lack of reference to the role of the authorities, such as the police, in labelling individuals as offenders (see below on labelling) and the assumption that juvenile offending is the preserve of young working-class males with no explanation offered for the offending of young females or of middle-class criminality. In evaluating these theories, Williams (2004) highlights Box's (1981) argument that they suffer from a basic implausibility in that 'lower', working-class boys are seen as being frustrated because they cannot attain middle-class goals, while such approaches also seem to argue that such boys do not really aspire to such goals anyway. It might be that those boys who just miss out on middle-class goals (rather than those who are miles away from them!) will suffer a greater disappointment and frustration.

CONTROL THEORY – TREVOR HIRSCHI

The explanations looked at so far have argued that conformity is normal behaviour and criminal behaviour is abnormal in some way; and that it follows that there must be something different, even abnormal, with those individuals who do commit crimes. These differences or abnormalities may be the result of biological, psychological or social factors; but some factor must be present in the individual which encourages their nonconformity.

The central argument of what have become termed 'control theories' is that crime is natural and conformity is the area that requires explanation. As Williams (2004) suggests in her introduction to control theories, conformist behaviour is the result of particular circumstances and criminal behaviour occurs when those circumstances change or break down. For instance it is not natural to form orderly queues when waiting for tickets yet most people will do so. Indeed throughout our lives, and particularly while growing up, we are learning what behaviour is acceptable and what is not. As Williams puts it, 'Parents at home, teachers at school and other individuals in the community . . . spend a lot of time and effort in controlling each of us'. She sees the essence of control theories as offering explanations for why people conform to rules and accept the social order as it is. Criminal behaviour is, then, the breakdown of the socialization process.

From this brief introduction control theories could be seen to cover a very broad range of explanations; indeed most sociological theorizing, from Durkheim's approach onwards, could be said to include notions of socialization and control. However this area of theorizing is often connected with the more recent work of Hirschi, who, along with Gottfredson in his earlier work, focused on the individual rather than external aspects of control, developing what has been termed a 'social bond' version of control theory. They focused on self-control based on early socialization, and especially on the role of the family. Williams cites two key aspects to their approach – the lack of self-control in an individual and the opportunities for committing crime: 'If the opportunity to commit a crime arises then the person with low self-control will commit it, whereas the person with high self-control will not.' Essentially self-control refers to the degree to which an individual is vulnerable to temptations.

The key issue that Hirschi tries to address is that of why (the majority of) people choose to follow the law. His original argument was that those people who break laws either do not have close attachments to others or do not have aims, aspirations and beliefs that bind them toward law-abiding behaviour. So young people who engage in delinquency do so because they are not strongly tied to the conventional social order – they have less self-control. As Hirschi and Gottfredson put it:

> The theory (of self control) simply stated, is this: Criminal acts are a subset of acts in which the actor ignores the long-term negative consequences that flow from the act itself (e.g. the health consequences of drug use), from the social or familial environment (e.g. a spouse's reaction to infidelity), or from the state (e.g. the criminal justice response to robbery). All acts that share this feature, including criminal acts, are therefore likely to be engaged in by individuals unusually sensitive to immediate pleasure and insensitive to long-term consequences . . . The evidence suggests to us that variation in self-control is established early in life, and that differences between individuals remain reasonably constant over the life course.
>
> (1994, 151)

In suggesting that law-breaking, rather than law-abiding, behaviour is natural, Hirschi is not restating the 'classical' theoretical position that crime is an expression of free will – people are not born wicked or 'criminal'. However, at birth children do not know what is acceptable and not acceptable and follow their natural desires until they are socialized into the activities of their own community. Socialization is seen as the process by which individuals learn about and consider the consequences of their behaviour. Once they have learnt and accepted this, there is little need for further reinforcement. As suggested above, the key issue or mystery then is how some people are able to ignore the consequences of their behaviour and carry on as if such consequences do not exist. It is very easy for people to steal, for instance, yet self-control will stop the majority of people from doing so. Hirschi also suggests that people are neither permanently law-abiding nor law-breaking – they may take part in criminal activities at certain periods while following a law-abiding lifestyle at others, depending on the controls that are affecting their lives at particular times.

Williams (2004) highlights four elements that Hirschi sees as vital 'social bonds' that are associated with law-abiding people as 'their attachments with other people; the commitments and responsibilities they develop; their involvement in conventional activity; and their beliefs'. To elaborate on these elements:

- Attachments – with other people and institutions in the community. Strong social and psychological attachments make criminal behaviour less likely as they make individuals more aware of and sensitive to the opinions of other people. (Hirschi is aware that strong attachments to criminal groups would have the opposite effect and encourage criminal behaviour.)
- Commitment – the more an individual has 'invested' in partners, children, education, occupation, property ownership and so on the less likely will she or he risk losing it through law-breaking behaviour. Individuals who do not consider such commitments important or who have fewer of them are seen as relatively freer to commit criminal acts.
- Involvement – refers to the extent that the individual is involved in their legitimate lifestyle or activity; the range of conventional interests they have and pursue. Crime is less likely if being involved in conventional activities is an important part of the individual's life.
- Beliefs – in this context Hirschi is referring to things an individual chooses to accept, including the law, rather than deeply held convictions. As these beliefs can be changed (by the individual accepting different arguments, for instance) they need constant social reinforcement.

The presence of each of these elements is seen by Hirschi as helping to prevent criminal behaviour and encourage lawful behaviour.

This theoretical position can be criticized for its generality and vagueness. Socialization is a vast concept and the question is still left as to whether socialization affects some people differently or whether they are differently socialized. It is almost like arguing that one's whole upbringing – interacting with inherited traits – will make the person what she or he is. In similar vein the theory has been criticized for being tautological – it starts from a conception of crime (as acts in which people ignore the consequences of the behaviour) and derives a conception of the offender from this (a person who ignores the consequences of their acts). However, Hirschi and Gottfredson see this as a positive element of their theorizing:

> What distinguishes our theory from many criminological theories is that we begin with the act, whereas they normally begin with the actor. Theories that start from the causes of crime – for example, economic deprivation – eventually define crime as a response to the causes they invoke. Thus, a theory that sees economic deprivation as the cause of crime will by definition see crime as an attempt to remedy economic deprivation, making the connection between cause and effect tautological. What makes our theory peculiarly vulnerable to complaints about tautology is that we explicitly show the logical connections between our conception of the actor and the act, whereas many theories leave this task to those interpreting or testing their theory, but again we are not impressed that we are unusual in this regard . . .
>
> In a comparative framework, the charge of tautology suggests that a theory that is nontautological would be preferable. But what would such a theory look like? It would advance definitions of crime and of criminals that are independent of one another.

(1994, 156)

In spite of criticisms, Hirschi's central argument that those who engage in crime and delinquency feel cut off from typical societal bonds has been widely and generally accepted.

THE CRIMINAL AS 'NORMAL' – DAVID MATZA

As suggested in introducing social control theories above, most of the theorists looked at so far have examined how criminal behaviour is a response to particular social circumstances and have stressed how, in responding to those circumstances, criminals become distinct from the mainstream, non-criminal population. We will now turn to theoretical explanations which see the criminal as 'normal' and focus on how society defines certain individuals or groups as criminal. These explanations stem from a critique of what is seen as the determinism of structural and subcultural theories. In developing this critique the work of David Matza was of particular importance.

The notion of a delinquent subculture implies that working-class adolescents are committed to certain delinquent values. However, Matza points out that delinquents generally conform to certain traditions and values of society and reject others. They are not in opposition to or conflict with all aspects of the wider society – indeed they may often be quite conservative in their social and political views. Furthermore, most juvenile delinquents do not engage full-time in delinquent activity and 'give it up' in early adulthood – there are relatively few delinquents aged over 30. In Matza's view, adolescents from time to time act out delinquent roles, rather than become committed to permanent violation of the rules of conventional society. He argued that they drift into and out of delinquent activities rather than embrace them as a way of life – his approach is illustrated by the title of one of his major studies, *Delinquency and Drift*.

Matza accepted that adolescents can be part of subcultures whose members do engage in delinquency but did not see such behaviour as a permanent way of life. Indeed he pointed out that individuals could be part of a 'subculture of delinquency' without actually taking part in offending behaviour. As with other explanatory approaches which have criticized 'deterministic' theories of crime, Matza saw the process of becoming an offender in terms of stages. The first stage involves some form of opposition to mainstream values and culture and a desire to be accepted as a member of a group – this is likely to involve some form of criminal or rule-breaking behaviour as a means of gaining acceptance. The second stage comes after these original anxieties about acceptance have been overcome and involves a release from conventional forms of social control which allows the individual to choose to drift into delinquency. During this stage the individual has to adopt what Matza termed 'techniques of neutralization'. He identified five major types of neutralization – a typology that has become established in sociological theorizing about crime:

- The denial of responsibility ('I didn't mean to do it')
- The denial of injury ('I didn't hurt anyone')
- The denial of the victim ('S/he deserved it')

- The condemnation of the condemners ('They're just as bad')
- The appeal to higher loyalties ('I was helping my mates').

While such techniques are basically excuses, Matza argued that they also provide individuals with 'episodic release' from general moral and social constraints and enable the drift into delinquency.

The third stage is when the individual has drifted into delinquency. Such behaviour has been justified and this leads to the acceptance of responsibility for their delinquent and offending behaviour. As Burke (2005) describes it: 'They *know* their activities are against the law. They *know* that they may be caught. They *know* that they may be punished. They probably accept that they *should* be punished. It is one of the rules of the game' (13 – emphasis in the original).

As an aside, Burke (2005) highlights how Matza's theorizing has been applied to the study of business crime, where corporate offenders use the same techniques of neutralization to rationalize their illegal behaviour and assuage any feelings of guilt.

QUESTION BREAK

Matza suggests that there are three stages in becoming an offender

- opposition
- neutralization
- fully accepting their criminality.

Consider how those who engage in the following crimes might fit in with these three stages:

- Robbery
- Terrorism
- Fraud

You might also consider a range of other criminal behaviour and relate it to Matza's argument.

DIFFERENTIAL ASSOCIATION – EDWIN SUTHERLAND

The process of drift and the notion of stages in becoming a delinquent are central to the labelling perspectives on crime that came to dominate sociological theorizing in the 1960s and 1970s which we will consider below. Before doing so it would be useful to refer back to the social learning approach to explaining crime discussed as an example of psychological theorizing (pp. 70–1). Indeed, this highlights the difficulties of dividing theoretical approaches into neat categories – while useful for organizing a textbook it does not acknowledge the overlap and blurring between different approaches. The idea of learning to become an offender was central to the concept of differential association developed by Edwin Sutherland. Differential association explains criminal behaviour in terms of the contact, or association, with particular social groups and environments. It moves away from early theorizing that centred on the individual characteristics of offenders. Sutherland was one of a group of social scientists based at the University of Chicago in the 1920s and 1930s who challenged the individualistic explanations for crime.

Sutherland argued that crime was socially defined by powerful sections of society, but he did not lose sight of the individual and how particular individuals were drawn into crime. He felt that criminal behaviour was learned just as any form of behaviour is. This led to the question of how is criminal behaviour learned, which Sutherland answered in terms of differential association: individuals have differential associations with other people who are either more or less disposed to criminality. The essence of this approach is that criminal behaviour is learned; the learning occurs through association with other people; learning includes ways and means for carrying out crimes; and so the process involved in learning criminal behaviour is no different from that involved in learning any other type of behaviour. It can be seen from this brief account that Sutherland's theory is both sociological, in its acknowledgement of the powerful of social forces to define crime, and psychological, with its concern for the individual. And, as with Matza's work, Sutherland applied his theory of differential association to business crime or crimes of the powerful.

This emphasis on interactions indicates the influence of the notion of differential association on the labelling explanations that developed from the interactionist (sometimes known as symbolic interactionist) perspective within sociology.

INTERACTIONIST THEORIES

Partly in response to some of the problems associated with the structural and subcultural theories, a different theoretical approach was developed by the interactionist perspective that became particularly influential in sociology in the 1960s and 1970s. Rather than seeing crime and deviant behaviour as a response of people to their social situation – and a response which established them as distinct from the mainstream, 'normal' population – the interactionist position was that the criminal or deviant can be quite normal. The emphasis, therefore, should be on how society defines certain individuals and groups as criminal or deviant. As can be seen from this introductory paragraph, interactionists refer to both crime and deviance, and the terms are quite often used interchangeably. Essentially, crime can be defined as action that breaks the criminal law and can be followed by criminal proceedings, while deviance is not used in its literal sense (as anything that is different or deviates from the normal) but taken to refer to any behaviour that is outside the rules of society and that is generally disapproved of. These rules might be legal rules, such as laws, or social and moral rules, such as conventional rules about how people should behave in public, for instance. Below we will usually refer to crime and criminal behaviour when introducing labelling theory.

A major criticism of the earlier theories of crime, from both outside of and within sociology, was their tendency to see such behaviour as relatively straightforward and easily recognizable – as behaviour that breaks the law. Such approaches imply that a general consensus exists within society as to what is right and wrong behaviour. Interactionist work questions this assumption. Numerous studies, plus our common-sense understanding, tell us that most people have broken the law, and that many people do so frequently without ever being recorded as criminals. Given this, it becomes difficult to argue that criminals are somehow different from the rest of society.

QUESTION BREAK

Which of the following crimes have you committed? How often have you done so?

- Taking stationery or similar from the workplace
- Keeping money if you received too much in change
- Keeping money found in the street
- Buying goods that may have been stolen
- Stealing from a shop
- Drinking in a pub while under age
- Taking illegal drugs
- Using a television set without a licence
- Taking 'souvenirs' from a hotel, pub or similar.

All of these actions break the criminal law.

- What would stop you committing those actions?

Labelling

Labelling theory is perhaps the key element of interactionist theorizing on crime and deviance. The focus is on the relationship, or interaction, between the criminal and those groups or individuals who define him or her as such. Essentially, the argument is that the criminal or deviant is an individual who has been labelled by society. The approach is associated with the work of a number of post-Second-World-War American sociologists. Perhaps the most famous and quoted statement defining the labelling approach is found in Howard Becker's collection of essays *Outsiders*:

Social groups create deviance by making rules whose infraction constitutes deviance and by applying those rules to particular people and labelling them as outsiders. From this point of view deviance is not a quality of the act a person commits, but rather a consequence of the application by others of rules and sanctions to an offender. The deviant is one to whom that label has been successfully applied; deviant behaviour is behaviour that people so label.

(1963, 9)

This comment indicates that labelling is a process by which individuals and/or groups classify and categorize certain types of behaviour and certain individuals. The focus on labelling raises the obvious question of 'who does the labelling?' – with the actions and motives of the labellers a key concern. Indeed consideration of the labellers highlights issues of who has the power to impose their definitions on others and of the extent to which there is a selective enforcement of the law. This is a concern articulated by Giddens:

The labels applied to create categories of deviance thus express the power structure of society. By and large, the rules in terms of which deviance is defined, and the contexts in which they are applied, are framed by the wealthy for the poor, by men for women, by older people for younger people and by ethnic majorities for minority groups.

(1993, 128)

Selective enforcement of the law

Laws and rules are seen as essentially political products that reflect the power some groups in society have: a power which enables them to impose their ideas about right and wrong on the rest of society. Of course it might be pointed out that the criminal law applies to everyone in society, including the rich and powerful, but interactionists would argue that those laws are less frequently and less vigorously applied to some groups and some individuals rather than others.

In his study of the administration of juvenile justice in the USA, Cicourel (1968) looked at the actual process of how delinquency and criminality are defined and applied to certain individuals and groups. His study followed a cohort of juveniles 'from their first contact with the police through their disposition by probation officials or juvenile court'. Essentially, Cicourel found that white, middle-class youths were less liable to be identified by the police and probation officers as having committed or being likely to commit a crime. The police were more likely to react toward those groups and individuals whom they saw as being prone to criminal activity, often labelling them before they actually commit any criminal action. The police, like most people, were seen as having stereotypical views as to the 'typical' criminal or delinquent. In the procedures of arresting and charging individuals and in their treatment in court, Cicourel found clear differences across the middle/working-class divide; and these serve to reinforce the public's (and police's) perception that certain groups are inclined to criminality. For instance he found that probation and social workers believed that delinquent behaviour was caused by factors such as 'broken homes', 'poor parenting' or 'poverty' and so juveniles who were seen as coming from such backgrounds 'were seen as the likeliest candidates for a delinquent career and were often, albeit unwittingly, launched upon one' (Burke 2005, 146). In contrasting the treatment of juveniles from different class backgrounds, Cicourel's research included case studies of youths from middle-class backgrounds who had been involved in 'juvenile offences'. In these situations, he found that both law-enforcement officers and family members managed to preserve ideal images of the family unit. The following quotation illustrates this differential reaction to young middle-class offenders and Cicourel's argument that certain groups are selected, processed and labelled as criminals:

> When parents challenge police and probation imputations of deviance, when parents can mobilize favourable occupational and household appearances . . . law-enforcement personnel find it difficult (because of their own commitments to appearances – lack of a broken home, 'reasonable' parents, 'nice' neighbourhoods etc.) to make a case from criminality in direct confrontation with family resources and a 'rosy' projected future. Imputations of illness replace those of criminality, or the incidents are viewed as 'bad' but products of 'things' done by 'kids' today.
>
> (1976, 243)

QUESTION BREAK

Cicourel's research on selective law enforcement was conducted over thirty years ago.

- Give more recent examples of how the police and others who work in the criminal justice system might stereotype different individuals and groups.
- What sort of groups and individuals are most likely to 'suffer' from such stereotyping? Why is this?

Consequences of labelling

We have not got the space here to consider the various examples of labelling theorizing. However in terms of the consequences of labelling for the individual it would be useful to refer to Lemert's conceptualization of primary and secondary deviance and to the notion of deviance amplification. In an early and pioneering work on the labelling of deviant behaviour, Lemert (1951) posed a theoretical distinction between primary and secondary deviation. As he put it in a later paper, he devised this distinction to highlight 'how deviant behaviour originates . . . [and] how deviant acts are symbolically attached to persons and the effective consequences of such attachment for subsequent deviation on the part of the person' (1967, 17). Primary deviance (although Lemert used the term deviation) refers to the initial act – and can be of a very tentative nature and occur in a wide variety of contexts. As such the initial act has only 'marginal implications for the psychic structure of the individual'. As Burke (2005) puts it, 'in short, primary deviants do not view their deviance as central to themselves and do not conceive of themselves as deviants'. It is the social reaction to the primary deviance that can lead to the offender becoming labelled as a criminal or deviant of some sort. In this situation the individual offender is faced with a crisis which, for some, can be resolved by accepting a deviant status and by becoming a secondary deviant, which will lead him or her to 'organise their life and identity around the facts of deviance' (Burke 2005). To use Lemert's own words:

> Secondary deviation is deviant behaviour, or social roles based upon it, which becomes a means of defense, attack or adaptation to the overt and covert problems created by the social reaction to primary deviation. In effect the original 'causes' of the deviation recede and give way to the central importance of the disapproving, degradational and isolating reactions of society.
>
> (1967, 17)

Lemert sees the distinction between primary and secondary deviation as a key factor in trying to develop a complete understanding of such behaviour. Crime and deviance are seen as the end products of a process of human interaction – primary deviance may or may not develop into secondary deviance depending on the extent and strength of the reaction that it engenders.

> A sociological theory of deviant behaviour must focus specifically on the inter-actions which not only define the behaviour as deviant but also organize and activate the application of sanctions by individuals, groups and agencies. For in modern society the socially significant differentiation of deviants from non-deviants is increasingly contingent upon circumstances of situation, place, social and personal biography and bureaucratically organized agencies of social control.
>
> (1967, 17–18)

In terms of what happens to the individual once she or he is labelled as a criminal or deviant, the process by and extent to which the label becomes fixed (its degree of permanence perhaps) is important to consider. Labelling an individual will mark them out, and knowing a person has been labelled will be liable to influence the behaviour of other people towards them. Knowing that someone has been convicted of theft, for example, might well influence how other people react and respond – keeping a closer eye on their possessions perhaps! Furthermore, the individual who has been labelled will be likely to view himself or herself in terms of the label and act accordingly. This leads to what is know as the process of amplification or snow-balling – an individual is caught and labelled a criminal, she or her sees herself or himself so and acts in that way, as a result the label becomes more widely applied and firmly fixed and the individual more attached to it.

This amplification process can occur on a wider, societal level, as well as at an individual level. Jock Young's work on hippies and the police in London during the 1960s and 1970s illustrated this wider application. Young (1971) found that the harder the police tried to stamp out drug use amongst hippies the more it actually grew. He suggested that the police themselves acted as amplifiers of this illegal behaviour. The police attempted to control drug use through the formation of drug squads; however this had the effect of spreading and amplifying such drug use. The drug squads discovered more cases of drug use because that was what they were searching for; this led to more police time and money being invested in dealing with it; this led to even more drug use being discovered – in other words there was a 'spiral of amplification'. Furthermore, Young argued that the way in which the police acted against hippies, stereotyping them as dirty, idle drug fiends and harassing them, helped to unite drug users and led to the development of a sort of group identity and ethos: 'drug taking becomes of greater value to the group as a result of the greater police activity'.

The interactionist approach to explaining crime implies that for the purpose of studying such behaviour there is a correlation between being a criminal and being seen to be a criminal. It makes no real difference whether the 'criminal' is innocent or guilty – for the purpose of theoretical explanation such a distinction is essentially irrelevant. In other words, being found guilty has the same consequences for the individual(s) as being guilty. Now of course common sense would tell us that there is a significant difference between a murderer or bank robber and someone who has been wrongfully convicted of murder or bank robbery. And it could be argued that there is a clear moral and philosophical difference between the 'innocent' and the 'guilty' criminal. However, this difference is not likely to have any effect on the way in which the two 'criminals' are treated. The wrongfully convicted prisoner will be treated identically to any other prisoner by prison officers. Furthermore, protesting one's innocence will be viewed as the kind of thing that everyone does and will gain little sympathy – indeed it may annoy and antagonize prison staff.

So being convicted involves being identified publicly as a criminal and it is in this context that we can say that being found guilty is the same as really being guilty – in terms of how the individual is treated and responded to by others. Thus being known as a criminal is the same as being one. It is these arguments that led interactionists to stress how labelling is crucial to the understanding of criminal and deviant behaviour – the labelling process publicly identifies individuals as guilty of criminal acts and leads to the consequences we have considered above.

QUESTION BREAK

- What groups of people are most likely to be labelled as criminals? Why is this?
- How might protesting one's innocence make life more difficult for a prisoner?

Look up examples of recent miscarriages of justice. Examples could include Stephen Downing (the 'Bakewell murder') or the Hickeys (murder of Carl Bridgewater).

- What led to the uncovering of the miscarriage?
- Did the individual's protesting of his or her innocence have any effect?

■ CASE STUDY BOX 4.1 LABELLING AND MENTAL ILLNESS

Of course the concept of labelling is not limited to criminal and deviant behaviour but occurs in all walks of life. For instance in schools and colleges teachers label pupils and pupils will also label teachers; and once a label is given it is difficult to lose it, for instance once a child is labelled as 'thick' or a 'troublemaker', or indeed positively as 'bright', he or she will tend to be responded to by others in terms of that label. At work bosses label their employees and vice versa, while workers will similarly label their colleagues in work. In the area of mental health, an area often examined as a form of deviance, the application of labels has been common-place and a number of studies have examined the effects of this labelling. Such studies have looked at the labelling of particular forms of behaviour as mental illness at different periods of time to illustrate the extent and power of labelling as a process.

For instance, from 1952 until 1980 in the United States, homosexuality was listed and accepted as a mental disorder, and people identified as homosexuals were expected to go for treatment. It was on the Diagnostic and Statistical Manual of Mental Disorders list – the official list of mental disorders. And in the mid nineteenth century women who expressed their frustrations through anger or crying were regularly classified as suffering from hysteria – and confined to their beds for treatment. One particularly famous piece of research was carried out by Rosenham in the early 1970s in the USA and reported in his paper 'On being insane in sane places'. He persuaded eight 'normal' people to try and gain admittance to psychiatric hospitals by claiming to hear voices in their heads. Once they had done this they behaved as they would usually – and although they tried to get discharged as soon as possible it took them on average 19 days to be discharged (with one 'pseudo-patient' being kept in for 52 days). Indeed their usual behaviours – such as writing notes – were diagnosed as 'exhibiting obsessive writing behaviour'. Clearly the hospital staff assumed the patients were mentally ill and responded to them as such – interpreting all of their behaviour as evidence of their illness.

Interactionist approaches – a brief critique

As mentioned above, interactionist theories of crime and deviance, centred on the notion of labelling, became particularly influential in the 1960s and 1970s. The focus on the meanings that such behaviour held for those engaged in it, and specifically the interaction between the criminal and agents of social control, seemed to offer a new direction for the sociology of crime and deviance. These developments attracted a good deal of debate and criticism as well – so much so that in 1973, ten years after the original publication, Howard Becker added an extra, final chapter to his famous study *Outsiders*, entitled 'Labelling theory reconsidered', in which he addressed some of the major concerns that had been raised about this perspective.

Labelling theory was criticized for implying that criminals were powerless and passive victims who have just had the misfortune to be labelled criminal and have not been able to do much about it. This seemed to ignore the fact that criminals might often choose to become so – people engage in fraud, smuggling and other crime because they want to. Too great an emphasis is given to the social reaction, thereby minimizing the role of the individual criminal or deviant. Linked with this, labelling theory has been seen as ignoring the origins of criminal behaviour – there is little explanation as to why certain people break laws and others do not. Criticisms, then, highlight what is seen as an over-emphasis on the social reaction and argue that there is no real explanation as to why some actions are made illegal, and of who makes the laws and why.

In 'Labelling theory reconsidered', Becker started by suggesting that the term 'labelling theory' was in itself inappropriate. His original work, and that of others, did not warrant being seen as a full-blown theory – a point which critics had, he argued, not recognized. His original position did not attempt to propose solutions as to the origin of criminal behaviour – the etiological question as he put it. Rather he and others had more modest aims: 'to enlarge the area taken into consideration in the study of deviant phenomena by including in it activities of others than the allegedly deviant actor' (179) and 'labelling theory . . . is, rather, a way of looking at a general area of human activity; a perspective whose value will appear, if at all, in increased understanding of things formerly obscure' (181).

Becker responded to the suggestions that individual criminals were seen as powerless and passive victims by pointing out that 'the act of labelling . . . while important, cannot possibly be conceived as the sole explanation of what deviants actually do. It would be foolish to propose that stick-up men stick people up simply because someone has labelled them stick-up men' (179) and 'To suggest that defining someone as deviant may under certain circumstances dispose him to a particular line of action is not the same as saying that mental hospitals always drive people crazy or that jails always turn people into habitual criminals' (180).

In summary, interactionist approaches concentrate on the specific 'drama' of crime without examining in depth the inequalities of power that underlie the defining and treating of criminal behaviour. It is these issues around decision-making and the distribution of power that are central to conflict- and Marxist-based theories of crime which we look at below.

CONFLICT-BASED AND MARXIST-BASED THEORIES

Marxist-based explanations of crime encompass a range of different approaches with different emphases and nuances, which have been categorized under various headings including critical criminology, radical criminology, left realism and left idealism. Before introducing some of these developments we will consider the common core underpinning these theoretical explanations and diversions.

Neither Marx nor his collaborator and colleague Engels proposed a full-blown theory of crime; and it has been later social theorists working within a Marxist framework who have developed a Marxist theory of crime. This work has centred on an examination of how crime relates to the power structure of society. From a Marxist perspective crime is largely the product of capitalism, and the relatively high rate of crime in capitalist societies is an indicator of the contradictions and problems that are inherent to such a system. Thus many forms of crime are to be expected under a capitalist system. This is due, in part, to the ability of the powerful to criminalize that which threatens their interests; and to the fact that basic motivations of capitalist societies, such as materialism and self-enrichment, can be pursued illegally as well as legally. In relation to crime one of the crucial questions for Marxists is not 'why does crime occur?' but rather 'why doesn't it occur more often?'.

A Marxist analysis of crime cannot be considered in isolation from the broader Marxist analysis of society. In a key example of a Marxist-based, conflict perspective on crime, Quinney (1977) points out that 'an understanding of crime in our society begins with the recognition that the crucial phenomenon to be considered is not crime per se, but the historical development and operation of capitalist society' (39). He argues that understanding crime necessitates an examination of fundamental aspects of capitalism, such as alienation, inequality, poverty and the economic crisis of the capitalist state. In focusing on work, alienation and exploitation – key features of class struggle in the Marxist analysis – Quinney suggests that as work is a central life activity, when it is thwarted 'the way is open for activity that is detrimental to self and others'. He goes on to argue that 'activity of a criminal nature becomes a rational and likely possibility under the conditions of capitalism' and that 'crime is a by-product of the political economy of capitalism'.

Later on in his study Quinney (1977) responds to the functional argument of Durkheim that crime is necessary and inevitable. The fact that many people are employed in dealing with crime in one way or another merely demonstrates that crime is generated within the capitalist mode of production. However even within capitalism this does not make crime functional: 'it results from the contradictions of capitalism, and it contributes further to these contradictions'.

As mentioned, Marxist explanations of crime cannot be considered apart from the broader Marxist analysis of society. This analysis holds that there is a basic distinction between the economic base of society, which determines the organization and structure of society, and the superstructure, the cultural, legal, religious and political aspects of society. These aspects of the superstructure support and reflect the economic base. Therefore, the law will be in line with and reflect the interests of the dominant economic class, and, as an instrument of this dominant class, the state will pass laws which support its interests. The various social control agencies of the state, such as the police, courts and prisons, will also perform in a way that is consistent with the interests of the powerful and against the interests of other less powerful groups, particularly the working classes.

So the criminal law is assumed to express and reflect the interests of the powerful. As evidence for this Marxists point out that much of the law is about the protection of property; and highlight the vast increase in the range of behaviour that has become subject to criminal law in capitalist societies. In their introduction to *Critical Criminology*, a key text in the development of Marxist, critical criminology, Taylor, Walton and Young (1975) point out that old laws have been reactivated and new ones created in order to control and contain an ever widening range of what is perceived as socially problematic behaviour. New laws that, for example, regulate industrial dissent and the right of workers to organize can create new criminals who do not fit the picture of the 'typical criminal' – the young working-class male. In view of this, Taylor and colleagues argue that criminological theorizing has to examine rule-making and breaking in relation to the distribution of power in society.

However, power in capitalist societies is not just about formal and institutionalized control and includes the ability to influence the way people think through controlling knowledge and ideas. Marxists argue that there is a dominant ideology from which the standards of acceptable and 'normal' behaviour, and as a consequence behaviour that is problematic and criminal, are defined. An illustration of this is the way in which the law, the media and public opinion would seem to view benefit frauds, 'fiddling the dole', as being more serious and costly than, say, tax evasion, which costs the exchequer billions of pounds, far in excess of the costs of benefit fiddling. The notion that the law reflects economic interests and protects the dominant classes from threatening or disruptive behaviour, and indeed enables the powerful to get away with exploiting the less powerful without actually breaking the law, is highlighted in Marxist-based studies of white-collar and corporate crime.

Such studies have helped move the focus away from the powerless and marginalized in society. Frank Pearce (1976) has argued that organized crime in the USA is dominated by business; and that the criminal activities of American business corporations involved far more money than did conventional crime. In line with a Marxist argument, Pearce felt that such criminal activity was rarely prosecuted as to do so would 'subvert the ideology that the bulk of crime is carried out by the poor, and would create a crisis of legitimacy for the capitalist system' (Tierney 1996). In similar vein, William Chambliss (1978), in a detailed study of crime in Seattle, Washington, demonstrated the interconnections between organized crime and the ruling groups in society. Of course the cost of crime is very difficult to even estimate, but a recent survey of one hundred major British companies carried out by consultants RSM Robson Rhodes (2004) in conjunction with the Home Office and Fraud Advisory Panel concluded that economic crimes such as fraud and corruption were costing British business £40 billion a year, equivalent to about 4 per cent of Britain's gross domestic product – and they suggested that this could be just the tip of the iceberg.

Another key way in which the criminal law reflects the interests of the powerful is the assumption that the 'crime problem' refers to working-class crime, often of a relatively trivial nature, and not the more costly area of white-collar and business crime. And that the law is enforced selectively in the interests of the dominant and powerful groups. Put simply, the Marxist argument is that the law, by largely ignoring white-collar/business crime, gives the impression that criminals are mainly from the working classes; and that this serves to direct attention away from 'ruling-class crime'. Examples of the differential treatment of 'conventional' from business crime are provided in the following question break.

QUESTION BREAK

The following extracts describe the manner in which two different types of criminal activity – burglary and business fraud – and two different offenders were treated by the criminal justice system in the USA. The first refers to the case of Martha Stewart, celebrity 'lifestyle guru', who was convicted of four counts of conspiracy, obstruction of justice and lying to the government about the sale of shares worth £250,000 in December 2001 and jailed for five months in 2004. The second refers to a shoplifter and burglar who was jailed for 25 years under California's 'three strikes and you're out' law.

Martha Stewart starts prison term

Martha Stewart, the US lifestyle guru convicted of lying to federal investigators about a suspicious share sale . . . was sentenced to five months imprisonment in July, after being found guilty of conspiracy and obstruction. Her website revealed that she had started her prison term at a minimum-security jail in West Virginia on Friday. Stewart earned millions from a business empire based on selling domestic items and lifestyle advice . . .

Although she stepped down as chairwoman and chief executive of her firm, Martha Stewart Omnimedia, the domestic icon remains the biggest shareholder in the business. She is expected to resume working for the firm after her release from prison.

(BBC News, 8 October 2004, www.news.bbc.co.uk)

Buried alive under California's law of 'three strikes and you're out'

Brian A. Smith didn't know the two women who were shoplifting. They were caught on security cameras stealing sheets at Los Cerritos mall in Los Angeles and received a two-year sentence. But Smith was seen standing near the shoplifters as they committed their crime. Despite having no stolen goods, he was convicted of aiding and abetting them. Under California's three strikes law, which marked its 10th anniversary on Sunday, the 30 year old received a 25-year-to-life sentence.

Smith's crime was to have two previous convictions, one 11 years earlier and the second six years before the shoplifting incident. Those convictions . . . earned him the dubious honour of being one of the first criminals to be sentenced under the California law . . .

Under the three strikes law, 25 years means 25 years: prisoners have no chance of parole. The law was voted for in March 1994, under California's proposition system, in which the electorate votes directly for specific policy initiatives. But unlike the three strikes laws operating in some other states, California's version does not restrict the initiative to violent crimes. Sixty-five per cent of those imprisoned under three strikes in California were convicted of non-violent crimes; 354 of them received 25-years-to-life sentences for petty theft of less than $250.

(Guardian, 8 March 2004)

- What factors do you think played a part in the treatment and sentencing of the two offenders?
- How might a Marxist or conflict theory of crime interpret the two extracts?

Strands of Marxist criminology – left realism and left idealism

As we have indicated, Marxist-based explanations do not constitute a unified perspective. In particular, and partly as a reaction to the new Marxist critical criminology of the 1970s, two different approaches or strands developed in the 1980s under the headings of left realism and left idealism.

Left realism developed as a criticism of the Marxist emphasis on crime as a response to class inequalities and to the patriarchal nature of advanced industrial societies. It is a realistic approach in that the reality of crime for ordinary working-class people is recognized. The fact that victims of crime are overwhelmingly from poor, working-class backgrounds – and that much crime is committed by the working class on the working class – is highlighted. The fear of crime is seen as based on the real experiences of people – as Tierney (1996) puts it, 'it is not the result of false consciousness created by media-induced moral panics'. Critical, 'left idealist' criminologists were seen as concentrating too much on crimes of the powerful and of underplaying the effects of crime carried out by working-class males – and indeed of having a somewhat romantic view of working-class crime as being a fight against the capitalist system.

The left realist approach involves examining all the basic components of crime – what one of the foremost proponents of this position, Jock Young, has termed the 'square of crime'. The square of crime includes four factors – the state, society, the offenders and the victims – and all need to be included in an analysis of all forms of crime and in any attempt to prevent and deal successfully with crime. This is summarized very clearly by Burke (2005):

> The square of crime is a reminder that crime is the result of a number of lines of force and that intervention to prevent it must therefore take place at different levels in order to be effective. Left realists propose that crime is a function of four factors. First, there is the state, principally through the capacity of its front-line agents to label individuals and groups as offenders. Second, there is the victim who may actually encourage offenders through inadequate defence or may even precipitate crime through his or her life-style or personality. Third, there is society, through which the various sources of social control are exercised. Fourth, there are the offenders themselves (their number, their rate of offending, the type of crime they commit etc.) . . . Fundamentally, all crime prevention efforts, of whatever type, involve some relationship between the four corners of the square.

(224)

The belief that crime should be taken seriously led left realists to become involved in research and policy issues, including the development of local victimization studies which asked people directly about the crimes they were troubled by and their views on police effectiveness. Such surveys (for instance the Islington Crime Survey of 1986) highlighted the greater burden of crime on the poor and ethnic minorities. The need to intervene to do something about crime was a central concern of the left realist position. It stressed the importance of both 'social' and 'situational' crime prevention; as Young (1971) himself put it, 'the ultimate task is to make fundamental changes in the social order whilst at the same time intervening on a day-to-day basis to protect the public . . . the central problem is to remain committed to change without being merely utopian'.

Left idealism is often contrasted with left realism – indeed left realism was essentially a reaction to what was felt to be the tendency for Marxist criminologists to idealize and romanticize the working-class criminal and not take enough account of the effect of crime on working-class people and communities. However, a number of British criminologists (including Gilroy, Scraton, Sim and Gordon amongst others) did not accept this left realist argument. They felt that left realism oversimplified the idealist position. Left idealists supported practical action by community groups to change and reform the criminal justice system – and supported those who questioned the way the criminal justice system operated. In Britain, they have supported and worked with groups involved in major political issues such as the Hillsborough disaster of 1989 and the inquiry into the death of Stephen Lawrence (1999).

FEMINIST CRIMINOLOGY

Other developments that can be seen as part of a more radical approach to explaining crime have come from feminist theorizing. Until the 1970s the study of crime had been a very male-dominated area – but the work of Smart and later Heidensohn highlighted the neglect of women in the study of crime. There had been some well-known (or perhaps infamous would be a better description) earlier explanations of female criminality. Lombroso, whose somewhat bizarre theories of crime and criminals were looked at earlier (see Chapter 2, pp. 23–4), in a famous study with Ferrero published in 1895 and entitled *The Female Offender*, offered a physiological explanations for the low rate of female crime, arguing that the physical characteristics that were linked with criminality were much rarer amongst females than males. He argued that women were 'congenitally less inclined to crime than men' and that those women who did commit crime were not feminine. Although largely discredited, the biological argument that women are naturally less inclined to crime and that female criminals are in some ways maladjusted has never been fully abandoned. In a variant of the biological explanation, in 1950 Pollak argued that female crime occurred to a much greater extent than crime statistics indicated but that female crime was much less likely to be detected, in part because of the naturally devious and cunning nature of women which enabled them to successfully conceal their crimes and avoid being caught. These early biologically based explanations have been criticized by feminists and social scientists more generally. Without detailing these criticisms, it is basically insulting to suggest that the female personality is biologically determined in a way that makes women incapable of rational action.

The feminist explanations in the 1970s came as a relief from these early deterministic theories and have been seen as part of a 'second wave' of feminism – the first having been at the turn of the nineteenth to the twentieth century, encompassing the move to universal suffrage. Carol Smart's book *Women, Crime and Criminology*, published in 1976, was the first major example of British feminist criminology and highlighted both the neglect of women in the study of crime and the weaknesses, and sexism, of explanations that had included women. Heidensohn, another noted British feminist and criminologist, considered why criminological research had been so male-dominated. She pointed to the fact that 'the discipline has been dominated by men, which affected such things as access to male gangs, cultural assumptions about masculinity and femininity, and a fascination with the macho, working class deviant' (Tierney 1996). Although the female crime rate is lower than the male rate, explanations for male crime based around structural factors such as poverty, inner city life, the mass media and so on did not explain why females faced with similar experiences apparently committed less crime. As Smart put it, a feminist approach should 'situate the discussion of sex roles within a structural explanation of the social origin of those roles' (quoted in Tierney 1996).

As well as examining female crime and reasons for differing rates of crime between men and women, feminist approaches have also considered issues around criminal justice. These issues include the treatment of women offenders by the criminal justice system – the police, courts and prisons in particular – and the ways in which women working within the system have fared, with regard to working practices, careers and promotions for instance. As regards the treatment of women by the criminal justice system, research and explanations have tended to polarize around the views that women are treated more leniently than men or that they are treated more severely because, as women, they are less expected to commit crime. These contrary views have become referred to as the 'chivalry versus doubly deviant' debate. The fact that far more men than women are convicted and the male prison population far outnumbers the female prison population does not necessarily mean that women are treated more leniently than men. Lloyd (1995) in her study *Doubly Deviant, Doubly Damned* examined the chivalry argument that women offenders are treated more leniently than males. She found that while this was the case for some women it was not for all. In particular, lenience or chivalry from the police and the courts seemed to be limited to certain types of women. Women who did not conform to a stereotypical picture of how women should behave were treated more strictly and with less understanding than male offenders – they were seen as offending against the law and against conventional notions of 'good women'. She found that domesticity was a key factor affecting the sentencing of women criminals – the family role and being a good mother was often an important aspect of mitigation pleas and the judiciary seemed to be influenced by the impact of sentencing on children. So 'conventional women', married women and mothers for instance, were treated with more leniency than others.

- What are the benefits for women offenders of being treated 'chivalrously'?
- What disadvantages might such treatment bring?
- List some arguments for and against motherhood affecting the sentencing of women offenders.

A further area where feminist criminology has been important is in highlighting the victimization of women. A major aspect of this area of feminist research has focused on women as victims of sexual crime and domestic violence and the massive under-reporting of such criminality.

This brief overview has considered feminism as a unified approach; however it is important to point out that feminism has a long history and, just as there are variations of feminism in general, so there are different feminist approaches to the study of crime. Daly (2004) suggests two major approaches – one based on liberal theory and one on critical social theory. The former focuses on role differences between men and women and suggests that women are denied the opportunities to do the same things as men, including taking part in crime. Critical social theory emphasizes gender power relations and focuses on how gender interacts with class and racial or ethnic differences. These and other aspects of feminist criminology are considered in greater depth in an examination of women and crime in Chapter 5.

RECENT DEVELOPMENTS – THE POSTMODERN INFLUENCE

In this chapter we have looked at explanations for crime going back over two hundred years. In concluding we will consider some of the recent and current areas of interest in theorizing about crime and consider their possible impact on criminological theorizing.

Changes in the social, political, cultural and economic arenas of life in the late twentieth century led theorists to suggest that Western societies in particular had reached a condition of 'postmodernity'. Some scholars have preferred to use terms such as 'late modernity' or 'high modernity' to describe the rapid transformations of recent years and have debated the extent to which there is a completely new postmodern world or whether there has just been a more rapid development of modernity. However, the different interpretations all highlight the myriad of new freedoms and associated new uncertainties that characterized late twentieth-century society. Some of the basic features of what has become known as postmodernism include a rejection of grand all-encompassing theories (metanarratives), a consequent acknowledgement that there is no such thing as an absolute truth and an extolling of variety and differences within cultural forms including the media, architecture, art and literature. While modernity is seen as characterized by moral certainty and a belief in the ability of theories to explain problems facing humanity, postmodernity is characterized by moral ambiguity and an acknowledgement that there are a range of truths and discourses that can be legitimate and acceptable at different times and for different people. Postmodernism's rejection of grand theory and the emphasis on diversity of explanations and on the role of the media in contemporary society have impacted on criminological theorizing.

QUESTION BREAK: GLOBALIZATION AND CRIME

As with postmodernism, globalization is a disputed term. In a limited sense it can be used to refer to the notion of a global economy and world financial markets. It can also be applied in a much broader manner to the blurring of the boundaries between nation states. As regards crime, it can be applied to the increasingly transnational character of organized crime. Technological developments in communication and transportation networks allow criminal operations to develop global networks and alliances. The old notion of crime being a local issue and problem is replaced with the need to understand 'the global contours of crime' (Burke 2005). However, Burke warns against over-romanticizing the past and points out that a good deal of crime in the past also relied on international markets and contacts – including slave and drug trading throughout history. Indeed the adage that 'there's nothing new under the sun' has always had a strong resonance in the study of crime.

Of course drug trafficking and pornography have been transformed by global transport and communications – including the World Wide Web – and new crimes such as e-piracy have appeared. And old ones have been updated – piracy is a crime that conjures up images of sailing ships and the Middle Ages, but it continues with faster speedboats and high-tech tracking devices enabling robbery on the high seas to become increasingly sophisticated.

- Consider a range of different types of crime – such as burglary, drug dealing, child abuse, fraud, football hooliganism, terrorism. How might developments in global transport and communications affect the form and the extent of such crimes?

Here we will consider how the emphasis on diversity of theories and explanations has impacted on how we think about and respond to crime. One, undoubtedly populist, approach might be to suggest that crime is a reality, a 'truth', to those who are victims and that rather than debating the different 'meanings' of crime the emphasis should be on better prevention of criminal behaviour and harsher punishment of those criminals who are caught. Of course, technological developments in surveillance and private security have enabled some groups to protect themselves from criminal activity to a far greater extent than others. In particular the affluent are able to protect themselves and their property by excluding the poor and marginalized from their areas and by using their influence to ensure that those offenders who are caught are more severely punished. Crime rates in major US cities have certainly declined in recent years but at the cost of a massive increase in the prison population. The number of prisoners in the USA rose to over two million in 2002 and the USA has the biggest prison population in the world – the highest number of prisoners as a proportion of its population. As a comparison, Russia, with a population of 144 million (compared to 286 million in the USA), had a prison population of 920,000 when the US number topped two million. Indeed the US prison population makes up almost a quarter of all the world's prisoners. And these figures have continued to rise – in June 2004 there were 2.1 million prisoners, a rise of over 48,000 from the previous year.

Another approach has been to focus on and manage the risks posed by crime and to emphasize the importance of risk management in relation to crime. The idea of a risk society developed by Beck (1992) and others goes well beyond the area of criminality and crime control. However in the area of crime, the notion that crime is a 'risk' that can be calculated, managed and possibly avoided has been influential. Crime has become a calculable risk for both offender and victim, and for criminal justice agencies. This view tends to see crime as an outcome of normal social inter-action, rather than something caused by biological, psychological or social factors that act on specific individuals and/or groups. So risk can be used to refer to decisions about whether to commit crimes and to decisions made by agencies of the criminal justice system. The latter is probably the more common way in which the concept of risk has played a role in criminological thinking. This can be seen in the basing of decisions on information and statistical probabilities about the re-offending of offenders. With or without detailed statistics, risk assessment is also involved in decisions around the security classification of prisoners, pre-sentencing reports prepared for the courts, whether to parole prisoners or keep them incarcerated and so on. Risk in crime goes beyond an application to criminal justice decisions – the design of streets, shopping centres and other community facilities is increasingly organized with risk of crime in mind. Concerns have been raised about the increased focus on risk in criminal justice. In particular that there is a possible net widening effect as people who are potential risks are targeted before they commit offences. And such a focus can increase feelings of insecurity and fear within communities – particular as those who cannot afford to protect themselves see better security techniques being used by those who can.

CRIME AND THE MEDIA – CULTURAL CRIMINOLOGY

A further influence of postmodernism that can be related to theorizing about crime concerns the spread of the media, including the scope this offers for new forms of criminal behaviour and the role it has played in the development of 'cultural criminology'. Particularly associated with the theorizing of American criminologist Jeff Ferrell, cultural criminology emphasizes the importance of image, style and representations and the way these have encouraged a mediated construction of crime and criminal justice. It takes on the postmodern position that 'style is substance' and that the meaning of something is based on its representation to suggest that crime can be best understood as part of an 'image driven media loop' (Ferrell 2001). Of the theoretical perspectives on crime looked at so far, this approach is probably closest to that of interactionism, with cultural criminologists emphasizing the symbolic aspect of 'symbolic interactionism', through examining the style of different types of criminal behaviour and the groups and subcultures associated with them. Ferrell (2001) points to a number of areas in which this new theoretical approach has developed. Firstly, crime is seen as a subcultural phenomenon organized around symbolic communication. It also examines the mediated construction of crime and the control of crime, considering the interconnections between the criminal justice system and the mass media, it looks at how certain activities come to be constructed as crimes and other do not. It looks at the everyday consumption of crime as drama and entertainment. To quote Ferrell (1999): 'The notion of cultural criminology references the increasing analytic attention that many criminologists now give to popular culture constructions, and especially mass media constructions, of crime and crime control.'

A good deal of research in cultural criminology has looked at 'subcultural style', seeing this style as defining the way deviants and criminals characterize their activity and also the way such activities are viewed and constructed from outside. It has also introduced the idea of 'culture as crime', whereby aspects of popular culture become criminalized: 'performers, producers, distributors, and retailers of rap and "gansta rap" music have likewise faced arrest and conviction on obscenity charges, legal confiscation of albums, highly publicized protests, boycotts, hearings organized by political figures and police officials, ongoing media campaigns and legal proceedings against them of promoting – indeed, directly causing – crime and delinquency' (Ferrell 1999).

In addition to framing how crime and criminal activities are viewed, the media also frame and determine our perceptions of crime control. With regards to the police, 'reality' policing programmes on television determine public perceptions of the police and will play a part in officer recruitment. To quote Ferrell (1999) again, 'From the view of cultural criminology, policing must in turn be understood as a set of practices situated, like criminal practices, within subcultural conventions of meaning, symbolism and style'.

The media and cybercrime

As well as cultural criminology highlighting the media as a key contributor to the perception of crime, another important aspect of the link between the media and crime is to examine the way that the media can cause crime. Indeed it could be argued that there has been a 'media revolution' in crime in recent years. This argument sees the media as a cause of an array of new crime in the sense that they used to commit criminal activity, such as cybercrime and internet crime.

Although cybercrime is a term that has become widely used of late, it is not always clear what it actually is. Wall (2004) points to the tendency to call any offence involving a computer a 'cybercrime', and offers a definition that embraces three different forms of such crime, which he suggests are at different positions on a 'cybercrime spectrum'. In general, 'cybercrimes are criminal acts transformed by network technologies' (Wall 2004); and the three different types can be placed at different points on the spectrum. At one end are acts which are called cybercrime but which are basically 'traditional' crimes where the internet has been used to help organize and carry out the crime (e.g. paedophilia). Without the internet the criminal behaviour will still exist using other forms of communication. In the middle are 'traditional' crimes which have 'benefited' from new global opportunities – which Wall terms 'hybrid' cybercrimes (e.g. frauds, global trade in pornography). Such crime would still exist without the internet but on a reduced scale. At the other end of the spectrum are 'true' cybercrimes which occur only as a result of the opportunities created by the internet (e.g. intellectual property theft, 'phishing'). Without the internet these last types of cybercrime would not exist.

We will look briefly at this last type of cybercrime – what Wall terms 'true' cybercrime. The dangers such crimes pose are often not immediately obvious. This might be because victims do not regard them as serious or because the danger they pose is as precursors for more serious crime in the future – for instance, identity theft from computers does not become serious until that information is used to harm the person whose identity is stolen. These hidden dangers are apparent in 'phishing' – a word that was coined to refer to scams in which computer hackers 'fish' for passwords for people's accounts on internet service providers such as AOL. In phishing scams, fraudsters target e-mail addresses requesting that the receivers of the e-mail provide personal details. They use very realistic logos and e-mail addresses in doing so – copying as closely as possible those of established banks and financial institutions. The extract illustrates how phishing scams can and do target major established banks and their customers.

CASE STUDY BOX 4.2 'PHISHING ATTACK ON NATWEST HALTS ONLINE SERVICE

Tens of thousands of bank customers have been targeted by online fraudsters.

One of Britain's biggest banks was forced to suspend some of its internet banking service yesterday after tens of thousands of its customers were targeted by fraudsters.

NatWest banned its one million online customers from setting up any new direct debits or standing orders yesterday in response to an escalating phishing scam, where fraudsters encourage customers to send personal banking details by e-mail.

The move was a recognition of the sharp rise in phishing attacks, and their increasing plausibility. The bank was also responding to comments from the City's chief watchdog, which gave warning last week that banks had to be more preventive in their measures against phishing.

The action by the bank could be followed by others, as it faces an onslaught from criminals who target customers by e-mail, demanding to know personal banking details. The bank said that it had stopped its online customers setting up accounts, servicing third parties to prevent money being switched out of the country . . .

In the phishing scam, fraudsters target e-mail addresses, demanding that the recipients of e-mails provide personal details. The criminals then arrange for money to be transferred out of the country.

(Caroline Merrell and Christine Seib, *The Times*, 18 November 2004)

An example of the way in which the internet can be used to encourage and increase crime is its use by race hate groups. Sutton (2002) argues that the internet has encouraged a growth in the race hate movement in recent years: 'The communications revolution has brought a new dimension to the hate movement. Racist websites provide an enabling environment in which hate can flourish both on-line and off-line in our towns and cities.' He cites the work of Back and his summary of the different ways in which the internet can assist racist activities. Photographs can be used to show and celebrate real instances of racial violence. This can promote an indifference towards victims. The internet provides a vehicle for selling racist paraphernalia and enables the downloading and saving of collections of racist materials. And it enables people to experience and indulge in racism without being directly and physically involved.

Sutton also points to the internet creating a new dimension in hate crime through bringing together a range of distinct racist groups from various countries, which helps create a 'powerful communications medium facilitating the development of neo-Nazi networks'. As well as racist groups using the internet, individuals are able to air and debate their own race hate on newsroom-type websites.

QUESTION BREAK: PROSECUTING GLOBAL CYBERCRIME

Child pornography is illegal in almost every industrialized nation. Just this Saturday, Italian investigators in Italy sought international warrants against almost 1600 individuals worldwide suspected of participating in online child pornography . . . The logistics to enable such a worldwide effort indicate the ferocity that some governments plan to take in regards to cybercrime.

An additional 1030 international warrants are being granted pending the completed investigations of the Italian police. Those additional 1030 international warrants are to be granted as soon as Internet users who entered a web site named 'childlovers' are identified.

In no way am I condoning child pornography, but to serve a warrant on someone who entered a site with the ambiguous name of childlovers just doesn't seem entirely fair. The name unto itself is not clearly pornographic in nature.

Your pregnant wife may have done a web search on children and clicked on a link to the childlovers site and I doubt she should qualify as a participant of online child pornography, nor should she suffer the indignity of discovering there's an international warrant in her name. Perhaps that website is clearly pornographic, but I'm not going there to find out.

(S. Underhill, 'Cybercrime prosecution is a nightmare', www.InfiniSource.com, 2 November 2000)

- Suggest other difficulties that face the policing and control of cybercrime across frontiers.

Finally, the media can affect the victims of crime, to the extent of victimizing victims even further. This is not to say that victims of crime are always treated badly by the media; some victims might in fact gain some comfort from seeing their situation getting media attention. As Mulley (2001) points out, the media can give victims the chance to tell their side of the story and 'set the record straight'. Also, people who have been victims of crime or family members or friends of victims often feel that bringing attention to the crime through the media will help to give strength to others who have suffered from similar experiences. However, she also highlights how media attention can become a form of secondary victimization. She reviewed research by Victim Support into the concerns and problems experienced by crime victims and witnesses which found that unwanted and intrusive media attention was complained of by 50 out of 80 families interviewed. Victims of the most serious crimes can find media attention extremely difficult, especially if media journalists are particularly persistent and assertive. And Victim Support has also detailed cases where victims have been harassed and intimidated by friends of an offender following media reporting which has provided personal details (anonymity is legally guaranteed only for child witnesses and victims of rape or sexual assault).

FURTHER READING

Burke, R. Hopkins (2005) *An Introduction to Criminological Theory*. Cullompton: Willan Publishing. A very thorough and up-to-date account of criminological theory covering all the major traditions and not limiting itself to sociological theorizing.

McLaughlin, J., Muncie, J. and Hughes, G. (eds) (2003) *Criminological Perspectives: Essential Readings*, second edition. London: Sage. There's nothing like the real thing, and reading extracts from original sources can give a flavour of the work and writing of key criminological thinkers. This reader contains examples of the core perspectives and early theorists, including Beccaria, Bentham, Durkheim and Becker, and of recent theorizing, including global and cultural criminology. The introductions to the different sections and readings provide particularly helpful guides.

Tierney, J. (1996) *Criminology: Theory and Context.* Harlow: Longman. An excellent and accessible overview that explores the history and growth of criminology and examines the major criminological theories that have developed as a result.

WEBSITES

www.crimetheory.com is a site run from the University of Ohio in the USA and includes archives of early criminological texts written or translated into English.

Explaining the Criminal Behaviour of Women

INTRODUCTION

Recent statistics show that women's involvement in crime is rising. In the last decade the number of women in prison has almost doubled, yet their involvement in crime is still minimal compared to that of males. The focus of this chapter will be to discuss the traditional, biological, psychological and sociological explanations for women's involvement – or rather lack of involvement – in crime. Traditional explanations look to religion and naturalistic phenomena. Biological and psychological explanations focus on the individual characteristics – and consider, for example, whether female crime is pathological; or whether women are less biologically evolved than men; or does PMT (premenstrual tension) offer a feasible account for most female crime? Sociological explanations look at the structure of society and how it affects individuals or groups. Questions that the sociological approach raises include: are girls socialized differently? does the family make girls passive? has the women's liberation movement led to a generation of 'laddettes' who emulate men even in relation to criminal behaviour? This chapter explores these and other explanations and the associated issues and tries to make sense of women's involvement in crime and how this involvement has changed over time.

In October 2005 the British prison population stood at (another) new high of 77,774; and of this number 4,621 were females (National Offender Management Service data). So it is clear that that women make up only a small percentage of those imprisoned – roughly 6 per cent. However, the rate of female imprisonment has risen quite dramatically in recent years. The number of women in prison has risen by 175 per cent since 1992 – while the corresponding figures for men during the same period is 50 per cent (Roxanne Escobales, *Guardian*, 12 March 2004). This new trend has led to claims by criminologists, the media and politicians alike that society is now faced with a 'new female criminal'; and there has been close to a moral panic surrounding the dawn of the 'laddette' – the violent female girl gang member who can be just as dangerous as her male counterpart.

QUESTION BREAK

- Why do you think that men outnumber women so dramatically in the prison population figures?
- Why do you think the number of female prisoners has risen faster than that of male prisoners in recent years?
- After you have read this chapter, return to consider your initial responses in the light of the material you have looked at.

Feminist criminologists have argued that history has been constructed through a masculine narrative of crime – crime being the province of men and women merely the recipients. The focus, then, has been on women as victims of criminal behaviour. When looking at women as victims the figures remain unusually high. It has been estimated that 70 per cent of female murder victims worldwide are killed by their male partner (WHO 2002) and Seager points out that this amounts to two women per week killed by their partner. In 2002 UNICEF stated that 25 per cent of women in Britain would be punched or slapped by their male partner or ex-partner in their lifetime. The estimated statistics for sexual violence are just as depressing. One in five women will become victims of rape in their lifetime (WHO 1997) and according to UNIFEM (2002) each year two million girls between the ages of five and 15 are introduced into the commercial sex market. In the face of such victimization and oppression it would perhaps make more sense to ask the question, 'why don't women commit as much crime as their male counterparts?' Indeed this is an issue that will be returned to later in the chapter.

HISTORY

It is clear that women are capable of, and have been found responsible for, all types of criminal and deviant behaviour. Also, despite recent moral panics around women's increasing criminality, history provides us with information which demonstrates that women's criminality has always existed and is not a relatively recent phenomenon.

Historically the focus for women and crime has centred on those crimes deemed 'feminine by nature'; in other words crimes which can be attributed to a transgression of female norms and values. Infanticide and prostitution for example have in the past been (and still are today) considered to be crimes predominantly committed by women. However throughout history women have also been capable of crimes which are beyond the realms of supposedly 'natural' female behaviour and, one might argue, have committed what might be labelled 'naturally masculine' crimes. Famous cases include Cleopatra, the last of the pharaohs, who ruled from 69 to 30 BC, and Boadicca, who led the Celts to a glorious but bloody defeat by the Roman Empire between 61 and 63 AD: both women leaders of great empires who were guilty of crimes against humanity and sanctioned (and in the case of Boadicca took part in) the genocide of innocent people. Mata Hari, a dancer and entertainer, is perhaps the most famous spy of all time – she was executed by the French in 1917 after being found guilty of spying for Germany, although it is claimed that she was a double agent. More recently, the cases of Myra Hindley in the 1960s and Rosemary West in the 1980s involved horrific examples of child abuse and murder.

Those cases of female crime that do fall into the category of being essentially or completely female include prostitution and infanticide, and we will discuss infanticide in some detail as an example of a uniquely female crime.

Infanticide

By definition the crime of infanticide can be committed only by a woman. As a consequence it is not only a heinous criminal behaviour but also a crime which questions female morality and the maternal instinct. The problem of infanticide is not new: throughout history it has taken many guises, from religious and supernatural child sacrifice to a solution for mothers in poverty and to concerns about overpopulation. This type of crime has been attributed to a number of things but for feminist criminologists and social historians alike this crime has been linked to patriarchy and social control over women's bodies.

For example, within the Victorian period (an era renowned for its strict moral sensibility) infanticide reached epidemic proportions and women found guilty were severely punished. Statistics provided in a study by H. R. Jones (1894) show the rate of homicide in England and Wales during the period 1863–87. On interpretation of the data Rose (1986) concludes that children under one year of age accounted for: '61% of all homicide victims compared to 2.5–3% of the population'. Partly as a consequence of the growing number of child deaths and partly owing to a sympathetic response from judges, in 1922 the Infanticide Act was introduced to the United Kingdom and was further refined and revised in 1938. The act was introduced partly as a response to the worrying child death rates highlighted above and partly because judges were reluctant to pass the sentence of death on mothers who killed their children, and felt there needed to be a legal means of dealing with such women. As already illustrated, child deaths had reached epidemic proportions in the late nineteenth century and it was believed that this would further be exacerbated by the social and economic problems and conditions that many mothers faced such as poverty and desertion by the child's father.

The 1922 Act defined infanticide as 'the act of a mother who kills her new born child'. However the act also stipulated that puerperal psychosis (severe mental disorder relating to childbirth) should be carefully considered. Normally the killing of a child led in the charge of murder and at the time the death penalty; however the 1922 Act effectively abandoned the death penalty for such cases. As mentioned, in 1938 the Act was refined further; the age range was extended from newborn child to 12 months old and the Act allowed for a plea relating to the balance of the mind in partial defence for murder. The 1938 Act extended this defence to cases where 'at the time of the act or omission the balance of her mind was disturbed by reason of her not having fully recovered from the effect of giving birth to the child or by reason of the effect of lactation consequent upon the birth of the child'. In 1957 the notion of diminished responsibility was introduced into the British justice system which further allowed for a more appropriate sentence than mandatory life imprisonment for a mother found guilty of killing her infant.

Infanticide, of course, is still a problem for society and has been related to the cultural norms of some societies and the economic and mental health problems of women. Sex-related infanticide is also very common in areas such as China and regions of India where male children are prized over females. Closely related to the problem of infanticide is the rate of abortion. Prenatal sex-determination techniques such as ultrasound have led to an increase in the abortion rates of female foetuses.

In Britain the phenomena of infanticide has become a major issue as a result of high profile cases of women accused of the crime. Sally Clark (1999) and Angela Cannings (2002) were accused and convicted of infanticide. Both women, like others, later had their convictions quashed on appeal in part because of the 'unscientific and unreliable' evidence and testimony of pediatrician Professor Roy Meadow. In his book *The ABC of Child Abuse*, Meadow establishes and defends the principle that 'two [cases of child death] is suspicious and three murder unless proved otherwise . . . is a sensible working rule for anyone encountering these tragedies'. However, partly as a result of appeals in these high-profile cases, it is now widely believed that many cases of what was once thought to be infanticide may be more appropriately attributed to Sudden Instant Death Syndrome (SIDS), more commonly known as cot death, which can help to explain deaths, including multiple deaths, in families.

From a criminological point of view infanticide is an interesting topic for debate as it medicalizes women's criminal behaviour (an issue we will return to when looking at biological perspectives) and furthers the idea that women's crime is related to biology and psychology. For those who are genuinely affected by their biology, and in this case by postnatal depression, the law does seem sympathetic but there is also cause for concern that many women use and take advantage of this notion for their own ends. Secondly, as indicated earlier, the idea of infanticide may be said to be an example of leniency towards women within the criminal justice system as this form of 'killing' is differentiated from murder (an issue which will be discussed below in relation to the notion of the 'chivalry factor'). Of course the idea of leniency also raises questions about the true level of female crime within the confines of the family. The following extract highlights the current debate around infanticide laws within the judiciary.

QUESTION BREAK

Scrap outdated infanticide law, say judges

Three Court of Appeal judges have called for a review of the 'outdated and unsatisfactory' law on infanticide after upholding the conviction of a mother for the murder of her baby.

They raised concerns that vulnerable, mentally ill women are being given mandatory life sentences for killing their babies when they should have been treated more leniently.

The judges had rejected an appeal by 29-year-old Chaha'Oh-Niyol Kai-Whitewind against her conviction for murdering her 12-week old baby Bidziil . . .

She was convicted in 2003 of suffocating Bidziil when, the prosecution said, she became frustrated with his refusal to breastfeed and depressed at her failure to bond with him . . .

Ms Kai-Whitewind, who changed her name after adopting native American culture, had told a psychiatric nurse she had thought about killing the baby, who was conceived as a result of rape. Blood was found in the boy's nose and mouth, and his mother had delayed calling an ambulance after he stopped breathing.

But she denied having anything to do with his death, claiming it was from natural causes. She refused to give evidence or plead guilty to infanticide or manslaughter on the grounds of diminished responsibility.

Under the 1938 Infanticide Act, a woman who kills her child when it is less than a year old and 'while the balance of her mind was disturbed by reason of the fact that she had not fully recovered from the effect of giving birth', should not be found guilty of murder.

Of the 49 women convicted of infanticide between 1989 and 2000, only two were jailed; the rest were given probation, supervision or hospital orders.

But because Ms Kai-Whitewind did not admit her guilt and refused to undergo psychiatric reports, she was convicted of murder and given a life sentence.

Giving their ruling yesterday, the deputy chief justice, Lord Justice Judge, sitting with Mrs Justice Hallett and Mr Justice Leveson, said her conviction was 'safe'. But Lord Justice Judge added: 'The law relating to infanticide is unsatisfactory and outdated. The appeal in this sad case demonstrates the need for a thorough re-examination.'

He said a 'particular area of concern' was that the infanticide defence was restricted to a mother being affected by the actual birth and not subsequent events, such as a lack of bonding. He added: 'The second problem arises when the mother who has in fact killed her infant is unable to admit it.

'This may be because she is too unwell to do so, or too emotionally disturbed by what she has in fact done, or too deeply troubled by the consequences of an admission of guilt on her ability to care for any surviving children. When this happens, it is sometimes difficult to produce psychiatric evidence relating to the balance of the mother's mind.

'Yet, of itself, it does not automatically follow from denial that the balance of her mind was not disturbed: in some cases it may indeed help to confirm that it was.'

About five infanticide convictions a year are handed down in England and Wales. One in 500 new mothers suffers from puerperal psychosis, a severe form of mania which can result in them harming themselves or their babies. Most cases are now spotted before a tragic incident occurs.

But lawyers say some of the most vulnerable women are still being jailed by the criminal justice system. Helena Kennedy QC, who has defended several women accused of killing their children, said in an interview last year: 'The problem in these cases is that unless a woman says "I did it", you can't mount a psychiatric defence. You can't go behind her back and get a psychiatric report.

'The problem is that these women can't admit it to themselves, and they certainly can't admit it to their partners. The problem for the lawyer is getting the woman to acknowledge it herself. It's complex.'

Until 1922, the killing of a child was a capital offence, but juries had become so sympathetic to women accused in such cases that the first infanticide law was brought in to cover newborn babies. In 1938, it was extended to the killing by a mother of babies up to a year old.

(Maxine Frith, 20 May 2005)

- The article argues that 'vulnerable and mentally ill women' who kill their babies should be treated more leniently. What support can you find in the article for this view?

PATTERNS AND TRENDS

Patterns and trends in terms of criminal behaviour suggest that men still commit the majority of crime. In general terms, roughly 80 per cent of those convicted for serious offences in England and Wales are male. Suggested explanations for this gender bias range from exploring the inherently different natures of men and women to focusing on the socially constructed gender roles that play a part in men's and women's lives. Also, it is suggested that statistics do not reflect the hidden nature of women's criminal behaviour; that female crime is allowed to continue unchecked owing to the chivalrous nature of the criminal justice system.

What is clear is that in the last ten years or so more women are being apprehended and charged. Table 5.1 compares female and male offenders found guilty at all courts or cautioned by sex and type of offence at various periods between 1994 and 2002 in England and Wales. The statistics reflect a steady increase in female involvement in crime. During this period women's involvement in crime increased in the areas of

Table 5.1 Offenders found guilty in all courts or cautioned by sex and type of offence, England and Wales, excluding motoring offences (thousands)

Sex and type of offence	1994	1996	1998	2000	2001	2002
Males						
Indictable offences						
Violence against the person	51.5	43.9	51.7	47.1	47.0	51.8
Sexual offences	7.4	6.4	6.2	5.2	5.0	5.5
Burglary	47.5	40.5	37.2	31.0	29.4	30.4
Robbery	5.1	6.0	5.6	5.9	6.7	7.3
Theft and handling stolen goods	169.0	153.7	152.6	142.1	137.8	131.5
Fraud and forgery	19.1	17.6	19.1	17.6	16.7	16.2
Criminal damage	13.0	11.7	12.4	12.0	12.5	12.5
Drug offences	65.1	72.8	96.0	76.5	76.1	84.1
Other	37.6	41.6	48.1	42.9	42.1	45.7
Total indictable offences	428.2	405.1	437.3	387.5	380.6	393.7
Summary offences	392.0	414.2	430.1	387.5	393.5	420.5
All offences	820.2	819.3	867.4	816.2	774.1	813.2
Females						
Indictable offences						
Violence against the person	9.7	7.9	8.9	8.1	7.8	9.5
Sexual offences	0.1	0.1	0.1	0.1	0.1	0.1
Burglary	2.0	1.8	2.0	1.8	1.8	2.1
Robbery	0.4	0.5	0.6	0.6	0.7	0.9
Theft and handling stolen goods	63.4	54.5	56.8	53.5	52.7	50.1
Fraud and forgery	6.9	6.2	8.0	7.8	7.3	7.3
Criminal damage	1.3	1.2	1.3	1.4	1.6	1.6
Drug offences	7.0	8.7	11.5	9.3	8.9	9.8
Other (excluding motoring offences)	4.4	4.8	6.5	6.1	6.1	6.7
Total indictable offences	95.7	86.3	96.1	88.9	87.5	88.6
Summary offences	161.4	169.6	128.9	150.0	134.6	149.0
All offences	257.1	255.9	225.0	239.0	222.1	237.6

Source: Adapted from Home Office: Criminal Statistics England and Wales 2002

burglary, robbery, fraud, criminal damage, drugs and 'other' crimes. Men on the other hand (although still committing the bulk of crime) have seen decreases in involvement in the areas of sexual offences, burglary, theft and handling of stolen goods, fraud and forgery, and criminal damages.

QUESTION BREAK

- What are the most 'popular' crimes for males and for females?
- Summarize the changes in the patterns of crime for males and for females between 1994 and 2002.
- Can you suggest any explanations for the patterns and changes?

Apart from new trends in the level of crime there have been some changes in the types of crimes women are prepared to commit (or have been caught involved in). Female crime has traditionally been associated with women's sexuality and gender. The focus has therefore been on what have conventionally been seen as 'female' crimes, such as prostitution and infanticide. Women are still over-represented in terms of these 'feminine crimes'. Statistics for those found guilty reflect this traditional pattern of women's criminality. For example figures for the year 2003 show that women outnumbered men within seven categories of which four reflect the feminine – cruelty to or neglect of children, concealing of birth, brothel keeping and offence by a prostitute.

However, recent data suggest that a change has occurred and is continuing in terms of female crime. Women have become more involved in what can be described as 'masculine' crime. Analysis of England and Wales Crown Court data in 2003 shows that the two most popular indictable (essentially the more serious) offences for women were violence against the person and drug offences. These data may go some way to explaining the moral panic surrounding the new violent female and the problems of drink and drugs amongst young women in particular.

It is worth mentioning that any phenomena subject to statistical analysis must be approached with caution. Crime and female crime in particular is subject to the political, cultural and social context within which criminal behaviour takes place. Therefore perceptions and definitions of crime are socially constructed. Arguably, girls and women are and have been subject to what might be seen as 'stronger' methods of social control – for instance girls are expected to conform to a stricter morality than boys by their parents, they are likely to be allowed less freedom to go out and stay out. Of course, we cannot assume that all girls are more closely controlled and supervised by their parents than boys are. None the less, it seems reasonable to suggest that there is a tendency for this to be the case; and if so this is likely to reduce to some degree the opportunities for girls to become involved with criminal behaviour.

While the patterns and trends of female crime clearly suggest that women crim-inals are still the minority, there has also been a considerable increase in female crime over the last few years. It is worthwhile here exploring the types of crime that have been traditionally associated with women and compare them with current Home Office statistics which highlight the recent figures in terms of men and women found guilty of indictable and summary offences.

Female crime has also been related to women's position in the social structure and their relationship to the economy. Women tend to be over-involved in 'survival crime', that is crimes which have an economic basis such as theft, shoplifting, prostitution and drug importing – Pat Carlen (1988) stated that this could be attributed to the 'feminisation of poverty'. The nature of women's criminal behaviour is highlighted by a recent study entitled *Working With Women Prisoners* (November 2003). The study found that the most frequent offences committed by women prisoners were theft and handling (2,599), drug offences (847), violence against the person (666), fraud and forgery (472), burglary (272) and robbery (228).

So in contemporary society women appear in all categories of crime. It is still the case, though, that certain types of offences are dominated by women more than others. As mentioned, around 80 per cent of those convicted of serious offences in England and Wales are male. And it is still the case that women are particularly likely to be arrested for relatively trivial offences. In 2003 women were most likely to be found guilty of crimes involving theft and handling, of which theft from shops accounted for 19,042 (approximately 38 per cent of such crimes).

QUESTION BREAK

The statistics in Tables 5.1 and 5.2 show offenders found guilty at all courts or cautioned by sex and types of offence. Study the statistics and highlight the trends in terms of female and male crime.

- What possible explanations are there for the trends in both tables?
- What possible explanations can you put forward for the increase in drug offences for women?
- Why has there been a significant decrease in men being cautioned or found guilty of sexual offences?
- Why has there been a significant increase in men being cautioned or found guilty of violent crime since 1996?

The social characteristics of female criminals

So who are these women criminals – and especially those few thousand who end up within the prison system? Using prison data as a starting point, in general terms, the majority of women prisoners are likely to be unemployed young women who belong to an ethnic minority group. It has long been established that a rise in the unemployment rate often corresponds with an increase in crime rates; and this has led to the argument that poverty or economic inequality can cause crime. Given that women are especially prone to poverty and or economic inequality owing to gender bias within society, it would be logical to suggest that women would be particularly prone to crime.

In terms of poverty the social and political situation for women within the last decade shows an increase in social and economic deprivation. The Social Exclusion Unit (2002) found that 40 per cent of women in prison had not worked for at least

Table 5.2 Offenders found guilty of, or cautioned for, indictable (more serious) offences: by sex, type of offence and age, England and Wales, 2003 (rates per 10,000 population)

	10–15	16–24	25–34	35 and over	All aged 10 and over (thousands)
Males					
Theft and handling stolen goods	81	162	96	18	124.3
Drug offences	18	156	62	10	86.2
Violence against the person	34	78	34	10	55.7
Burglary	26	45	21	2	29.3
Criminal damage	14	19	7	2	13.2
Robbery	7	13	4	–	6.8
Sexual offences	3	4	3	2	5.6
Other indictable offences	10	101	62	13	72.1
All indictable offences	193	577	288	56	393.2
Females					
Theft and handling stolen goods	52	62	32	6	49.3
Drug offences	3	15	9	2	10.6
Violence against the person	13	13	6	2	11.1
Burglary	3	3	1	–	2.0
Criminal damage	3	2	1	–	1.8
Robbery	2	1	–	–	0.9
Sexual offences	–	–	–	–	0.1
Other indictable offences	3	19	14	3	15.4
All indictable offences	78	116	64	12	91.2

Source: Adapted from Home Office

five years before entering prison and only 39 per cent had any educational quali-fications; 39 per cent of women prisoners had not worked outside the home in the year prior to imprisonment and 23 per cent had not worked for over five years. At the very least, such figures indicate that those women convicted of offences serious enough to warrant a custodial sentence are from relatively poor and economically deprived backgrounds.

As regards ethnic background, in a recent study (Working With Women Prisoners Nov 2003 HM Prison Service) 31 per cent of women prisoners were from ethnic minority background and a further 21 per cent were foreign nationals, of whom 83 per cent would be classified as ethnic minorities, 50 per cent as Afro-Caribbean and 6 per cent as Nigerian.

CRIMINOLOGICAL PERSPECTIVES

Demonic theory

Historically the origins of criminological thought have focused on religious and supernatural or demonical reasoning. In this context criminal and deviant behaviour is seen as beyond the control of the individual and society. The demonic perspective is therefore a pre-Enlightenment view and focuses on the idea that supernatural forces can control 'man's' behaviour through, for example, demonic possession. This perspective gained its authority and credulity through world religions which promote the idea of dualism – the idea that malevolent powers wrestle for the control of the universe. With regard to Christianity this malevolent power is described as Satan, Lucifer, the Devil etc.

In terms of women, the best example of the use of demonic theory came in the form of the witch craze of pre-industrial Europe in which the majority of those accused were women (Hughes 1965). The notions of demonization and demonic possession explain the fate which befell those women accused of witchcraft, especially during the sixteenth century. These 'witches' were said to be in league with the Devil who, in return for their loyalty, granted them supernatural powers which they used to cause death and destruction within society through illness and disease. In hindsight, different theories have emerged to explain this dark period. Economic and social change, crises within religion, mental illness and the role of King James I of England and of Scotland have been used to explain the actions of the accused and the accusers. Despite the underlying reasons, it is true that those who lived throughout this period (1500–1700) felt a real sense of a malevolent power wrestling with the forces of good for control of the universe.

We may argue that civilization and the rise of scientific reasoning and theory have rendered these ideas obsolete. Since the Enlightenment demonic notions of criminal behaviour have been criticized and superseded by social science. However in terms of human behaviour the religious model is still adhered to by many, and old demonic concepts have survived and are still used and accepted by society as explanation for criminal behaviour (for example the ritual abuse of children and the criminal activities of those who call themselves Satanists). Serious female crime in particular is seen as beyond human comprehension and is often described as 'evil' and 'unnatural'. In particular female child killers such as Myra Hindley and Rosemary West have been portrayed as demons.

A clear example of the persistence of demonic perspective in relation to women's criminal behaviour is the case of Aileen Wuornos. Aileen made headlines in Florida in the 1990s for the murder of five men. She was sentenced and was put to death through lethal injection in 2003. The case has been sensationalized using demonic language and was even dramatized in a feature film aptly named *Monster*. Trying to make sense of the crimes herself Aileen stated: 'I pretty much had them selected that they was gonna die. My evil came out because of what I was doing, the hitchhiking and hooking. I'm telling you, you have to kill Aileen Wuornos, 'cause she'll kill again (Nick Bloomfield documentary *Aileen*, (2003).

Naturalism

Naturalism rejects the notion that behaviour is controlled by supernatural forces and argues instead that events within the natural world explain human behaviour including criminal behaviour. The naturalistic approach developed out of the Enlightenment period (of the eighteenth century – often known as the 'age of reason' as it was characterized by a rejection of religious explanations for human behaviour and by greater value given to scientific enquiry). The idea of naturalism is grounded in ancient philosophy – a number of history's most revered scientists and philosophers have incorporated naturalism into their beliefs, including Aristotle (384–322 BC), Thomas Aquinas (1224–74) and John Locke (1632–1704).

In terms of criminology, naturalism requires a more scientific or objective rationale for criminal behaviour, which has influenced both classical and positivist criminology (see Chapter 4). Views of women and their involvement or lack of involvement in crime have in the past focused on common-sense assumptions of female behaviour – and they still do today. From an essentialist (naturalistic) point of view females have a different countenance to men. This naturalistic explanation renders anything that deviates from the female norm as 'unnatural'. The acceptable female norm is closely linked to female biology. For example women are seen to be closer to nature as they give birth and are subject to the menstrual cycle. It is widely assumed then that women are naturally caring, emotional and maternal. As the old nursery rhyme goes, girls are made of 'sugar and spice and all things nice'.

This essentially functionalist and conservative view of women (associated with the work of functionalist sociologists such as Talcott Parsons) has been criticized by many as assuming that what is natural (in their view) is also morally right and desirable. But even more important, especially to feminist thinkers, is the view that these attributes are natural and not socially constructed, that this evolutionary explanation naturalizes and justifies the continuation of sexist attitudes to and perceptions of female criminals. This naturalistic or essentialist approach can be seen to underpin much of more recent positivist theorizing which embraces biological and psychology approaches. Examples of these approaches are considered below.

Biological or physiological views

Lombroso

In the late Victorian period a revolutionary new theory was sweeping Europe which would change the way that 'man' viewed his world forever. Charles Darwin wrote *The Descent of Man* in 1884, which put forward the idea of evolutionary theory as an alternative explanation for 'man's' existence. These ideas influenced many theorists in different philosophical and academic areas. In the field of criminology it was Cesare Lombroso, often described as the founding father of criminology, who utilized Darwin's ideas and related them to criminal behaviour (see pp. 23–4).

Lombroso's ideas stem from the idea of atavism, which is based around the theory of evolution. Whilst most humans evolve, it was Lombroso's contention that criminals or deviants devolve, in other words they become primitive or atavistic. Criminals according to Lombroso were marked and identified by their atavistic stigmata. Atavistic stigmata may be reflected in the physical features or characteristics of a person, for instance the size of cranium, hands or ears.

The Female Offender (1895) was the first scientific text ever written on women and crime. Analysing data on female crimes throughout Europe and searching their anatomy for 'atavistic' elements, Lombroso (with Ferrero) deduced that women in general failed to reach the evolutionary progress of European males. On his scale white men were at the pinnacle of evolutionary progress and black women at the base. Normal women were amongst 'others' included in a group that held criminals, savages, and children in terms of their lack of evolutionary progress. Women had failed to evolve their moral senses; they often lied – a 'fact' deduced from the fact that women masked menstruation from men and sexual intercourse from children (la donna delinquent); they were unusually cruel and politically inept. Indeed the female offender was described by Lombroso to be as 'a man arrested in his intellectual and physical development'. In relation to their anatomy, Lombroso suggested that between European women there was a low degree of differentiation; and for him this strengthened the idea of the atavistic women. It was precisely the 'normality' of woman that pointed to her degeneracy – no variation pointed to a lack of progression.

So, if 'normal' females were less evolved, how could the idea of atavism be used to understand female criminality? Even at this time in history it was generally agreed that women were less involved in crime than their male counterparts, so how could this be reconciled with the idea that women were as primitive as criminals – why was their behaviour less criminal? If all women were evolutionary degenerates (as were criminals) shouldn't they be committing as much crime as if not more crime than their male counterparts? The answer to this question was seen to lie in atavistic stigmata.

The idea of stigmata was very important within Lombroso's study of women. Analysing criminal and non-criminal females in Sicily, he deduced that stigmata relating to female criminals manifested itself in a number of ways. The female born criminal was described as being short, with dark hair, moles and masculine features. It was noted by Lombroso that 'normal women' had a small cranium, which made them less intelligent and less passionate. On the other hand criminal women had a larger cranium which made them more like men. 'Normal' women were less intelligent than criminal women which lowered their capacity for reason. In place of natural female traits criminal women had 'strong passions and intensely erotic tendencies, much muscular strength and a superior intelligence for the conception and execution of evil' (Lombroso and Ferrero 1895, 150–2). They were 'born criminals' and 'monsters' who 'belong more to the male than to the female sex, combining the worst aspects of womanhood – cunning, spite, and deceitfulness – with the criminal inclinations and callousness of men' (Lombroso and Ferrero 1895, 152–53).

Further, Lombroso argued that sexual deviancy was the female equivalent of male crime – which is why women feature most heavily within the area of prostitution. To Lombroso, then, female offenders were dangerous because they lacked womanly

[handwritten margin note: pregnancy etc.]

qualities such as maternalism. He went so far as to describe female offenders as 'excessively erotic, weak in maternal feeling, inclined to dispassion, astute and audacious' (101).

Pollak

In a 1950 Otto Pollak published *The Criminality of Woman*. He emphasized the link between female biology and criminal behaviour. According to Pollak, women's crime was related to the biological phases that women endure during their lifetime, for example menstruation, pregnancy through to the menopause. These biological phases undermine women's inhibitions and can therefore influence female participation in criminal behaviour. Menstruation led to feelings of irritation and forced women to reflect upon their subordinate position in society, pregnancy led to emotional and physical imbalances and the menopause left women feeling insecure about their status within their marital relationships. All, according to Pollak, can lead to female offenders being what he described as 'deceitful, vengeful and unemotional'.

It would seem then that women are emotionally unbalanced for the most part of their lives. This raises the question as to why, according to the statistics of that time as well as today, female crime statistics are so low in comparison to men. Pollak suggests that the reason for a lack of crime could be related to the nature of crimes committed and the deceitfulness of women. Firstly, women did not appear within the statistics as they preferred to be involved in professions that rendered their crimes relatively undetectable. Traditionally female occupations focused upon jobs which were relatively private and isolated. He claimed, for example, that women prefer professions like maids, nurses, teachers and homemakers so they can engage in undetectable crime. In hindsight it is quite naive to state that these occupations were preferred – they were more likely to have been taken through necessity.

Not only were these types of crime 'undetectable' but they were also made invisible because women had superb skills of deceit and concealment. Pollak again attributed this to female biology. Deceit and secrecy were skills acquired through social reinforcement but which had their roots in female biology. To explain further, *[handwritten margin note: feminists argue that ✓]* women's crimes are masked by their art of deceit and this stems from their concealment of menstruation and ability to fake orgasm. Society, in particular male society, has therefore encouraged and allowed women to be deceitful, even in terms of the personal and biological.

W.I. Thomas

W.I. Thomas's early work highlighted the biological biases of the time at which he was writing – the early twentieth century. In *Sex and Society* (1907) he states, 'Morphologically the development of man is more accentuated than that of woman. Anthropologists . . . regard women as intermediate between the child and the man.' Therefore his early work pointed to the idea that women were biologically inferior to men. As his work progressed Thomas studied early matriarchal society and concluded that social rather than biological change had left women subject to male domination. 'In the earliest period of a society under the maternal system the woman had her own will more with her person; but with the formulation of a system of control, based on male activities, the person of women was made a point in the application of the male standpoint' (Thomas 1907, 158).

Thomas examined the problems of monogamy and, he argued, its resulting boredom, writing that 'It is psychologically true that only the unfamiliar and not-completely controlled is interesting' (1907, 56). Explaining the growth in female crime, Thomas argued that traditional society was going through what he considered 'social disorganization'. The social control of women had lessened and the deviant or criminal woman was emerging. Thomas understood this in terms of pathology rather than biologically inherited traits. Focusing on juvenile girls in *The Unadjusted Girl* (1923), he claimed that women committed crime out of 'wishes' for excitement and new experiences. These new experiences manifested themselves through women's sexuality. Confined under monogamy women's pent-up sexual energy was released in criminal acts.

Thomas's approach to theorizing was the basis of what later became known as symbolic interactionism – in examining the phenomenon of female crime he adopted a 'micro level' perspective. In order to understand deviant behaviour more fully Thomas developed the notion of 'definition of the situation', meaning that a situation is constructed through the context of the interaction and the consequences of the situation. The understanding or meaning of a situation is derived from contact between members of a group and the overall definition of the situation. However, a group defines the norms of particular situations and this determines whether or not a reaction to a situation is considered deviant. In one of the most sophisticated sociological analyses then available, he stated that women's behaviour was a function of definitions of the situation that were socially and culturally derived.

Contemporary applications

Despite the fact that many of these theories have been criticized for oversimplifying, generalizing and 'pathologizing' women, there has been a resurgence of biological theory in understanding the female offender. The idea that hormones affect behaviour has been with us for many years. High testosterone levels in men, for example, is said to lead to aggressive behaviour. For women hormone levels are said to fluctuate during pre-menses, postnatal and menopausal stages. Premenstrual syndrome, in particular, is said to cause irritability and mood swings in many women. Trimble and Fay (1986) point to the fact that the symptoms of PMS were noted by the ancient Greeks. The philosopher Simonides for example warned: 'One day she is all smiles and gladness. A stranger in the house seeing her will sing her praise . . . But the next day she is dangerous to look at or approach: She is in a wild frenzy . . . savage to all alike, friend or foe' (cited in Trimble and Fay 1986, 183).

Criminological studies into female crime have supported the idea that PMS can contribute to the female crime rate. Indeed, Lombroso and Ferrero (1895) concluded that, of 80 women arrested for 'resistance to public officials', 71 were menstruating

links to CHIVALRY as clearly courts are treating women differently

LUDICROUS

at the time, pointing to menstruation as a catalyst to deviant behaviour. In 1⟩ Dr K. Dalton (who coined the term premenstrual syndrome with Dr Raymond Greene in 1953), found that, of 156 British women imprisoned for theft, prostitution and public drunkenness, half the offences had committed during paramenstruum (four days prior to bleeding and the first three days of menstruation). Similarly Ellis and Austin (1971) found that 41 per cent of female inmates who had committed violent acts when in a North Carolina prison had been within the paramenstruum stage at the time. More recently Moiré and Jessel (1997) suggests that there is a link between suicide or aggressive behaviour in women and PMS. However in the modern medical community there is no consensus upon the origins or indeed existence of PMS.

In terms of criminal behaviour PMS has been used successfully within the courts as a mitigation to crimes such as shoplifting and murder. One of the most famous cases of a successful plea was the case of R *v* Craddock 1980 and R *v* Smith 1981 (Craddock and Smith are the same person). Craddock, a barmaid with thirty previous convictions, killed a co-worker. In court it was successfully argued that Craddock suffered from acute PMS and the judge accepted PMS as a mitigating factor. Probation and progesterone treatment were recommended. The following year (and on a reduced level of progesterone) Craddock (now Smith) attempted suicide and threatened to kill a police officer. Again the judge accepted PMS as a mitigating factor. Since this case, PMS has been raised successfully within the British court system both civil and criminal.

Psychological

In terms of women and crime Freud believed that all humans had criminal tendencies that were part of the natural human drives and urges. In the 'normal', these drives and urges were suppressed through the process of socialization, in which the individual developed 'inner controls'. Improperly socialized, however, a child will develop personality disorders and indulge in anti-social behaviour, which displayed inwardly would become neurosis and outwardly criminal. The genesis of criminal behaviour, then, could be traced back to early childhood trauma using psychoanalysis, and the most common cause according to Freud was faulty identification with parents. Psychological approaches overlap with the physiological theories looked at earlier. Indeed, Thomas's work (p. 147) embraces psychological and sociological factors as well as physiological. And Freud's early work was a major influence on the work of Pollak (p. 147).

Freud's analysis of women as criminals was built around the premise that women are anatomically inferior to men. As with many of the theories discussed above, in terms of women and crime Freud saw the cause of female criminality as sexual in nature. The criminal women is motivated by sexual neurosis. This idea is derived from what is commonly and famously known as 'penis envy'. According to Feud, as a female child develops she becomes aware that her sexual organs are incomplete and inferior to her male counterparts; as a result envy ensues and leads the girl to feel revengeful. 'Normal' women will, through socialization and 'inner controls', deal with these feelings and emotions. However the result will be a strong need for male love and approval which such women will gain through narcissism and exhibitionism, often resulting in an obsession with being physically beautiful. In a patriarchal society where male law takes precedence, females adhere to their given social roles as flouting them would mean the removal of male affection and love and protection.

According to Freud, however, criminal or deviant women reject this 'forced' passivity. They are driven by the desire to gain a penis – ultimately this type of women longs to be a man. Of course this want of a penis is futile and as a consequence the woman becomes neurotic and aggressive in a way which will predispose her to criminal behaviour.

Sociological and feminist perspectives

Introduction

Within traditional theories of criminology the focus has been on male offenders. To some extent this has been a rational response to the statistical evidence showing men as the overwhelming perpetrators of crime. Those theories discussed so far have been criticized for providing a one-dimensional view of female criminality and, particularly, making parenthetical reference to women and crime. Traditionally explanations for female crime (or lack of it) have their roots in the 'natural state of women'. Woman is caring, emotional and maternal and attached unequivocally to the private sphere – incapable practically and emotionally of committing serious crime. When she does move into the criminal arena, the woman is degenerate, failing to reach the same evolutionary stage as her male counterpart. Chronological perspectives then have centred upon women's inferiority to men and the sexual nature of her deviance or crime.

The 1960s and 1970s saw rapid social change within society. Older and traditional theories around human behaviour seemed out of touch with the reality of late twentieth-century life and in terms of criminology new theorists began to develop their ideas around the social construction of crime (for example, Becker 1963, Goffman 1968 and Foucault 1977). These ideas challenged traditional notions of how crime was defined and explained.

In general terms, the private and public arenas of women's lives were subject to accelerated economic, social and medical change. This led to a challenging of traditional definitions of and explanations for female behaviour. There was a need to re-evaluate the way in which criminal and deviant women had been researched and theorized. Feminist criminology in its various forms (given that feminism is not just one generally agreed position, with different categories or types of feminism including liberal feminism, socialist feminism and black feminism) placed gender at the heart of its investigations into criminal or deviant behaviour. Patriarchal ideology within society led to a male power base which led to differentials in equality affecting men and women in their experience of crime, both as the offender and the victim. This affected not only the likelihood of criminal behaviour but the way in which the criminal justice system was likely to respond to that behaviour.

male dominated a world.

This section aims to explore the various feminist viewpoints and go some way to rectifying the misrepresentation and exclusion of women and girls from traditional criminological theory. There is no doubt that feminist criminology has 'grown up' since the late 1960s. This has reflected the fact that the feminist experience has moved through stages, from the search for gender inequality and its removal from society to a realization that the concern may lie in the importance of epistemology in producing knowledge and truths (here the work of Foucault has been particularly important). For feminist criminologists, the general focus of research into criminality has fallen into two camps. There are first those who investigate the lack of female criminality compared to male and second and those who seek to answer the question of rising female crime statistics.

QUESTION BREAK

- What changes in the private and public areas of women's lives might affect the extent and type of female crime?
- How well do you think these changes explain the rise in the number of women committing crime?

So far our discussion has focused on the biological and psychological differences between men and women as being an important part of the explanation for women's relative lack of involvement in crime. From a feminist perspective the key lies in the social construction of gender identity and how this affects behaviour. Therefore male and female identity or characteristics are not the result of biological differences but the product of social and cultural processes. In 1972 Ann Oakley challenged the notion that men and women were two separate distinct biological categories. Oakley stressed the difference between sex and gender – sex being defined by the anatomical and physiological characteristics which determine maleness or femaleness and gender referring to the socially constructed notions of masculinity and femininity which are learned behaviours picked up through imitation of family and society in general (primary or secondary socialization). Behaviour patterns, then, are not universal, rather they will depend upon the society that the individual belongs to, as different societies vary in the ways that they define the social, cultural and psychological attributes of men and women.

The study of conformity and deviance is central to the exploration of criminal behaviour. How individuals react to social constraints and regulations is of great importance to the criminologist. For feminist researchers, gender and the rules and regulations attached to gendered identities can help to explain female crime patterns.

A key question within criminology is: what is it that makes one person go through life relatively crime-free compared to someone who immerses themselves within a criminal subculture? The answer, according to Hirschi, lies in control theory (see p. 107). According to Heidensohn (1996), women's behaviour is much more closely monitored than that of males and this control begins within the immediate family in early childhood. Expectations of behaviour begin at an early age. Boys are expected to conform to society's view of masculinity – they should be tough, independent and strong, whereas girls are expected to be emotional, passive and domesticated. These ideas are similar to the expected roles of men and women within the family put forward by functionalist sociologists such as Talcott Parsons (1951).

Ultimately the gender socialization process of females affords them fewer opportunities for exploration than boys. According to Smart (1976) a particularly important aspect is the fact that restrictions are placed upon girls' freedom in adolescence. For boys these restrictions are less stringent and their freedom of movement may aid in the discovery of delinquent behaviour. Girls on the other hand lack the opportunity to witness, learn about and engage in delinquency. Thus, this social control prevents women from entering the criminal arena as they lack such exposure and access to it. Therefore, from this feminist viewpoint the patriarchal male-dominated society controls women more effectively than men – these controls also operate within the public arena through work and leisure. Here controls are often in the form of invisible structures which prevent female freedom of movement and expression. Privately, women are physically and mentally controlled through domestic violence but it is threat of public violence towards women which forms a much more subtle form of control. Fear through the media's portrayal of 'stranger danger' keeps women physically off the streets and confined to their homes especially after dark. Over the last ten years the media have concentrated on women as victims rather than perpetrators.

Conformity is learned behaviour, and owing to their differential socialization women tend to conform to the 'norm' more than men. Conformity in women brings praise and rewards. According to Carlen (1988) women are controlled by two mechanisms in modern society: home and work. The socialization process in early childhood and the conformity impressed on them mean that the rewards of this conformity remain psychologically important to women. Hence the rewards of employment are more prized than entering the criminal arena. For women there are more moral sanctions attached to criminal behaviour, not least the threat to the stability and happiness of the family unit which prevents many women from turning to crime.

Of course not all women conform – a fact which is reflected in the rising female crime statistics. Conformity in women and girls may depend on a number of things. Firstly the structure of the family is an important indicator of the level of future conformity. Hagan (1990) points to changes in the family structure to explain levels of female crime. Since the late 1950s family style and structure has been changing. The patriarchal family was once the norm within society and was characterized by the father as the controlling influence and occupying the traditional 'breadwinner, head of the family role'. Mothers on the other hand occupied the domestic realm and were subordinate to her husband's position. Daughters, then, were closely supervised by mothers and expected to follow the female pattern of entering the 'cult of domesticity'. Therefore girls were socialized away from risk-taking behaviour, whilst boys were encouraged to 'experiment'. However changes in family structure (single parents, reconstituted families) and parenting styles have produced what Hagan calls the egalitarian family, which stresses greater fairness between the sexes and in turn greater independence for women, thereby providing a greater propensity for risk. Hagan further argues that female delinquency may have a class dimension. In terms of the egalitarian family Hagan argues that middle-class aspirations (such as autonomy, success and mobility) dominate and that children of both sexes are encouraged along these lines. The conclusion drawn is that daughters and sons now have the same (or at least getting close to the same) propensity towards delinquent behaviour.

Siegel (1992) suggests that:

Middle class girls are more likely to violate the law because they are less closely controlled than their lower class counterparts. And in homes where both parents hold positions of power, girls are more likely to have the same expectations of career success as their brothers. Consequently, siblings of both sexes will be socialized to take risks and engage in other behavior related to delinquency. Power control theory, then, implies that middle class youth of both sexes will have higher crime rates than their lower-class peers.

(207)

Of course this idea cannot explain the fact that the vast majority of women within the prison system are working class or underclass.

Secondly Heidensohn (1997) points to the fact that girls and women do not always live up to gendered stereotypes and therefore do not always conform to the social norm even if this was the expected behaviour within their family unit. Girls may resist and resent controlling techniques. After all if social control theory was to be an unflawed theoretical position, society would have no female crime!

Emancipation and crime

It was in the 1960s and 1970s that women began to emerge from their traditional roles of mother and housewife. Owing to social and economic changes women were no longer slaves to their biological make-up. The advent of the contraceptive pill allowed women to make their own choices regarding pregnancy and family size, affording them a new independence. As a result women began to enter the public arena which had previously been dominated by men. In terms of the employment sector, the growth of women in employment began under the first wave of feminism in the early twentieth century when the Suffragette movement began to gain momentum. In what has become known as the 'second wave' of feminism, the 1960s and 1970s, the Equal Pay Act (1970), the Sex Discrimination Act (1975) and the Employment Protection Act (1975) helped to establish women's social and legal rights as equals of men. During the period 1951–79 women's employment rates doubled (Reid and Wormald 1982). It seemed at this time that the women's liberation movement was beginning to gain ground in the fight for equality.

During this period female crime statistics had also shown a significant rise and it was not long before a link was made between rising female criminality and the 'new found' emancipation of women and their increased economic opportunities. The relationship between rising crimes and women's emancipation was the focus of Adler's major work *Sisters in Crime* (1975). In terms of equality and crime Adler wrote that 'women have lost their chains. For better or worse they have lost many of the constraints which kept them within the law' (24). Figures in her book stated that between 1969 and 1972 national arrest rates in the USA for major crimes showed a jump for boys of 82 per cent and for girls of 306 per cent. 'During the twelve-year period between 1960 and 1972 the number of women arrested for robbery rose by 277 per cent, while the male figure rose 169 per cent. Dramatic differences are found in embezzlement (up 280 per cent for women, 50 per cent for men), larceny (up 303 per cent for women, 82 per cent for men), and burglary (up 168 per cent for women, 63 per cent for men)' (Adler 1975, 16).

Rita Simon (1975) added to the debate through focusing on women's access to blue- and white-collar crime through their extended employment opportunities. She wrote: 'Women's participation in financial and white collar offences (fraud, embezzlement, larceny, forgery) should increase as their opportunities for employment in higher status occupations extend'.

Therefore the social control that women had been subjected to began to break down and, as they entered the workforce, their access to criminal subcultures increased. For instance, it is the case that more women are now involved in the higher echelons of big business, so providing more opportunity for fraud and embezzlement. One high-profile recent case was that of Martha Stewart. The American ex-stockbroker turned style guru was accused and charged with insider dealing in 2001. The case related to the sale of $225,000 of shares in the biotech firm Implone the day before it was announced that federal regulators had turned down a review of the cancer drug Erbitux (produced by Implone). Stewart's case was well publicized and she was sentenced to five months in prison in July 2004 for obstructing a federal securities investigation. Having served her sentence, Martha Stewart is back in the media spotlight with her career seemingly little affected by her imprisonment (see also p. 122).

The emancipation thesis does not relate only to women's position within the world of legitimate business. In recent years women's prominence within the underworld has been felt. Within the mafia, for example, as fathers and brothers are murdered or sent to jail, the women within the families are taking control. This situation has become known as the Godmother phenomenon and is considered in the question break.

QUESTION BREAK

Read the article on 'mafia godmothers' below. In what ways might the article be used to

- criticize the emancipation thesis?
- support it?

Mafia Godmothers Seize Control: Arrested at Dawn in Curlers and Pyjamas

Anti-Mafia police arrested mafia chieftan Concetta Scalisi after bursting in on her hideout on the slopes of Mt Etna in Sicily this week.

Having been on the run for eight months, Concetta is facing three murder charges, but more chillingly, she's one of a growing breed of Godmothers, who are proving as ferocious and cold-blooded as their male counterparts.

Cornered in a house where she was being harboured by two other females, Scalisi, whose sartorial style is as strict as her alleged control over the mob – no make-up, lipstick, earrings or other jewellery, white shirts, dark suits – greeted police by slashing her hands and stomach with a piece of glass, apparently in an attempt to be sent to hospital, rather than directly to prison.

Her ploy failed. Though it wasn't exactly what you'd have expected of Al Capone, its suddenness and Scalisi's rare ferocity of purpose left the officers shaken.

'To all intents and purposes,' said Inspector Alvaro Cavazza of the police in Catania, who arrested her at the end of a probe involving a mixture of old fashioned detective work and electronic eavesdropping devices, 'Concetta Scalisi is a man. Her gestures, way of acting and of talking are typical of the male Mafioso.'

It is not surprising. She took up the reins of her murdered father Antonio's clan following the arrest in March 1997 of a nephew who had been minding the shop . . .

Gone are the days when the place of a mobster's wife was in the cucina, rattling the pots and pans and daily making fresh pasta all'uovo, while her husband was busy refining heroin, collecting the pizzo or protection money and killing. Now, more and more often, it is the women who are forced to step in to run the 'firm' when their husbands or brothers are sent to jail or are killed by Mafia rivals.

The Godmother phenomenon first came to light a few years ago in Naples, where Rosetta 'Ice Eyes' Cutolo, the sister of the jailed former capo dei capi of the city Raffaele Cutolo, heads a line-up of feared Godmothers now behind bars. Clutching her handbag and often seen in the company of a priest, 'Ice Eyes' evaded the law for 13 years until her arrest in 1993, running her brother's criminal empire as he languished in jail doing seven life sentences. But the Code of Honour governing the behaviour of the Camorra or Neapolitan Mafia is much looser than its more organised and more fuddy-duddy Sicilian relation, whose strict rules barring women from true Mafia pursuits have only recently begun to yield to necessity and social pressure.

In Sicily, Catania and its lawless environs are proving to be the most fertile ground for the growth of the phenomenon of the 'Woman of Honour'. The area's, and Sicily's, first Godmother was arrested four years ago: although only 26 at the time, Maria Filippa Messina was accused of having taken over her husband Antonio's clan two years earlier, when he was jailed for 21 years for murder. The clan ran prostitution, drugs and extortion rackets.

Messina was arrested with seven men after they were overheard plotting the massacre of six members of a rival clan. She is now breaking stones – the only woman in Italy subject to Law41/BIS, which metes out extra harsh prison conditions for the most serious Mafia offenders.

Also in Catania two years ago Santa Puglisi, 23 and already a Mafia widow, was praying on her husband's grave in the city's cemetery when she was gunned down by assassins, believed to be from a rival Mafia family.

Santa's nephew Stefano, who is thought to have witnessed the execution, was also murdered. He was 14. Detectives believe that the reason for her death was that Santa, besides mourning her husband, had also taken up the reins of his business. Her killers have yet to be brought to justice.

(*Daily Telegraph*, 19 April 1999)

Since Adler's and Simon's studies many feminist criminologists have vehemently criticized the emancipation thesis. Chesney-Lind (1997) has argued that there is no evidence to suggest that emancipation in terms of criminal behaviour has occurred.

As indicated earlier by the data on the under-representation of women offenders, women's criminal behaviour is, on the whole, still marginal compared to that of men. Theoretically the emancipation thesis was born of liberal feminism and its emphasis on equality. This has led to framing criminal behaviour in gender-neutral terms, which assumes an equality and masks the patriarchal structures within which female crime occurs. For example in terms of female violence 'women's violence is profoundly threatening for a patriarchal society because it challenges the naturalness of the gender binarism on which that society depends' (Boyle 2005, 100).

During the 1980s researchers and theorists such as Naffine (1987, 1997) and Steffensmeier and Allan (1996) have rejected the idea that there has been a gender convergence in terms of criminal behaviour. Indeed Steffensmeir and Allan (1996) argue that between 1935 and 1990 the increase in female crime has actually been modest with the exception of larceny, fraud and embezzlement. Moreover increases in these crimes are in line with traditional gender roles. For example statistics for larceny probably relate to increases in shoplifting and fraud and embezzlement figures for women are dominated by welfare and credit card fraud.

Some have argued that the changing rate of female crime is related directly to the demise of 'chivalry' within the criminal justice system (see below). Chesney-Lind (1989, 1997) believes that women are now treated more punitively than men within justice agencies such as the police and the courts. Of course this leads directly to arguments that the increase in female crime rate is simply due to the fact that more women are being apprehended and charged than in previous years, that the 'dark figure' of female crime (crimes that remain hidden from public view and are not recorded in official crime statistics) is being illuminated by new policy and changing attitudes towards women and crime.

The chivalry hypothesis

Pollak, whose work we looked at in relation to biological explanations (see p. 147), argued that women do commit (much) crime yet the true level is masked by the existence of chivalry within the criminal justice system. The chivalry hypothesis – in contrast to the emancipation theory – argues that women have not achieved an equality with men in terms of crime or punishment. On the contrary this line of thought points to the chivalrousness of a patriarchal society permeating a criminal justice system that is prepared to treat women more leniently compared to men and so masks their true level of criminal behaviour.

ENDING

The chivalry argument effects woman in different ways. The idea of paternalism in the criminal justice system permeates all other explanations – women are viewed as submissive or passive and are therefore in need of a caring attitude. This paternal attitude also tends to view women as naive, which has ramifications for the way they are responded to – they will be seen as capable of being misled or of not understanding the gravity of the crime. This naivety also leads criminal justice personnel to believe that women are less dangerous and less capable of committing crime, compared to men.

Moreover the chivalry hypothesis points to the argument that chivalry may affect the type of punishment that women receive. On a practical and moral level judges may be reluctant to imprison women with children as incarceration leads to additional expense and upheaval when placing children in adequate care as well as long-term emotional or psychological turmoil that might affect the offender and her children.

EXAMPLE?

DOUBLY DEVIANT POINT.

As mentioned, these ideas emanate from Pollak's biologically based arguments which today have been criticized for being rather crude and without real evidence. One line of criticism suggests that a chivalrous response is afforded only to women who closely relate to the socially acceptable feminine traits. Ann Lloyd (1995), for example, agrees that chivalry does exist but only in respect of those who are seen to conform to gender stereotypes, in other words those women who engage successfully in female heterosexual behaviour. She goes as far as to argue that those who do not fit or refuse to fit gender norms are often treated more harshly as not only do they commit crime but they also transcend female norms. As the title of her book suggests, these women are seen to be doubly deviant and doubly damned. Indeed, Farrington and Morris (1983) were among the first to point to the fact that a female offender's background, such as marital status, was deemed important when sentencing women.

QUESTION BREAK

- To what extent do you think that factors such as child care should influence the sentencing of women (and men)?
- Find some recent press reports of criminal trials which involve male and female defendants. Can you find evidence for the chivalry thesis?

Evidence shows that different factors interact to produce different experiences for women within the criminal justice system. Pat Carlen for example points to the effects that class and race can have on a women's apprehension and eventual punishment and suggests that while 'women who break the law come from all kinds of backgrounds ... Those who land in prison are much more likely to have come from the lower socio-economic groups than from the higher ones' (Carlen 1985).

The marginalization thesis

Most contemporary research into women and crime has argued that a more plausible explanation for a rise in the female crime statistics is women's economic marginalization, that is the idea that women have suffered increased financial deprivation compared with men. In terms of crime, poverty – absolute and relative – has forced women into the criminal arena. As mentioned earlier it is the case that the most popular and fastest growing area of female crime can be termed 'survival crime' – this refers to crimes which are characterized by the need for financial gain, such as prostitution, shoplifting and acting as drug mules.

This raises the question as to what extent women turn to crime through reasons of economic marginalization rather than through an increased liberation from economic and social inequality.

Box was one of the first to claim a link between economic marginality and female crime. Analysing unemployment rates over the period 1951–80, he concluded that the rate of female employment had some bearing on female crime statistics. For instance, Box argued that:

> although some upper middle-class women have made inroads into formerly male professions, the vast bulk of women have become increasingly economically marginalised – that is, more likely to be unemployed, or unemployable, or if employed, then more likely to be in insecure, lower paid, unskilled, part-time jobs, where career prospects are minimal ... [and] the welfare state, on which proportionately more women than men depend, has tightened its definition of who deserves financial assistance and at the same time has become increasingly unable to index these payments in line with inflation.
>
> (1983, 197)

Feminist researchers (particularly those adopting a Marxist or conflict perspective) have referred to the 'feminization of poverty' thesis to explain women's position more specifically. Pat Carlen (1988), for example, focused on the policies of the Thatcher government in the 1980s to explore this notion of the feminization of poverty. Her study followed the criminal careers of 39 women and, in her conclusion, she argued that Thatcherite policies on employment, tax and social security benefit had had the effect of criminalizing women who found economic survival under such policies virtually impossible.

In recent years there has been an increase and improvement in women's position within the employment sector. However, while it may be true that women occupy a higher percentage of the employment sector than ever before, they still exist in disproportionately large numbers in low-paid, part-time positions which are more often than not lacking the protection of trade unions. For example, much of the increase in the number of women in paid work can be accounted for by the rise of part-time work. Between 1971 and 1993, 93 per cent of the total increase in women's employment was in part-time work (Court 1995).

The Equal Opportunities Commission states that that although 46 per cent of women are now part of the labour market, 44 per cent of women workers are in part-time employment compared to only one in ten male workers. Hourly earnings for women in full-time employment are 18 per cent lower than for men in equivalent employment, and for women in part-time employment the figures are significantly lower, at 40 per cent that of men.

QUESTION BREAK

Read the article below and answer the questions below.

Women Making Slow Progress in Pay Fight: Equality Campaigners Demand Urgent Action to Curb Female Poverty

The average income of men in Britain is almost double that of women, according to new government figures.

The latest statistics from the Department of Trade and Industry, covering the period from 1996/7 to 2003/4, show that while women are slowly narrowing the income gap – with single mothers moving fastest of all – the sexes remain far apart.

The biggest differences between male and female incomes are for those living in pensioner couples, where women's income is a mere 37% of that of comparable men.

But the gap is, predictably, smallest for single women without children, whose income stands at 93% of that for single childless men.

According to the data the median weekly total individual income for all women in 2003/4 was £161, just 53% of that for men at £303 . . .

Overall, women's total weekly incomes have gone up as a proportion of men's, from 46% to 53%. The largest increase in this comparison was for women in the 25-to-34 age group, those some way up the career ladder but not necessarily with children. They saw their income rise by 15 points, from 52% of men's to 67% . . .

Thirty years after the Equal Pay Act came into force female full-time workers earn almost a fifth less than men per hour, while the gap for the part-time sector, dominated by women, yawns far wider . . .

The report also makes clear the significant gender income gap within families. Just over two-thirds of the total family income of couples came from men, while the rest came from women. However, for a fifth of couples women's individual incomes contributed more than half of the family's total.

Kate Bellamy, senior policy officer at the Fawcett Society, said: 'These figures show once again that the pay gap is only part of the reason why women are much poorer than men. Lower pensions, greater reliance on benefits, responsibilities for unpaid domestic and caring work all play their part . . .

'Until the government makes gender equality an explicit target progress on the income gap will continue to be painfully slow.'

(Lucy Ward, *Guardian*, 18 May 2005)

- How might the evidence above be used to support the marginalization thesis with regard to women's criminality?
- What effect might the 'narrowing of the income gap' mentioned above have on rates of female crime?

This argument does not suggest that all women have become economically marginalized. However some have suggested that those who have gained from the women's liberation movement are middle-class white women – often in professional-type occupations. In terms of female criminality, such changes need to be related to the picture of the typical female criminal – who is not a mid-twenties to thirties professional worker.

Women offenders tend to be poor, members of minority groups with truncated educations and spotty employment histories. These were precisely the women whose lives were largely unaffected by the gains, such as they were, of the then white, middle class women's rights movement

(Chesney-Lind 1997)

FURTHER READING

Naffine, N. (1997) *Feminism and Criminology*. Cambridge: Polity Press. This study provides a clear and concise examination of how feminism has contributed to the study of criminal behaviour. Naffine demonstrates the wide range of feminist studies that have analysed crime and provides a corrective to the generally held view that feminists have had little impact in this area of study.

Walklate, S. (2004) *Gender, Crime and Criminal Justice*, second edition. Cullompton: Willan Publishing. This text provides a thorough overview of explanations as to why women do (and do not) commit crime and on the treatment women offenders receive from the criminal justice system. It considers women both as offenders and as victims; and also examines in some depth issues around the fear of crime and sexual violence.

WEBSITE

www.methodist.edu/criminaljustice/index.htm. This website is a general criminology one which contains a wealth of information on criminological theorizing. It discusses the work of many of the theorists we have looked at in examining the criminal behaviour of women, including Alder, Hirschi and Lombroso.

Explaining the Criminal Behaviour of Ethnic Minorities

INTRODUCTION

The idea of 'black crime' and more generally the relationship between race and crime are seen as recent phenomena, and, while our focus will be on explanations for current patterns of ethnic minority crime, it would be appropriate to start with a brief reminder that this is not a new issue. 'Scientific' approaches to the notion of racial differences and hierarchies are seen as originating at the time of the Enlightenment – with Enlightenment philosophers associating civilization with white European peoples and regarding other cultural and racial groups as less rational and moral than these white populations. Phillips and Bowling (2002) refer to Gobineau's 1853 essay on *The Inequality of Human Races* in which 'negroes' are described as having mental faculties that are 'dull or even non-existent' and as killing 'willingly, for the sake of killing'. Later in the nineteenth century, Lombroso (whose theorizing is examined more fully below) argued that there was a clear link between race and crime: 'many of the characteristics found in savages, and in the coloured races, are also to be found in habitual delinquents'.

Such theories and arguments legitimated ideas of white supremacy and practices of slavery. British merchants and traders sold their goods for black slaves from Africa who were taken to the West Indies to work in the British colonies there. Although slavery was abolished in the nineteenth century, the notion of the superiority of the white race and, in particular, the British empire have left a legacy of racist thinking. And such thinking was brought to the fore in the 1950s and 1960s when immigration from the British colonies was encouraged as a result of the labour shortage in Britain. While there was a clear need for immigrant workers in Britain, their arrival still encouraged racist sentiments and worries around the 'racial degeneration'. There was widespread hostility to the influx of 'coloured' immigrants to particular areas of Britain, the best-known example being Enoch Powell's 1968 speech predicting 'rivers of blood' on the streets of Britain as a result of immigration from Asia and the West Indies. Although Powell's comments were widely condemned, when Margaret Thatcher became Prime Minister in 1979 her sympathetic comments over white fears of being ' swamped' by 'alien cultures' reflected similar sentiments. In the early 1980s the inner-city disorders in many parts of Britain, most notably Brixton, Bristol, Liverpool and Manchester, lent support to the stereotype of black youths as disorderly and criminal.

Reports of the disorders of the early and mid-1980s highlighted the deprived social and economic conditions of the areas where there were high concentrations of ethnic-minority groups. Ethnic-minority groups were shown to be concentrated in the most deprived and depressed neighbourhoods; Afro-Caribbean boys, in particular, were over-represented in exclusions from schools; and unemployment rates were consistently higher among ethnic-minority groups than for the population as a whole. None the less, the basic link between crime and certain ethnic-minority groups was never far from media and public thinking. And, as we have indicated, this link has a long, undistinguished history. The rest of this chapter looks at the evidence and explanations for the link between race and crime. In recent years terrorist crimes have been committed by many different ethnic-minority groups in many countries including Britain. However, the focus of this chapter is on the criminal activities of black ethnic minorities in Britain.

THE EVIDENCE – PATTERNS AND TRENDS

QUESTION BREAK

Before reading this section consider the following questions and return to them later.

- Which crimes are commonly perceived as committed by Afro-Caribbeans; Asians?
- Which crimes do you associate with Afro-Caribbeans; Asians?
- Where have your ideas come from?

It is a common stereotype that young males, and especially young ethnic-minority, and particularly black, males, are especially prone to criminal behaviour. And a range of crimes are widely seen as typically committed by young black males. Since the 1960s, for instance, drug use and supply and 'mugging' or street robbery have been popularly associated with black people and more recently car-jacking and gangland violence have been characterized in a similar way. Illegal immigration and asylum

and Rutter and Giller suggested there was also evidence which suggested that many black teenagers appeared to be more committed to education than their white peers. With regard to different ethnic groups, Stevens and Willis (1979) found that Asian crime rates were substantially lower than white rates and found that Asian communities (at this time anyway) were generally law-abiding. By contrast, arrest rates for black groups (and especially West Indian) were much higher than for the white population for both adults and juveniles. In concluding their review, Rutter and Giller highlighted three distinct findings. Firstly, the delinquency rates for Asians had been and remained equal to or lower than those for the white population. Secondly, although the arrest rates for blacks in the 1950s and 1960s were similar to those for whites, they had risen substantially above that during the 1970s. Thirdly, most of the violent crime that did occur was between people of the same skin colour. Since the late 1970s and Rutter and Giller's study the position regarding Asian criminality has altered. The notion of young Asians as being essentially 'conformist' has been challenged by groups of Asian youths defending 'their territory' from racist white youths. As Phillips and Bowling (2002) comment, the idea of the 'Asian gang' was 'brought to the fore in 1994 by the murder of Richard Everitt in King's Cross by a group of Bangladeshi youths, the disorders in Manningham in Bradford in 1995, and again in the summer of 2001 with disorders in Oldham, Burnley and Bradford'.

More generally, what is the situation twenty years on from Rutter and Giller's work? Official Home Office statistics on race and the criminal justice system are produced annually under section 95 of the Criminal Justice Act 1991, which states that 'The Secretary of State shall in each year publish such information, as he considers expedient for the purpose of . . . [avoiding] discriminating against any persons on the ground of race or sex or any other improper ground'. These statistics provide a wealth of information across a range of areas including stop and search rates, arrest rates, prosecutions and imprisonment, as well as detailing the numbers and proportions of ethnic minority practitioners working in the different criminal justice agencies. The most recent report refers to figures for 2003/4 and covers England and Wales. As regards the percentage of the population from different ethnic groups, the 2001 census figures are used, with 2.8 per cent of the general population Black, 4.7 per cent Asian and 1.2 per cent 'Other'. These proportions need to be kept in mind when looking at the proportions of different ethnic minority groups involved with crime and criminal justice. There were 738,016 stop and searches recorded by the police in 2003/4, of which 15 per cent were of Black people, 7 per cent of Asian and 1 per cent of 'Other' ethnic origin; so relative to the general population figures, Black people were 6.4 times more likely to be stopped and searched than White people, and Asian people twice as likely. Of 1.33 million arrests for notifiable offences, 9 per cent were recorded as being of Black people, 5 per cent Asian and 1 per cent 'Other', with Black people over three times more likely to be arrested than White people. The report also breaks down these arrest figures for different offence groups, which show that the main differences between ethnic groups was a greater tendency for White people to be arrested for burglary and criminal damage, Black people for robbery and fraud and forgery and Asian people for fraud and forgery. Table 6.1 provides a summary of information on the ethnic background of those who come into contact with the criminal justice system at different stages.

Table 6.1 Proportion (%) of ethnic groups at different stages of the criminal justice process, England and Wales, 2003/4

| | Ethnicity | | | | | |
	White	Black	Asian	Other	Unknown/ not recorded	Total
General population (aged 10 & over) @ 2001 Census	91.3	2.8	4.7	1.2	0.0	100
Stops and searches[1]	74.3	14.7	7.3	1.5	2.3	100
Arrests[2]	84.3	8.8	4.8	1.4	0.7	100
Cautions[2]	84.2	6.7	4.7	1.2	3.2	100
Youth offences	83.5	6.3	3.1	2.9	4.3	100
Crown Court[3]	76.8	12.2	7.4	3.6	*	100
Prison receptions[4 5]	80.5	9.7	4.8	2.9	2.1	100
Prison population[5]	77.1	15.5	3.1	4.1	0.1	100

Note: Figures may not add to 100% due to rounding.
1 Stops and searches recorded by the police under section 1 of the Police and Criminal Evidence Act 1984 and other legislation.
2 Notifiable offences.
3 Information on ethnicity is missing in 35% of cases, therefore, percentages are based on known ethnicity.
4 'Other' includes those prisoners who classified their ethnicity as 'Mixed'.
5 Sentenced.

Source: Adapted from 'Statistics on Race and the Criminal Justice System 2003–4', London: HMSO, 2005

QUESTION BREAK

Summarize the information in the table and try to offer explanations for the over-representation of the different non-White ethnic groups at the different stages of the criminal justice system.

The proportions of ethnic-minority groups in prisons are massively greater than would be expected by the general population figures. In February 2003, Black and minority ethnic groups accounted for 24 per cent of the male prison population (16 per cent Black, 3 per cent Asian and 5 per cent Other) and 31 per cent of the female prison population (25 per cent Black, 1 per cent Asian and 5 per cent Other). However, these figures included foreign nationals, who made up 12 per cent of the male and 21 per cent of the female prison populations.

- How could you account for the massive discrepancy in prison figures between Black, White and Asian populations?
- Why do you think 25 per cent of female prisoners are Black?

Finally, with regard to people working in the criminal justice system, the most obvious finding is the under-representation of ethnic-minority groups. While these figures do not relate to Black and non-White people committing crime, they are worth mentioning in relation to the treatment and perceptions of treatment of ethnic-minority groups by the criminal justice system, and to the related issue of bias (or not) within the system. In 2003–4 the proportion of Black and ethnic-minority officers with the 43 police forces in England and Wales was 3.3 per cent; however, the figure dropped to 2 per cent for those at Inspector or Chief Inspector level. None the less this was an increase on previous years, and a similar increase was found in the number of Black and ethnic-minority prison officers, with 4.1 per cent from Black and ethnic-minority backgrounds. However when it comes to the judiciary, the proportion of non-White people reaching the more senior positions is virtually negligible. Of the 105 High Court Judges and 36 Lord Chief Justice none was from ethnic-minority backgrounds; amongst the 564 Circuit Judges, one was Black and three Asian (*Statistics on Race and Criminal Justice System*, London: Stationery Office, 2004).

So far we have considered the data and patterns around race and crime. The next section turns to the theoretical explanations for the links between ethnic group background and criminal behaviour.

EXPLANATIONS

There are two basic explanations for the heavy over-representation of ethnic-minority groups in the crime statistics: firstly, that ethnic minorities, and especially black people, do commit more crime than the white population and the reasons for this 'fact' need to be explored and established; secondly, that ethnic-minority groups do not commit any more crime than the rest of the population but the criminal justice agencies, such as the police and courts, work in a way which is biased against them – so that they are more likely to be recorded as committing crimes. This second line of explanation examines issues of racism within the criminal justice system. Firstly, though, we will, look at black crime as a social reality. This basic division – which suggests a sort of either/or in terms of whether ethnic-minority populations commit more crime than the white population or whether such groups face discriminatory treatment by the criminal justice system and so are over-represented in crime statistics – has been criticized by recent commentators (Phillips and Bowling 2002). Such a distinction, it is argued, ignores or underplays the experience of ethnic minorities as victims of crime. While acknowledging this is an important issue, the focus in this chapter is on why particular groups of people do or do not commit crime and in order to keep this focus we will consider different explanations under the two basic explanations for the disparity in crime statistics between the black and white populations suggested above.

Black crime as social reality

We have been using the terms 'ethnic minority' and 'black' and it is important to be aware that such terms cover very broad categories that need to be broken down when looking at explanations for criminal behaviour. The stereotypical black criminal has been based around African or Caribbean groups – who have been seen for centuries as having characteristics that predisposed them to criminality. In contrast, Asian criminality has been viewed in a very different way – the popular image of Asian communities has been one which has not highlighted criminality, but rather passivity, family-centredness, tradition and conformity. Although this image has been challenged in recent years, with examples of Asian youths turning to criminal and violent behaviour, the basic stereotypical division remains (see p. 166 above).

Biological explanations

The earliest criminological theorizing that attempted to explain the link between crime and race offered individualistic solutions – focusing on the biological and/or psychological characteristics of offenders. These approaches, which emerged in the nineteenth century, adopted the methods of the natural sciences and were particularly influenced by the work of Charles Darwin and other 'Darwinists'. Cesare Lombroso is generally regarded as the most influential of the early scientific criminologists and as the 'founder' of modern criminology. In his book *L'uomo delinquente* (The Criminal Man), published in 1876, he developed a complex description of what he called the 'born criminal', who could be recognized by a variety of physical characteristics, in particular facial characteristics – for example large jaws and high cheek bones. In the medical faculty at the University of Rome there are portraits of splendidly ugly delinquents who were used by Lombroso to illustrate his theory. For Lombroso criminals were throwbacks to an earlier evolutionary form of species. To use his own language:

> Thus were explained anatomically the enormous jaws, high cheek bones, prominent superciliary arches, solitary lines on the palms, extreme size of the orbits, handle-shaped or sessile ears found in criminals, savages and apes, insensibility of pain, extremely acute sight, tattooing, excessive idleness, love of orgies and the irresistible craving for evil for its own sake.

Lombroso believed there was a clear link between racial origin and criminality. As he put it, 'many of the characteristics found in savages, and among the coloured races, are also to be found in habitual delinquents'. Among these common characteristics were thinning hair, receding foreheads, darker skin, curly hair and large ears. By contrast the white race were the most evolved species and 'represent the triumph of the human species'.

Lombroso's ideas were developed in Britain and the United States and played a part in the eugenics movement and its advocating of selective policies to improve the human race – through, for instance, encouraging elite groups to have children and discouraging the less intelligent. Although Lombroso's work has been widely criticized and rejected by social scientists, the attempt to identify biological explanations for crime and to link this with race has continued and will be explored briefly here.

While most advocates of biologically based theories do not express themselves in the same bizarre language and style as Lombroso, such approaches to explaining crime are not merely historical relics that died with Lombroso. In a major study of institutionalized delinquents in the USA in the 1950s, Sheldon and Eleanor Glueck found that delinquent boys were twice as likely to have a mesomorphic build – a chunky muscular physique – compared to non-delinquent boys. Similarly, Herrnstein, writing in the 1990s, concluded that mesomorphic people were more likely to become criminals. With regard to the links between criminal behaviour and inherited characteristics, other theoretical explanations have suggested an association between criminality and personality. Such approaches might be termed 'psychological positivism' and see the most usual psychological 'cause' of crime to be low intelligence, as measured by IQ tests. Again, the work of Herrnstein (1995) has been at the forefront of such theorizing, arguing that the fact that criminals have lower IQs is 'among the prime discoveries of criminology'. Herrnstein and Charles Murray (see next section) wrote *The Bell Curve*, which, as well as being a best-selling book, excited massive controversy in the scientific community. It explored the role of intelligence in understanding social problems in America, the term 'bell curve' referring to the bell-shaped graph that a normal distribution of IQ scores would show. Herrnstein and Murray argue that there has been a rise of a 'cognitive elite', a stratum of highly intelligent people who have the greatest chance of success in life. However, the book became (in)famous for its discussion of the links between race and intelligence and its examination of the role IQ plays in determining the social and economic differences between ethnic groups. The authors argue that intelligence is largely inherited and that genetic differences in intelligence are increasingly contributing to social and economic differences among individuals. The claims that white ethnic groups had more (natural) intelligence than other ethnic groups attracted the most controversy, with the subsequent debate and defence largely centred on the work and ideas of Murray, as Herrnstein died in the early 1990s before *The Bell Curve* was published. Indeed the debate around the book led the American Psychological Association to set up a task force to investigate the claims made in it. Essentially its report was noncommital, stressing that there was no definite evidence that the black–white differences in test scores were due to genetic differences between the groups. It concluded that 'the question (as to whether there were genetic explanations for differences in intelligence) has no scientific answer'.

QUESTION BREAK

- If it could be proved that the causes of criminal behaviour could be found in physical (bodily) or mental characteristics that some people were born with, what sort of policies might be suggested to deal with crime?
- What problems or dangers could you foresee if such explanations were widely accepted?

Look also at the discussion of biological explanations in Chapter 2.

These biological and psychological based theories do not focus solely on race; however it is never far from the surface and is regularly linked with crime through its association with supposedly inherited characteristics such as intelligence or extra-version. A major problem faced by approaches that suggest a link between genetic make-up and criminality is the difficulty of separating genetic and environmental effects. While genetic influences certainly exist, just what is inherited is very difficult to measure.

Cultural explanations – the importance of economic and social conditions

Moving away from the individualistic, physiological explanations for criminal behaviour, cultural theories take a sociological approach to explaining crime. Crime cannot be considered apart from its social context; crime and the criminal can be understood only in relation to the social structure and to the social conditions and opportunities that impact on individuals' lives. Sociological explanations for crime were considered in Chapter 4, and in this section we will try and relate these sort of theoretical approaches to the issue of race and crime. Cultural theories focus on the lifestyles of different groups within society – and offer different perspectives on them. Bowling and Phillips (2002) suggest three major variants of cultural theory – conservative, liberal and radical – which we will introduce briefly here.

Conservative cultural theory offers a right-wing approach that suggests there is an 'underclass' whose poor position, in terms of poverty, is largely its members' own fault and a result of their own inadequacy and lack of drive. Although the notion of an 'underclass' has been around for many years (with the 'dangerous classes' regularly referred to in the eighteenth and nineteenth centuries) Charles Murray 'rediscovered' and applied the term in the 1980s and 1990s, suggesting that in modern Western societies there was a growing group of people who inhabit a 'different world' to the decent and respectable majority (1990). He saw crime as heavily focused in underclass neighbourhoods where young males are socialized from an early age to seeing crime as a normal activity. Although, it is not just a 'race' issue, conservative, 'underclass' theorists see ethnic-minority groups as not assimilating into the majority white culture but rather as holding on to their own values and norms, and have argued that there is a strong tendency for ethnic-minority communities, especially black communities, to fit into the 'underclass'. Such an approach, which essentially sees criminal behaviour as a matter of choice, takes no real account of the ways in which individuals' and groups life chances are structured by social and economic forces that are largely beyond their own control.

Liberal cultural theory suggests that crime (and, more generally, disorders such as riots) is a collective demonstration of despair by those who are marginalized in modern society. Crime, then, is largely a result of social position, with class and ethnic background being key factors that affect such position. With regard to race, the Chicago school of social researchers, writing between the 1920s and 1940s, noted the tendency of ethnic immigrant groups to become concentrated in poorer inner-city areas. The Chicago researchers defined 'zones of transition' in the city in which immigrant groups were particularly likely to settle. Some groups managed to move out of these 'zones' and become assimilated into the wider cultural life of the city. Others were not able to escape these socially disorganized areas which were characterized by crime and poverty. These ideas were applied in a famous study of race and class by Rex and Moore (1967) to Britain and the settling of immigrant groups in the Sparkbrook area of Birmingham in the late 1960s. This approach sees black groups as prone to criminality because of their poor economic, social and geographical position within white society. In response to the conditions they face, deviant and criminal subcultures are formed, and black and Asian groups have been seen as particularly likely to form such subcultures as a way of coping with what they perceive as a hostile wider society. As Lea and Young (1984) put it, 'the economic alienation of young black people gives rise to a culture with a propensity for crime' (quoted in Bowling and Phillips 2002).

Radical or critical cultural theory does not see crime as basically a part of black culture. Rather it focuses on the conditions which drive black people to commit crime. Social and economic conditions encourage black cultures to develop which challenge their oppressed position. The law, both immigration and criminal, discriminates against black groups and, indeed, serves to 'criminalize' them; and the police response to black youth and black crime is seen as exacerbating the sense of oppression felt by such groups. One response to this situation, for black youth in particular, has been to turn to illegitimate avenues for economic and social fulfilment.

QUESTION BREAK

Read the following extracts and consider the questions below

The Underclass

There are many ways to identify an underclass. I will concentrate on three phenomena that have turned out to be early-warning signals in the United States: illegitimacy, violent crime, and drop out from the labour force . . . I

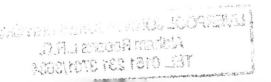

begin with illegitimacy, which in my view is the best predictor of an underclass in the making.

Illegitimacy and the Underclass

Why should it be a 'problem' that a woman has a child without a husband? . . . Why is raising a child without having married any more of a problem than raising a child after a divorce?

. . . Illegitimacy has been sky-rocketing since 1979 . . . From the end of the Second World War until 1960 Britain enjoyed a very low and even slightly declining illegitimacy ratio . . .

The sharp rise is only half the story. The other and equally important half is that illegitimate births are not scattered evenly among the British population . . . The increase in illegitimate births is strikingly concentrated amongst the lowest social class . . .

'It's mainly a black problem.' . . . The statement is correct in this one, very limited sense: blacks born in the West Indies have much higher illegitimacy rates – about 48% of live births is the latest number – than all whites.

Crime and the Underclass

Crime is the next place to look for an underclass for several reasons. First and most obviously, the habitual criminal is the classic member of an underclass. He lives off mainstream society without participating in it . . . To the extent that many people in a community engage in crime as a matter of course, all sorts of the socializing norms of the community change, from the kind of men that the younger boys chose as heroes to the standards of morality in general.

Unemployment and the Underclass

If illegitimate births are the leading indicator of an underclass and violent crime a proxy measure of its development, the definitive proof that an underclass has arrived is that large numbers of young, healthy, low-income males choose not to take jobs . . .

My hypothesis . . . is that Britain is experiencing a generation gap by class. Well-educated young people from affluent homes are working in larger proportions and working longer hours than ever. The attitudes and behaviour of the middle-aged working class haven't changed much. The change in stance toward the labour force is concentrated among lower-class young men in their teens and twenties. It is not a huge change. I am not suggesting that a third or a quarter or even a fifth of lower-class young people are indifferent to work. An underclass doesn't have to be huge to become a problem.

(Murray 1990)

Zones of Transition

As we saw above, the idea of a zone of transition comes from the Chicago School of sociologists and specifically Ernest Burgess. It was a zone in his division of the city into a series of concentric circles or zones which had differing usages. The zone of transition was an area between the central business unit and the outer rings of working and middle class residence; it contained run down housing which was gradually being displaced as the business areas of the city moved outward. The zone was largely inhabited by the poor and by ethnic minority groups (with the two often overlapping of course). In modern cities the term inner city is roughly what Burgess referred to as the zone of transition. Such an area has a shifting population with little sense of community and a high crime rate.

- How might Murray's notion of an underclass be particularly applied to ethnic-minority groups?
- What criticisms can you make of Murray's argument and hypothesis?
- Think of your region, town or city – can you recognize a 'zone of transition'? How closely does it fit the Chicago school's idea?

These different explanations have been introduced only in a very sketchy manner to highlight the structural and cultural approaches. A problem with such arguments is that they take little account of human agency – of the way in which structure is mediated by the role of the individual. The tendency to see poor, oppressed and marginalized people as almost forced into criminality seems to ignore the fact that there are massive differences in how particular marginalized, ethnic groups respond to their situations. This indicates a more obvious point about over-generalizing, which is illustrated by the fact that one member of a family may engage in theft or violent crime while another, in a similar environment, will not.

Race, crime and bias – black crime as over-exaggerated by the crime statistics

The criminal justice system and racial bias

The argument that the various agencies of the criminal justice system work in a manner that discriminates against ethnic minorities is potentially a major reason for the higher number of ethnic minority offenders. In looking at patterns and trends in criminal statistics earlier, we saw that members of ethnic-minority groups, and especially black people, were more likely to be stopped and searched, arrested and end up in prison than the white population. Here we will consider evidence and arguments that there is bias against ethnic-minority groups. It is important to bear in mind that bias can, and perhaps most often does, result not from deliberate discrimination but through unconscious prejudice and stereotyping. As Cavadino and Dignan put it: 'Bias can operate at any and every stage of the criminal process, stages which include investigation and charge by the police, prosecution decisions by the Crown Prosecution Service, bail decisions, court verdicts and sentencing decisions' (2002, 309). In this brief review, we will look at bias and the potential for bias in the three major criminal justice agencies – the police, the courts and prisons.

Firstly we will consider the extent to which the greater likelihood of black and Asian people being stopped and searched and arrested than white people is evidence of prejudice and/or discrimination within the British police. This raises the question of whether police culture and practice is racist. Various studies (Smith and Gray 1983, Reiner 2000, Holdaway 1996) have found that police culture is inherently conservative. In part this is because of the nature of police training and practice – the whole process of becoming a police officer happens in a very institutionalized manner, with probationers at the bottom of a rigid hierarchy that emphasizes discipline and following orders. Probationers are placed under the guidance of experienced officers from whom they pick up the 'real' world of day-to-day policing and the common-sense discourse on crime and criminals. Indeed the nature of police work involves developing methods for recognizing certain types of people as 'typical' criminals and encourages the adoption of stereotypes. Furthermore, the nature of police work encourages a distrust with the outside world and a feeling of 'them versus us' expressed in terms such as 'the thin blue line' to describe the police as guardians of respectability against the forces of crime and disorder. The police, then, are likely to feel a sense of isolation from society owing to the special nature of their job (enforcing the law) and this encourages a strong degree of solidarity within the police; and such solidarity helps breed a strong internal working culture.

One element of this essentially conservative culture is racism. As we saw earlier, there are relatively few black police officers, especially in the more senior ranks; this in itself does not mean there is a racist element to police culture, but it may be indicative. The Policy Studies Institute report, *Police and People in London* (Smith and Grey 1983), examined the work of the Metropolitan police force in London and, when published in 1983, was the most detailed study of a British police force yet produced. In looking at the relationship between the police and people in London it provided a good deal of information on police culture and racism. It found that racist language was used in a casual and almost automatic way, even over radio links that were picked up by all officers. For instance, the researchers heard an inspector say, 'Look I've got a bunch of coons in sight'. It is, of course, debatable whether people who use racist language behave in a racist manner. One young officer told the researchers, Smith and Gray, 'I know that PCs call them spooks, niggers and sooties, but deep down the majority of PCs aren't really against them, although there are some who really hate them . . . I call them niggers myself now but I don't really mean it.'

The PSI report found that there was some racism within 'the Met' but that it did not lead to black people being treated in a biased or inferior way, although there was some evidence that the police tended to link crime and black people and so be more suspicious of ethnic minority groups. In general terms the report found that a lack of confidence in the police was quite widespread among Londoners, and especially amongst young black Londoners, with almost two-thirds (62 per cent) of black 15–24-year-olds thinking the police often used threats or unreasonable behaviour. However, while this demonstrated a degree of criticism of the police, the vast majority of young black people also said they wanted a police force and did use its services like anyone else.

QUESTION BREAK

One aspect of policing that the PSI report referred to above considered was the relationship between the police and black people. Read the brief extract below and answer the questions after it.

> Police officers often use racialist language (among themselves) for effect, but it is the more casual and automatic use of such language that is most telling . . . racialist language is quite commonly used over the personal radio. For example, JG [J. Gray] heard the inspector of the relief with which he was working say over the personal radio, 'look I've got a bunch of coons in sight'. The inspector was standing in a public place at the time, and of course this message came up over the radios of all police officers on the Division . . .
>
> Although the terms by which police officers refer to black people are in common use in various other social contexts, they seem to be more commonly used within the Met than in most other groups: there can be few other groups in which it is normal, automatic, habitual to refer to black people as 'coons', 'niggers' and so on . . .
>
> (Smith and Gray 1983, 111–15)

- What effects might this language have on black people's view of the police and the law?
- Should police officers be disciplined for using racist language?

(More generally, you might consider whether police officers should have to follow more stringent rules of behaviour than other people in society, given their unique position of authority.)

So, to what extent are the PSI findings relevant over twenty years on? The Macpherson Inquiry report (1999) into the murder of the black teenager Stephen Lawrence in 1993, highlighted the continued existence of 'institutional racism' within the Metropolitan police – it concluded that the Met operated an 'unwitting' form of racism. In gathering its material, Macpherson took evidence from the Chief Constable of Manchester, David Wilmot, who accepted that institutional racism existed in his force, saying 'we have a society that has got institutional racism. Greater Manchester Police, therefore, has institutional racism . . . and it is our responsibility to try and make sure it is eradicated.' And in a follow-up survey to these remarks, the *Independent* (16 October 1998) found that 'twelve police forces admit racism', with the Chief Constable of Sussex, Paul Whitehouse, for example, stating, 'Yes, there is institutional racism within Sussex police'.

One of the recommendations of the Macpherson report was to step up efforts to recruit more ethnic-minority officers. Cashmore (2001) considered the issue of under-recruitment in examining the experiences of ethnic-minority officers in Britain. Since the 1960s the British police have been encouraged to recruit more officers from ethnic-minority backgrounds; indeed in 1965 there were only three such officers in the whole British police force. In 1981 the Scarman report into the Brixton disorders urged more ethnic-minority recruitment to the police. However, the lack of success in this regard was shown by the fact that the Macpherson report almost twenty years later was again highlighting the police's failure to recruit enough ethnic minorities. Cashmore's research, which was undertaken in the twelve months after the Macpherson report was published (February 1999), investigated this persistent failure to recruit through interviewing already serving ethnic-minority officers to try to understand their experiences. One area he focused on was the extent to which racism in the police service might explain the under-recruitment. The notion of institutional racism raised by Macpherson was felt by Cashmore to emphasize 'institutional aspects' of police work and ignore the everyday talk and banter which seemed part and parcel of police life. Ethnic-minority officers referred to racist talk which they felt they had to accept, almost as if they were being tested to 'see if they could take a joke'. Other studies of the police's occupational culture have suggested that the day-to-day racism within the police is due to the nature of their work (Chan 1997, Holdaway 1997). Indeed as one officer interviewed by Cashmore said: 'I've got colleagues who subscribe to the philosophy that, if you see four black youths in a car it's worth giving it a pull, at least one of then is going to be guilty of something or other.' And if the police are under pressure to get arrest figures, the officers will be tempted to perform more searches based on their stereotyped views as to who is likely to be a 'good arrest'.

As to why this sort of racist talk is not challenged, the nature of police work necessitates black and white officers working as a team, which can lead to a reluctance to 'rock the boat', and for ethnic-minority officers to avoid 'getting a reputation'. Police work is a potentially dangerous occupation and ethnic-minority officers will want their (white) colleagues to be 'there when they need them'. As one Asian officer put it: 'If I call for assistance that means I need somebody there now, not in ten minutes . . . If I've taken somebody to task for a racial remark or whatever, months or weeks later that some bobby might be the one who's called out for me . . . it would put some doubt in your mind.' In concluding, Cashmore suggested that ethnic-minority officers don't challenge racism because of their career ambitions and orientations and, particularly, because of the special nature of police work which can, unlike most jobs, involve life-threatening situations.

There is less research on race, racism and the courts and prisons than with regard to the police. However, one of the most startling of all criminal justice statistics is the massive over-representation of ethnic-minority populations who are sentenced to prison. Although making up just over 6 per cent of the British population, ethnic minorities account for a much higher proportion of the prison population. Data gathered by the Institute of Race Relations showed that in June 2000 ethnic minorities accounted for 19 per cent of the male prison population and 25 per cent of female prisoners (Institute of Race Relations 2002). This over-representation is even more noticeable for specific ethnic groups. While fewer than 2 per cent of the population are classified as of Afro-Caribbean origin, 12 per cent of male prisoners and 19 per cent of female prisoners are Afro-Caribbean (Institute of Race Relations 2002). Since then there has been an increase in the proportion of both male and female black prisoners. Official Home Office statistics on race and the criminal justice system (see p. 167 above) show that in February 2003 16 per cent of male prisoners and 25 per cent of female prisoners were black; and the black prison population increased by 138 per cent between 1993 and 2003, compared to a 48 per cent increase for white and 73 per cent increase for Asian prisoners. The question such figures raise is whether the differences can be explained by a higher crime rate among ethnic-minority groups or whether other factors, including bias in the system, can offer an explanation. One point to bear in mind is the high number of foreign nationals who are imprisoned for drug smuggling – a factor which skews the female prison figures as a high proportion of such prisoners are black. In addition demographic and social factors will have an influence – such as the lower average age of the ethnic-minority population and the tendency for Afro-Caribbean groups in particular to have other characteristics associated with higher offending, such as higher unemployment, lower educational attainment and living in areas with high crime rates.

However these points do not tell us if the court system works differently for the different ethnic-minority groups it deals with. Differential treatment in court is likely to occur as a result of the tendency for black offenders to plead not guilty – for example 48 per cent of young black offenders plead not guilty in crown courts, compared to 30 per cent of young white offenders. And as offenders are given heavier sentences if found guilty after not guilty pleas (as a consequence of the discount on sentence given for pleading guilty), this can lead to more black offenders being imprisoned, and for longer.

Hood's study for the Commission for Racial Equality (1992) examined and tried to explain the over-representation of ethnic minority prisoners. In considering whether ethnic minority offenders were sentenced according to the same criteria as white offenders a number of relevant factors were highlighted. A higher proportion of black people were charged with offences that were deemed to be more serious and that could be dealt with only by the Crown Court. For instance, many more were charged with robbery and, although robbery is a nasty crime, it could be questioned whether it is any more serious than housebreaking or grievous bodily harm (GBH), both of which can be dealt with summarily by magistrates' courts if both parties consent. As regards the classifying of offences, black offenders were disproportionately charged with supplying drugs – and the insistence that offences involving trading in small or moderate amounts of cannabis should be committed to Crown Court is also likely to influence the rate of imprisonment for black offenders. As well as being more likely to plead not guilty (see above), black defendants were found to be more likely to be remanded in custody by magistrates: a factor which can, again, lead to a greater likelihood of a custodial sentence.

Hood's research suggested that ethnic-minority, and particularly black or Afro-Caribbean, defendants were subject to forms of indirect discrimination at least. The implications of a practice that favours so strongly those who plead guilty and the ways in which different offences are ranked in terms of where they should be tried, for example, would seem to work against the interests of ethnic-minority offenders. Hood acknowledges that it is a complex issue but on the basis of the detailed sample of almost three thousand Crown Court cases it would seem that some discrimination does occur in courts.

More recently, Hood, along with Shute and Seemungal, has examined the extent to which ethnic minorities get a fair hearing in the criminal courts (Shute et al. 2005). The focus of the study was on perceptions of unfair treatment, which, it is argued, can be as important as unfair treatment itself – if people are treated fairly they will have positive perceptions and increased confidence in the system. The research examined how defendants and witnesses experience their treatment, and was based on a very detailed interview schedule carried out in 2001 and 2002, with defendants, witnesses, court staff, solicitors, magistrates and judges interviewed – all in all 1,250 interviews were carried out by the team of researchers (including ethnic-minority interviewers). As with the police, but even more so, there is massive under-representation of ethnic-minority people in judicial and court positions, and especially amongst the higher ranks of the judiciary (see p. 168 above). Shute et al. found that the proportion of black and Asian defendants who felt they had been treated unfairly owing to their race was lower than expected, with one in five black defendants feeling their treatment had been influenced by racial bias. However, amongst those black and Asian defendants who thought they had been given a heavier sentence than others, more than half put it down to their ethnicity rather than what they had done or said in court; and seemed to believe that there was a sort of institutional racism present. As a 19-year-old Caribbean male who had lived in Britain all his life said after being sentenced to five years in prison: 'If I was a different colour a light sentence would have been given . . . the judge wanted to take another black face off the street . . . I was treated as a black offender.' To summarize their findings: the majority of defendants did not think they had been unfairly treated in court; of the minority who did feel unfairly treated, more than half attributed this to racism, and it was black defendants in Crown Courts who were most likely to feel they had been treated unfairly. It could be argued that even if only a minority hold this view, it is not satisfactory that many come away from court feeling they have been subject to racial bias.

Finally, we turn to what happens in prison and whether ethnic-minority prisoners receive differential treatment from white prisoners. We saw above the massively disproportionate numbers of ethnic-minority groups, and especially black people, in prison in Britain; here we will focus on what happens within prison.

There has been long-standing concern over the treatment of ethnic-minority prisoners, particularly since studies of racist attitudes amongst prison staff in the

1970s and 1980s (Phillips and Bowling 2002). Genders and Player's (1989) widely cited research in the 1980s found clear evidence of racial discrimination in prisons, and this seemed to affect the sort of prison jobs such prisoners were given and the extent to which they were allocated to open prisons. Black prisoners were also found to be more likely to be placed on disciplinary charges than white prisoners (McDermott 1990). A Home Office survey in 1994 found that prison officers held stereotypical views on ethnic-minority prisoners, describing them as arrogant, hostile to authority and as 'having a chip on their shoulders'.

The issue of racism within prisons is still high on the agenda. The murder of Zahid Mubarek by his cellmate Robert Stewart, a known and violent racist, at the Feltham Young Offenders Institution, West London, in 2000 and the subsequent investigations into it have highlighted the extent of such racism. Mubarek died seven days after he was beaten in his cell by his cellmate Stewart, who has since been sentenced to life for murder. The investigation into Mubarek's murder has uncovered damning evidence of continuing racism within prisons. In his comments to the Inquiry, Duncan Keys (Assistant General Secretary of the Prison Officers Association) said that warders at Feltham youth jail 'thought it would be funny to see what would happen when they put a young Asian lad in with someone who wanted to kill Asians'. He claimed that Mubarek died because he was placed in a cell with a white racist psychopath for the 'perverted pleasure' of officers. He referred to a game of what officers called 'Gladiator' which involved pitting inmates against one another and betting on who would win in a fight. White inmates would routinely be placed with black prisoners and bullies would be placed together to try and spark a conflict.

The investigation showed that the Mubarek case was not an isolated incident. The Prison Service's first race equality adviser, Judy Clements, told the inquiry that racism was rife at Feltham, saying she had heard numerous reports of ill-treatment of black and ethnic-minority prisoners. In a statement cataloguing racist abuse throughout the system, she said, 'In most areas, prison staff and management were . . . in complete denial that prisoners were subjected to any form of racism'. In every prison she visited, she found that black and ethnic-minority prisoners were 'disproportionately over-represented in the prison discipline regime'. Looking beyond Feltham, the prison service's own internal report found racist language and jokes to be widespread. At Portland jail a staff member told a black member of the investigating team that 'we're being overrun by you lot'.

Since Mubarek's murder evidence of racism amongst prisoner staff continues to be uncovered. Two prison officers were suspended in July 2001 for allegedly intimidating black staff. They have been on full pay for three years after Nazi memorabilia, neo-fascist literature and 'nigger-hunting licences' were found in police raids on their homes, where one room was decorated as Hitler's bunker. In July 2004 a Home Office Inquiry finally admitted that it was not acceptable for prison officers to keep such items on display and recommended that both officers be charged with serious unprofessional conduct. In commenting on this case, the prison service said it was committed to rooting out racist prison staff and had dismissed 15 people since 2001; however this particular case had been delayed while the police were deciding whether to prosecute it as a criminal case.

QUESTION BREAK

- Earlier we asked you to consider whether police officers should be dismissed for using racist language. Do you think prison officers should be dismissed for racist language? Give reasons for your answer.
- To what extent do you think that the studies and evidence looked at above support the argument that there is racial bias in the criminal justice system? What points might be made to argue against that view?

In concluding this section and as a final comment on racism within prison, we will refer to the recent report from the Commission for Racial Equality on 'Race Equality in Prisons' (CRE 2003). This report looked for evidence of racial discrimination other than that which related to Mubarek's murder (on which a separate report has been published); it examined three prisons – Brixton, Parc and Feltham. The evidence found ranged from acts of intimidation and serious racial harassment to issues to do with whether prison meals fitted particular dietary requirements. The investigation found many areas of 'failure' with regard to race and equality, which are too numerous to list here. The two general overall findings the Commission highlighted were, firstly, that prisoners from ethnic-minority backgrounds were not provided with equivalent protection (to white prisoners) from racial violence and, secondly, the prison service failed to provide race equality in its employment or custodial practices. Some of the key problems and issues are detailed in the box.

CASE STUDY BOX 6.1 SUMMARY OF FINDINGS OF CRE REPORT *RACE EQUALITY IN PRISONS* (2003)

The General Atmosphere in Prisons

Prison 'culture' among prison staff meant race equality procedures could be ignored, staff operated in a discriminatory way, and racist attitudes and behaviour were tolerated. Racist abuse and harassment and the presence of racist graffiti were persistent features of prison life for many staff and prisoners.

Treatment of Prison Staff

Ethnic minority staff had to work in an atmosphere of racist taunting and intimidation. Ethnic minority staff who spoke up about these matters were subsequently victimized.

continued

Treatment of Prisoners

Complaints of racial discrimination raised within the prison by prisoners were often not investigated.

Access to Goods, Facilities and Services

Meals provided for prisoners and goods available in prison shops often did not meet the needs of ethnic-minority prisoners.

Discipline for Prisoners

Prison statistics clearly suggested a consistent over-representation of black male prisoners in the prison disciplinary system.

Access to Work

Allocation to prison jobs (or in some cases work outside prison) tended to be at the discretion of individual officers, and was a long-standing source of complaint by black prisoners.

Black and Asian prisoners were consistently under-represented in work parties at Brixton and Feltham.

Protection from Victimization

Prisoners who made race complaints were punished or victimized for making the complaint.

FURTHER READING

Bowling, B. and Phillips, C. (2002) *Race, Crime and Justice*. Harlow: Longman. This is a comprehensive text that focuses exclusively on racism and the criminal justice process. It examines and discusses theorizing on the link (or not) between race and crime and issues around the treatment of ethnic-minority groups by the criminal justice system – including the police, courts, probation and prison service.

Shute, S., Hood, R. and Seemungal, F. (2005) *A Fair Hearing? Ethnic Minorities in the Criminal Courts*. Cullompton: Willan Publishing. This is an interesting and readable example of a piece of first-hand research that looks into a little-researched area of criminal justice – the treatment of ethnic minorities by the court system.

WEBSITE

www.homeoffice.gov.uk. The Home Office website provides masses of statistical information on crime in general and by accessing the section on crime and victims and narrowing the search to race provides a wealth of data relevant to our examination of ethnic-minority criminality.

REFERENCES

AACAP (1997) 'AACAP official action. Practice parameters for the assessment and treatment of children and adolescents with conduct disorder', *Journal of the American Academy of Child and Adolescent Psychiatry*, 36 (supplement), 122–39.

Adler, F. (1975) *Sisters in Crime*. New York: McGraw-Hill.

Ainsworth, M., Blehar, M., Waters, E. and Wall, S. (1978) *Patterns of Attachment: A Psychological Study of the Strange Situation*. Hillsdale, NJ: Erlbaum.

Allen, G. (1976) 'Scope and methodology of twin studies', *Acta Genetica Medicae Gemellolgiae*, 25, 79–85.

American Psychiatric Association (1997) 'Biological reductionism said to be linked to economic reductionism', *Psychiatric News* http://www.psych.org/pnews/97-12-05/scully.html. Last accessed 12 November 2004.

Andersen, S.L. (2003) 'Trajectories of brain development: point of vulnerability or window of opportunity?' *Neuroscience and Biobehavioural Reviews*, 27, 3–18.

Anderson, S., Bechara, A., Damasio, H., Tranel, D. and Damasio, A. (1999) 'Impairment of social and moral behaviour related to early damage in human prefrontal cortex', *Nature Neuroscience*, 2, 1032–7.

Appel, R. (1995) 'Mother Simpson', *The Simpsons*. Production code 3F06.

Bandura, A. (1990) 'Selective activation and disengagement of moral control', *Journal of Social Issues*, 46, 27–46.

Barrett, L., Dunbar, R. and Lycett, J. (2006) *Human Evolutionary Psychology*. London: Palgrave Macmillan.

Baumrind, D. (1978) 'Parental disciplinary patterns and social competence in children', *Youth and Society*, 9, 238–76.

Beccaria, C. (1963 (1764)) *On Crimes and Punishment*. Indianapolis: Bobbs-Merrill Educational.

Beck, U. (1992) *Risk Society: Towards a New Modernity*. London: Sage.

Becker, H.S. (1963) *Outsiders: Studies in the Sociology of Deviance*. New York: Free Press.

Becker, H.S. (1973) 'Labelling theory reconsidered'. In: *Outsiders: Studies in the Sociology of Deviance*, second edition. New York: Free Press.

Begley, S. (2002) 'Genes don't give humans edge over their primate relations', *Wall Street Journal*, April 2.

Berry-Dee, C. *Talking with Serial Killers*. London: John Blake.

Blackburn, R. (1993) *The Psychology of Criminal Conduct: Theory, Research and Practice*. Chichester: Wiley.

Blackburn, R. (1999) *The Psychology of Criminal Conduct: Theory, Research and Practice*. Chichester: Wiley.

Blass, T. (ed.) (2000) *Obedience to Authority: Current Perspectives on the Milgram Paradigm*. Mahwah, NJ: Lawrence Erlbaum Associates.

Bohman, M., Cloninger, R., Sigvardsson, S. and von Knoring, A. (1982) 'Predisposition to petty criminality in Swedish adoptees. I Genetic and environmental heterogeneity', *Archives of General Psychiatry* 39, 1233–41.

Boland, F.J., Burrill, R., Duwyn, M. and Karp, J. (1998) *Fetal Alcohol Syndrome: Implications for Correctional Service*. Research Report R-71. Ottawa, ON: Correctional Service of Canada.

Bond, M. (2004) 'The making of a suicide bomber', *New Scientist* 182, issue 2447, 15 May.

Bowlby, J. (1946) *Forty-Four Juvenile Thieves: Their Character and Home Life*. London: Hogarth.

Bowlby, J. (1951) *Maternal Care and Mental Health*. Geneva: WHO monograph series.

Bowling, B. and Phillips, C. (2002) *Race, Crime and Justice*. Harlow: Longman.

Box, S. (1981) *Deviance, Reality and Society*, second edition. Eastbourne: Holt, Rinehart and Winston.

Box, S. (1983) *Power, Crime and Mystification*. London: Tavistock.

Boyle, K. (2005) *Media and Violence*. London: Sage.

Breggin, P. (1995) 'Campaigns against racist federal programs by the center for the study of psychiatry and psychology', *Journal of African American Men*, 1, 3–22. http://www.breggin.com/racist fedpol.html.

Bridges, G.S. and Stone, J.A. (1986) 'Effects of criminal punishment on perceived threat of punishment: toward an understanding of specific deterrence', *Journal of Research in Crime and Delinquency*, 23, 207–39.

Britton, P. (1997) *The Jigsaw Man*. London: Corgi.

Brownmiller, S. (1975) *Against Our Wills: Men, Women, and Rape*. New York: Bantam.

Brunas-Wagstaff, J., Tilley, A., Verity, M., Ford, S. and Thompson, D. (1997) 'Functional and dysfunctional impulsivity in children and their relationship to Eysenck's impulsiveness and venturesomeness dimensions', *Personality and Individual Differences*, 22, 1 25–9.

Brunner, H., Nelen, M., van Zandvoort, P., Abeling, N., van Gennip, A., Wolters, E., Kulper, M., Ropers, H. and van Oost, B. (1991) 'X-linked borderline mental retardation with prominent behavioral disturbance: phenotype, genetic localisation and evidence for disturbed monoamine metabolism', *American Journal of Human Genetics*, 52, 1032–9.

Bufkin, J. and Luttrell, V. (2005) 'Neuroimaging studies of aggressive and violent behaviour: current findings and implications for criminology and criminal justice', *Trauma, Violence and Abuse*, 6, 176–91.

Burke, R. Hopkins (2005) *An Introduction to Criminological Theory*, second edition. Cullompton: Willan Publishing.

Burns, J. and Swerdlow, R. (2003) 'Right orbitofrontal tumor with pedophilia symptom and constructional apraxia sign', *Archives of Neurology*, 60, 437–40.

Canter, D. (1994) *Criminal Shadows*. London: HarperCollins.

Carlen, P. (1985) *Criminal Women*. Oxford: Polity Press.

Carlen, P. (1988) *Women, Crime and Poverty*. Milton Keynes: Open University Press.

Cashmore, E. (2001) 'The experience of ethnic minority police officers in Britain: under-recruitment and racial profiling in a performance culture', *Ethnic and Racial Studies*, 24, 4.

Cavadino, M. and Dignan, J. (2002) *The Penal System*, third edition. London: Sage.

Cavior, N. and Howard, L. (1973) 'Facial attractiveness and juvenile delinquency among black and white offenders', *Journal of Abnormal Child Psychology*, 1.

Cernkovich, S.A. and Giordano, P.C. (1987) 'Family relationships and delinquency', *Criminology*, 25, 295–321.

Chambliss, W. J. (1978) *On the Take: From Petty Crooks to Presidents.* Bloomington: Indiana University Press.

Chan, J. (1997) *Changing Police Culture: Policing in a Multicultural Society.* Cambridge: University Press.

Chesney-Lind, M. (1989) 'Girls' crime and women's place: toward a feminist world of female delinquency', *Crime and Delinquency,* 35.

Chesney-Lind, M. (1997) *The Female Offender.* Thousand Oaks, CA: Sage.

Christiansen, K. (1977) 'A preliminary study of criminality among twins'. In: S. Mednick and K. Christiansen (eds) *Biosocial Bases of Criminal Behavior,* 89–108. New York: Gardner Press.

Cicchetti, D. and Barnett, D. (1991) 'Attachment organization in maltreated preschoolers', *Development and Psychopathology,* 3, 397–412.

Cicourel, A.V. (1968) (second edition 1976) *The Social Organisation of Juvenile Justice.* New York: Wiley.

Claes, L., Vertommen, H. and Braspenning, N. (2000) 'Psychometric properties of the Dickman Impulsivity Inventory', *Personality and Individual Differences,* 29, 27–35.

Cloninger, C. and Gottesman, I. (1987) 'Genetic and environmental factors in anti-social behaviour disorders'. In: S. Mednick, T. Moffitt and S. Stack (eds) *The Causes of Crime: New Biological Approaches.* Cambridge: Cambridge University Press.

Cloninger, C., Sigvardsson, S., Bohman, M. and von Knorring, A. (1982) 'Predispositions to petty criminality in Swedish adoptees: II. Cross-fostering analysis of gene-environment interactions', *Archives of General Psychiatry,* 39, 1242–7.

Cloward, R. and Ohlin, L. (1960) *Delinquency and Opportunity.* London: Collier Macmillan.

Coccaro, E., Kavoussi, R., Coper, T. and Hauger, R. (1997) 'Central serotonin activity and aggression: inverse relationship with prolactin response to d-fenfluramine, but not CSF 5-HIAA concebtration in human subjects', *American Journal of Psychiatry,* 154, 1430–5.

Cohen, A.K. (1955) *Delinquent Boys: The Culture of the Gang.* New York: Free Press.

Cohen, L.E. and Felson, M. (1979) 'Social change and crime rate trends: a routine activity approach', *American Sociological Review,* 44, 588–608.

Commission for Racial Equality (2003) *Racial Equality in Prisons.* London: CRE.

Cook, P.J. (1980) 'Research in criminal deterrence: laying the groundwork for the second decade'. In: M. Tonry and N. Morris (eds), *Crime and Justice: An Annual Review of Research.* Chicago: University of Chicago Press.

Cornish, D. and Clarke, R.V. (1987) 'Understanding crime application of rational choice theory', *Criminology,* 25, 933–47.

Court, G. *Women in the Labour Market: Two Decades of Change and Continuity,* IES Report 294, 1995.

Cox, D., Hallam, R., O'Connor, K. and Rachman, S. (1983) 'An experimental study of fearlessness and courage', *British Journal of Psychology,* 74, 107–17.

Dalgaard, O. and Kringlen, E. (1976) 'A Norwegian twin study of criminality', *British Journal of Criminal Psychology,* 16, 213–32.

Dalton, K. (1961) 'Menstruation and crime', *British Medical Journal,* 2, 1752.

Daly, K. (1989) 'Gender and varieties of white collar crime', *Criminology,* 27 (November).

Daly, M. and Wilson, M. (1988) 'Evolutionary social psychology and family homicide', *Science,* 242, 519–24.

Daly, M. and Wilson, M. (1998) *The Truth about Cinderella.* London: Wiedenfeld & Nicolson.

Daly, M. and Wilson, M. (1999) 'Human Evolutionary psychology and animal behaviour', *Animal Behaviour,* 57, 509–19.

Daly, M. and Wilson, M. (2002) 'The Cinderella Effect: parental discrimination against stepchildren', *Samfundsøkonomen* 4, 39–46.

Damasio, A. (2003) *Looking for Spinoza: Joy, Sorrow and the Feeling Brain.* New York: Harvest.

Darwin, C. (1850/1964) *On the Origin of the Species by Means of Natural Selection: The Preservation of Favoured Races in the Struggle for Life.* Chicago: University of Chicago Press.

Darwin, C. (1871) *The Descent of Man.* London: Murray.

Davidson, R. (2001) 'Towards a biology of personality and emotion', *Annals of the New York Academy of Sciences*, 935, 191–207.

Dawkins, R. (1976) *The Selfish Gene.* Oxford: Oxford University Press.

Deno, D. (1996) 'Legal implications of genetics and crime research'. In: G. Bock and J. Goode (eds), *Genetics of Criminal and Antisocial Behavior*, 248–56. Chichester: John Wiley & Sons.

Dickens, C. (1897) *Oliver Twist.* Re-issued 2004. Harmondsworth: Penguin Books.

Dickman, S.J. (1990) 'Functional and dysfunctional impulsivity: personality and cognitive correlates', *Journal of Personality and Social Psychology*, 58, 95–102.

Dobzhansky, T. (1973) 'Nothing in biology makes sense except in the light of evolution', *American Biology Teacher*, 35, 125–9.

Dolan, M., Deakin, W., Roberts, N. and Anderson, L. (2002) 'Serotonergic and cognitive impairments in impulsive aggressive personality disordered offenders: are there implications for treatment?', *Psychological Medicine*, 32, 105–17.

Dostoyevsky, F. (1886) *Crime and Punishment.* Re-issued 1997. Harmondsworth: Penguin Books.

Douglas, K. (2006) 'Are we still evolving?', *New Scientist* 2452, 11 March.

Durkheim, E. (1960 (1893)) *The Division of Labour in Society.* New York: Free Press.

Durkheim, E. (1964 (1895)) *The Rules of Sociological Method.* New York: Free Press.

Ebstein, R., Novick, O., Umansky, R., Priel, B., Osher, Y., Blaine, B., Bennett, E., Nemanov, L., Katz, M. and Belmaker, R. (1996) 'Dopamine D4 receptor (D4DR) exon iii polymorphism associated with the human personality trait of novelty seeking', *Nature Genetics*, 12, 78–80.

Einstadter, W. and Henry, S. (1995) *Criminological Theory: An Analysis of its Underlying Assumptions.* Fort Worth: Harcourt Brace College.

Eisenberg, L. (2005) 'Violence and the mentally ill: victims not perpetrators', *Archives of General Psychiatry*, 62, 825–6.

Eley, T., Lichenstein, P. and Stevenson, J. (1999) 'Sex differences in the etiology of aggressive and nonaggressive antisocial behavior: results from two twin studies', *Child Development*, 70, 155–68.

Elliott, D.S. and Voss, H.L. (1974) *Delinquency and Dropout.* Lexington, MA: Lexington Books.

Ellis, D. and Austin, P. (1971) 'Menstruation and aggressive behavior in a correctional center for women', *Journal of Criminal Law, Criminology and Police Science*, 62, 388–95.

Ellis, L. (2005) 'A theory explaining biological correlates of criminality', *European Journal of Criminology*, 2, 287–315.

Emsley, C. (1996) *Crime and Society in England 1750–1900*, second edition. Harlow: Longman

Eron, L.D. (1987) 'The development of aggressive behaviour from the perspective of a developing behaviourism', *American Psychologist*, 42, 435–43.

Evansburg, A. (2001) '"But your honour, it's in his genes." The case for genetic impairments as grounds for a downward departure under the federal sentencing guidelines', *American Criminal Law Review*, 38, 1565–87.

Eysenck, H.J. (1974) *Crime and Personality*, third edition. London: Paladin Press.

Eysenck, H.J. (1987) 'Personality theory and the problems of criminality'. In: B.J. McGurk, D.M. Thornton and M. Williams (eds), *Applying Psychology to Imprisonment: Theory and Practice*, 29–58. London: HMSO.

Eysenck, S.B.G. and Eysenck, H.J. (1971) 'Crime and personality: item analysis of questionnaire responses', *British Journal of Criminology*, 11, 49–62.

Faraone, S., Doyle, A., Mick, E. and Diederman, J. (2001) 'Meta-analysis of the association between the dopamine D4 gene seven-repeat allele and attention deficit hyperactivity disorder', *American Journal of Psychiatry*, 158, 1052–7.

Farrington, D.P. (1972) 'Delinquency begins at home', *New Society*, 21, 495–7.

Farrington, D.P. (1992) 'Explaining the beginning, progress, and ending of anti-social behaviour from birth to adulthood'. In: J. McCord (ed.), *Facts, Frameworks, and Forecasts: Advances in Criminological Theory (Vol. 3)*. New Brunswick: Transactional Publishers.

Farrington, D.P. (1995) 'The development of offending and antisocial behaviour from childhood: key findings in the Cambridge Study in Delinquent Development', *Journal of Child Psychology and Psychiatry*, 36, 929–64.

Farrington, D.P. and Morris, A. (1983) 'Sex, sentencing and reconviction', *British Journal of Criminology*, 23, 229–48.

Farrington, D.P., Barnes, G.C. and Lambert, S. (1996) 'The concentration of offending in families', *Legal and Criminological Psychology*, 1, 47–63.

Ferrell, J. (1999) 'Cultural criminology', *Annual Review of Criminology*, 25, 1.

Ferrell, J. (2001) 'Cultural criminology'. In: E. McLaughlin and J. Muncie (eds), *Sage Dictionary of Criminology*. London: Sage.

Foglia, W. (2000) *Sigmund Freud: Encyclopaedia of Criminology and Deviant Behaviour*. Blacksburg, VA: Taylor & Francis.

Foucault, M. (1977) *Discipline and Punish: The Birth of the Prison*. London: Allen Lane.

Fowles, J. (1999) *The Case for Television Violence*. Thousand Oaks, CA: Sage.

Freedman, B.J., Rosenthal, L., Donahoe, C.P., Schlundt, D.G. and McFall, R.M. (1978) 'A social behavioural analysis of skills deficits in delinquent and non delinquent adolescent boys', *Journal of Consulting and Clinical Psychology*, 46, 1448–62.

Freeman, R.B. (1983) 'Crime and unemployment'. In: J.Q. Wilson (ed.), *Crime and Public Policy*. San Francisco: ICS Press.

Freud, S. (1953) 'Criminals form a sense of guilt'. In: S. Freud, *The Standard Edition of the Collected Works of Sigmund Freud*, vol. 14. London: The Hogarth Press (pp. 332–3).

Freund, K. (1994) 'In search of an etiological model of pedophilia', *Sexological Review*, 2, 171–84.

Galen, E. (2000) 'US chemical pollution threatens child health and development', *World Socialist Website*. http://www.wsws.org/articles/2000/oct2000/poll-o06.shtml. Accessed 28 October 2005.

Garland, D. (1997) 'Of crimes and criminals: the development of criminology in Britain'. In M. Maguire, R. Morgan and R. Reiner (eds) *The Oxford Handbook of Criminology*, second edition. Oxford: Oxford University Press.

Gelles, R. (1997) *Intimate Violence in Families*. Thousand Oaks, CA: Sage.

Genders, E. and Player, E. (1989) *Race Relations in Prison*. Oxford: Clarendon Press.

George, C. and West, M. (1999) 'Developmental vs social personality models of adult attachment and mental ill health', *British Journal of Medical Psychology*, 72, 285–303.

Gesch, C.B., Hammond, S.M., Hampson, S.E., Eves, A. and, Crowder, M.J. (2002) 'Influence of supplementary vitamins, minerals and essential fatty acids on the antisocial behaviour of young adult prisoners. Randomised, placebo-controlled trial', *British Journal of Psychiatry*, 181, 22–8.

Giddens, A. (1993) *Sociology*, second edition. Cambridge: Polity Press.

Gilligan, C. (1993) *In a Different Voice: Psychological Theory and Women's Development*, second edition. Cambridge, MA: Harvard University Press.

Glover, V. and O'Connor, T. (2002) 'Effects of antenatal stress and anxiety: implications for development and psychiatry', *The British Journal of Psychiatry*, 180, 389–91.

Glueck, S. and Glueck, E. (1950) *Unraveling Juvenile Delinquency.* Cambridge, MA: Harvard University Press.

Goddard, H.H. (1914) *Feeble-Mindedness: Its Causes and Consequences.* New York: Macmillan.

Goffman, E. (1968) *Asylums: Essays on the Social Situation of Mental Patients and Other Inmates.* Harmondsworth: Penguin.

Goring, C. (1913) *The English Convict: A Statistical Study.* London: HMSO.

Gottfredson, M.R. and Hirschi, T. (1990) *A General Theory of Crime.* Stanford: Stanford University Press.

Groza, V., Ryan, S.D. and Cash, S.J. (2003) 'Institutionalisation, behavior and international adoption: predictors of behavior problems', *Journal of Immigrant Health*, 5, 1, 5–17.

Hagan, J. (1990) 'The structuration of gender and deviance: a power-control theory of vulnerability to crime and the search for deviant role exits', *The Canadian Review of Sociology and Anthropology*, 27 (2), 137–56.

Hall, C. (2005) 'New look at dangers of drinking in pregnancy', *Daily Telegraph*, 24 October.

Hare, R. (1996) 'Psychopathy and anti-social personality disorder: a case of diagnostic confusion', *Psychiatric Times*, 13, 39–40. Available at http://www.psychiatrictimes.com/p960239.html. Accessed 28 October 2005.

Hare, R.D. (1980) 'A research scale for the assessment of psychopathy in criminal populations', *Personality and Individual Differences*, 1, 111–19.

Harlow, H. (1962) 'The heterosexual affectional system in monkeys', *American Psychologist*, 17, 17–19.

Hart, N. (1993) 'Famine, maternal nutrition and infant mortality: a re-examination of the Dutch Hunger Winter', *Population Studies*, 47, 1.

Heidensohn, F. (1996) *Women and Crime*, second edition. Basingstoke: Macmillian.

Heidensohn, F. (1997) 'Gender and crime'. In: M. Maguire, R. Morgan and R. Reiner (eds), *The Oxford Handbook of Criminology*, second edition. Oxford: Oxford University Press.

Herbert, W. (1997) 'Politics of biology: how the nature vs nurture debate shapes public policy – and our view of ourselves', *US News and World Report*, 27 April. Accessed 28 October 2005.

Herrnstein, R.J. (1995) 'Criminologicla traits'. In: J.Q. Wilson and J. Petersilia (eds), *Crime*. San Francisco: ICS Press.

Herrnstein, R. J. and Murray, C. (1994) *The Bell Curve: Intelligence and Class Structure in American Life.* New York: Free Press.

Hirschi, T. (1969) *Causes of Delinquency.* Berkeley, CA: University of California Press.

Hirschi, T. (1995) 'The family'. In J.Q. Wilson and J. Petersilia, *Crime*. San Francisco: San Francisco Institute for Contemporary Studies.

Hirschi, T. and Gottfredson, M. (1994) *The Generality of Deviance.* New Brunswick, NJ: Transaction.

Hirschi, T. and Hindelang, M.J. (1977) 'Intelligence and delinquency: a revisionist review', *American Sociological Review*, 42, 571–87.

Hoffman, M.L. (1977) 'Moral internalisation: current theory and research'. In: L. Berkowitz (ed.), *Advances in Experimental Social Psychology (Vol. 10).* New York: Academic Press.

Holdaway, S. (1996) *The Racialisation of British Policing.* London: Macmillan.

Holdaway, S. (1997) 'Some recent approaches to the study of race in criminological research: race as social process', *British Journal of Criminology*, 37, 3.

Hollin, C. (1989) *Psychology and Crime: An Introduction to Criminological Psychology.* London: Routledge.

Hollin, C.R. (1992) *Criminal Behaviour: A Psychological Approach to Explanation and Prevention*. London: The Falmer Press.

Holmes, B. (2005) 'Here's looking at you, chimp', *New Scientist*, 2531.

Holmes, R.M. and Holmes, S.T. (1996) *Profiling Violent Crimes: An Investigative Tool*, second edition. CA: Sage.

Hood, R. (1992) *Race and Sentencing*. Oxford: Clarendon Press.

Hooten, E. (1939) *The American Criminal*. Cambridge, MA: Harvard University Press.

Hucklesby, A. (1993) 'Women, crime and deviance'. In: S. Jackson and S. Scott *Women's Studies: A Reader*. London: Harvester Wheatsheaf.

Hughes, P. (1965) *Witchcraft*. Harmondsworth: Penguin.

Hyder, K. (1995) 'Black marks', *Police Review*, 14 July.

Inman, M. (2005) 'Human brains enjoy ongoing evolution', NewScientist.com news service, http://www.newscientist.com/article.ns?id=dn7974. Accessed 4 March 2006.

Institute of Race Relations (2002) *The Criminal Justice System*. www.irr.org.uk.

Jeffery, C.R. (1977) *Crime Prevention Through Environmental Design*. Beverly Hills, CA: Sage Publications.

Jensen, P., Mrazek, D., Knapp, P., Steinberg, L., Pfeffer, D., Schowalter, J. M.D. and Shapiro, T. (1997) 'Evolution and revolution in child psychiatry: ADHD as a disorder of adaptation', *Journal of American Child & Adolescent Psychiatry*, vol. 36.

Johnson, A.G. (1989) *Human Arrangements: An Introduction to Sociology*. New York: Harcourt Brace Jovanovich

Johnson, J.G. and Smailes, E. (2004) 'Anti-social parental behaviour, problematic parenting and aggressive offspring behaviour during adulthood: a 25-year longitudinal investigation', *British Journal of Criminology*, 44, 915–30.

Jones, H.R. (1894) 'The perils and protection of infant life', *Journal of the Royal Statistical Society*, March.

Jones, S. (2005) 'Darwinism and genes'. In: J. Stangroom, *What Scientists Think*. London: Routledge.

Jones, S. (2006) *Criminology*. Oxford: Oxford University Press.

Julien, R. (2004) *A Primer of Drug Action*, second edition. New York: Worth.

Kanazawa, S. (2003a) 'A general evolutionary psychological theory of criminality and related male-typical behaviour'. In: A. Walsh and L. Ellis (eds) *Biosocial Criminology: Challenging Environmentalism's Supremacy*. Hauppauge, NY: Nova Science.

Kanazawa, S. (2003b) 'Why productivity fades with age: the crime-genius connection', *Journal of Research in Personality*, 37, 257–72, at http://www.lse.ac.uk/collections/methodology Institute/ pdf/SKanazawa/JRP2003.pdf.

Katz, L. (2000) *Evolutionary Origins of Morality*. Thorneston: Imprint Academic.

Kerr, D.C. and Lopez, N.L. (2004) 'Parental discipline and externalizing behaviour problems in early childhood: the roles of moral regulation and child gender', *Journal of Abnormal Child Psychology*, 32, 4.

Kiehl, K., Smith, A., Hare, R., Mendrek, A., Forster, B., Brink, J and Liddle, P. (2001) 'Limbic abnormalities in affective precessing by criminal psychopaths as revealed by functional magnetic resonance imaging', *Biological Psychiatry*, 50, 677–84.

Kohlberg, L. (1978) 'Revisions in the theory and practice of moral development', *Directions for Child Development*, 2, 83–8.

Krueger, R.F., Schmutte, P.S., Caspi, A. and Moffitt, T.E. (1994) 'Personality traits are linked to crime among men and women', *Journal of Abnormal Psychology*, 103, 328–38.

Kurtzberg, R. Mandell, W., Levin, M., Lipton, D. and Shuster, M. (1978) 'Plastic surgery on offenders'. In: N. Johnston and L. Savitz, *Justice and Corrections*. New York: McGraw-Hill.

Ladd-Taylor, M. and Umansky, L. (1998) *'Bad' Mothers: The Politics of Blame in Twentieth Century America*. New York: New York University Press.

Lahey, B.B., Hart, E.L., Pliszka, S., Applegate, B. and McBurnett, K. (1993) 'Neurophysical correlates of conduct disorder: a rationale and a review', *Journal of Clinical Child Psychology*, 22, 141–53.

Lambert, J.R. (1970) *Crime, Police and Race Relations*. London: Oxford University Press.

Lavater, J. (1775) *Physiognomical Fragments*. Leipzig: Weidmann.

Lawson, W. (2003) 'Fighting crime one bite at a time: diet supplements cut violence in prisons', *Psychology Today*.

Lawton, G. (2004) 'Urban legends', *New Scientist*, 183 (issue 2465), 18 September, 32–5.

Lea, J. and Young, J. (1984) *What Is to Be Done about Law and Order?* Harmondsworth: Penguin.

Lemert, E.M. (1951) *Social Pathology*. New York: McGraw-Hill.

Lemert, E.M. (1967) *Human Deviance, Social Problems and Social Control*. Englewood Cliffs, NJ: Prentice-Hall.

Leonard, M. (1995) 'Masculinity, femininity and crime', *Sociology Review*, vol. 94.

Lewontin, R., Rose, S. and Kamin, L. (1984) *Not in Our Genes*. London: Penguin.

Lloyd, A. (1995) *Doubly Deviant, Doubly Damned: Society's Treatment of Violent Women*. Harmondsworth: Penguin.

Loeber, R. and Farrington, D.P. (1994) 'Problems and solutions in longitudinal and experimental treatment studies of child psychopathology and delinquency', *Journal of Consulting and Clinical Psychology*, 62, 887–900.

Lombroso, C. (1876) *L'uomo delinquente*. Milan: Hoepli.

Lombroso, C. and Ferrero, W. (1920 (1885)) *The Female Offender*. London: Unwin.

MacLeod, M. (n.d.) Charles Whitman: the Texas Tower sniper. *Court TV's Crime Library*. http://www. crimelibrary.com/notorious_murders/mass/whitman/index_1.html. Accessed 28 October 2005.

Macmillan, M. (1999/2005) The Phineas Gage Information Page. http://www.deakin.edu.au/hbs/GAGEPAGE/index.html. Accessed 10 April 2005.

Macmillan, M. (2000) *An Odd Kind of Fame: Stories of Phineas Gage*. Cambridge, MA: MIT Press.

Macpherson, W. (1999) *The Stephen Lawrence Inquiry: Report of an Inquiry by Sir William Macpherson*. London: HMSO.

Margolin, G. and Gordis, E.B. (2000) 'The effect of family and community violence on children', *Annual Review of Psychology*, 51, 445–79.

Martens, W. (2002) 'Criminality and moral dysfunctions: neurological, biochemical, and genetic dimensions', *International Journal of Offender Therapy and Comparative Criminology*, 46, 170–82.

Matza, D. (1964) *Delinquency and Drift*. New York: Wiley.

Mayr, E. (1982) *The Growth of Biological Thought: Diversity, Evolution, and Inheritance*. Cambridge, MA: Belknap Press.

McCord, J. (1979) 'Some child-rearing antecedents of criminal behaviour in adult men', *Journal of Personality and Social Psychology*, 37, 1477–86.

McCord, J. (1982) 'A longitudinal view of the relationship between parental absence and crime'. In: J. Gunn and D.P. Farrington (eds), *Abnormal Offenders, Delinquency and the Criminal Justice System*, (Volume 1). Chichester: Wiley.

McDermott, K. (1990) 'We have no problems: the experience of racism in prison', *New Community*, 16, 2.

McEwen, B. (1999) 'Development of the cerebral cortex XIII: Stress and brain development – II', *Journal of the Academy of Child and Adolescent Psychiatry*, 38, 101–3.

McGinn, L.K. (2000) 'Cognitive behavioral therapy of depression: theory, treatment, and empirical status', *American Journal of Psychotherapy*, 54, 254–60.

McGurk, B.J. and McDougall, C. (1981) 'A new approach to Eysenck's theory of criminal personality', *Personality and Individual Differences*, 2, 338–40.

McMillan, T. and Rachman, S. (1987) 'Fearlessness and courage: a laboratory study of paratrooper veterans of the Falklands war', *British Journal of Psychology*, 78, 375–83.

Mcnally, R. (1995) 'Homicidal youth in England and Wales 1982–1992: profile and policy', *Psychology, Crime and Law*, 1, 333–42.

Meadow, R. (ed.) (2000) *The ABC of Child Abuse*. London: BMA.

Mealey, L. (1995) 'The sociobiology of sociopathy: an integrated evolutionary model', *Behavioral and Brain Science*, 18, 523–99.

MedlinePlus (2005) Pregnancy and substance abuse. http://www.nlm.nih.gov/medlineplus/pregnancy andsubstanceabuse.html. Last accessed 29 October 2005.

Mednick, S., Gabrielli, W. and Hutchings, B. (1984) 'Genetic factors in the etiology of criminal behaviour'. In: S. Mednick, T. Moffitt and S. Stack (eds) *The Causes of Crime: New Biological Approaches*, 74–91. Cambridge: Cambridge University Press.

Mendez, M., Chow, T., Ringman, J., Twitchell, G. and Hinkin, C. (2000) 'Pedophilia and temporal lobe disturbances', *Journal of Neuropsychiatry and Clinical Neuroscience*, 12, 71–6.

Merton, R.K. (1938) 'Social structure and anomie', *American Sociological Review*, 3, 672–82.

Miethe, T.D., Stafford, M.C. and Long, J.S. (1987) 'Social differentiation in criminal victimisation: a test of routine activities/lifestyle theories', *American Sociological Review*, 52, 184–94.

Milgram, S. (1983) *Obedience to Authority: An Experimental View*. New York: HarperCollins.

Miller, B., Darby, A., Benson, D., Cummings, J. and Miller, M. (1997) 'Aggressive, socially disruptive and antisocial behaviour associated with frontotemporal dementia', *British Journal of Psychiatry*, 170, 150–5.

Miller, G. (2001) *The Mating Mind*. London: Vintage.

Miller, W. (1958) 'Lower class culture as a generalising milieu of gang delinquency', *Journal of Social Issues*, 14, 3.

Mirels, H.L. (1970) 'Dimensions of internal and external control', *Journal of Consulting and Clinical Psychology*, 34, 226–8.

Moffitt, T., Bramner, G., Caspi, A., Fawcett, J., Raleigh, M., Yuwiler, A. and Silva, P. (1998) 'Whole blood serotonin relates to violence in an epidemiological study', *Biological Psychiatry*, 43, 446–57.

Moffitt, T.E. (1990) 'Juvenile delinquency and attention deficit disorder: boys' development trajectories from age 13 to age 15', *Child Development*, 61, 893–910.

Moffitt, T.E. (1993) 'Adolescence-limited and life-course-persistent antisocial behaviour: a developmental taxonomy', *Psychological Review*, 100, 674–701.

Moiré, A. and Jessel, D. (1997) *Brainsex: Real Difference Between Men and Women*. London: Mandarin.

Motluk, A. (2004) 'Life sentence', *New Scientist*, 2471.

Mulley, K. (2001) 'Victimized by the media', *Criminal Justice Matters*, 43.

Murray, C. (1990) *The Emerging Underclass*. London: Institute of Economic Affairs.

Naffine, N. (1981) 'Theorizing about female crime'. In: S. Mukherjee and J.A. Scutt (eds), *Women and Crime*. North Sydney: Allen & Unwin.

Naffine, N. (1987) *Female Crime: The Construction of Women in Criminology*. Boston: Allen & Unwin.

Naffine, N. (1997) *Feminism and Criminology*. Cambridge: Polity Press.

Newson, J., Newson, E. and Adams, M. (1993) 'The social origins of delinquency', *Criminal Behaviour and Mental Health*, 3, 19–29.

Oakley, A. (1972) *Sex, Gender and Society*. London: Temple Smith.

Parens, E. (2004) *Genetic Differences and Human Identities*. A supplement to the Hastings Centre Report, January–February.

Parsons, T. (1951) *The Social System*. London: Routledge & Kegan Paul.

Passer, M.W. and Smith, R.E. (2001) *Psychology: Frontiers and Applications*. Boston, MA: McGraw-Hill.

Patterson, G.R. and Dishion, T.J. (1985) 'Contributions of families and peers to delinquency', *Criminology*, 23, 63–79.

Pavlov, I.V. (1960) *Conditional Reflexes*. New York: Dover.

Pearce, F. (1976) *Crimes of the Powerful*. London: Pluto Press.

Pearson, G. (1983) *Hooligans: A History of Respectable Fears*. London: Macmillan.

Pearson, J. (1972) *The Profession of Violence: The Rise and Fall of the Kray Twins*. London: Weidenfeld and Nicolson.

Pellegrini, A. and Bartini, M. (2001) 'Dominance in early adolescent boys: affiliative and aggressive dimensions and possible functions', *Merrill-Palmer Quarterly*, 47, 142–63.

Pennington, B. and Bennetto, L. (1993) 'Main effects or transactions in the neuropsychology of conduct disorder? Commentary on "The neuropsychology of conduct disorder"', *Development and Psychopathology*, 5, 153–64.

Phillips, C. and Bowling, B. (2002) 'Racism, ethnicity, crime and criminal justice'. In: M. Maguire, R. Morgan and R. Reiner (eds) *Oxford Handbook of Criminology*, third edition. Oxford: Oxford University Press.

Pinker, S. (2005) 'Evolutionary psychology and the blank slate'. In: J. Stangroom, *What Scientists Think*. London: Routledge.

Pollak, O. (1950) *The Criminality of Women*. New York: A S Barnes.

Poole, M. (1994) 'A critique of aspects of the philosophy and theology of Richard Dawkins', *Science and Christian Belief*, 6, 41–59.

Power, M.J., Alderson, M.R., Phillipson, C.M. and Morris, J.N. (1967) Delinquent schools? *New Society*, 10, 542–3.

Quay, H.C. (1987) 'Intelligence'. In: H.C. Quay (ed.), *Handbook of Juvenile Delinquency*. New York: Wiley.

Quinney, R. (1977) *Class, State and Crime*. Harlow: Longman.

Quist, J., Barr, C., Schachar, R., Roberts, W., Malone, M., Tannock, R., Basile, V., Beitchman, J. and Kennedy, J. (2000) 'Evidence for the serotonin HTR2A receptor gene as a susceptiblilty factor in attention deficit hyperactivity disorder (ADHD)', *Molecular Psychiatry*, 5, 537–41.

Rafter, N. and Heidensohn, F. (eds) (1995) *International Feminist Perspectives in Criminology: Engendering a Discipline*. Buckingham and Philadelphia: Open University Press.

Raine, A. (1993) *The Psychopathology of Crime*. New York: Academic Press.

Raine, A. (2002a) 'Annotation: the role of prefrontal deficits, low autonomic arousal, and early health factors in the development of antisocial and aggressive behaviour in children', *Journal of Child Psychology and Psychiatry*, 43, 417–34.

Raine, A. (2002b) 'Biosocial studies of antisocial and violent behaviour in children and adults: a review', *Journal of Abnormal Child Psychology*, 30, 311–26.

Raine, A., Lencz, T., Taylor, K., Hellige, S., Bihirle, S., Lacasse, L., Lee, M., Ishikawa, S. and Colletti, P. (2003b) 'Corpus callosum abnormalities in psychopathic antisocial individuals', *Archives of General Psychiatry*, 60, 1134–42.

Raine, A., Mellingen, K., Liu, J., Venables, P. and Mednick, S. (2003a) 'Effects of environmental enrichment at age 3–5 years on schizotypal personality and antisocial behavior at ages 17 and 23 years, *American Journal of Psychiatry*, 160, 1–9.

Rankin, J.H. and Kern, R. (1994) 'Parental attachments and delinquency'. *Criminology*, 32, 495–515.

Reid, I. and Wormald, E. (1982) *Sex Differences in Britain*. London: Grant MacIntyre.

Reiner, R. (2000) *The Politics of the Police*, third edition, London: Harvester Wheatsheaf.

Ressler, R.K., Burgess, A.W. and Douglas, J.E. (1988) *Sexual Homicide: Patterns and Motives*. New York: Lexington Books.

Revere, C. (1999) 'Ticking bomb baby', *Tucson Citizen*, 29 April. Available at http://www.come-over.to/FAS/Citizen/part3_5.html.

Rex, J. and Moore, R. (1967) *Race, Community and Conflict*. Oxford: Oxford University Press.

Rhee, S. and Waldman, I. (2002) 'Genetic and environmental influences on antisocial behaviour: a meta-analysis of twin and adoption studies', *Psychological Bulletin*, 128, 490–529.

Ridley, M. (1996) *The Origins of Virtue*. London: Viking.

Rose, L. (1986) *Massacre of the Innocents: Infanticide in Great Britain 1800–1939*. London: Routledge & Kegan Paul.

Rose, S. (1997) *The Mismeasure of Man*, second edition. Harmondsworth: Penguin Science.

Rose, S. (2003a) *Lifelines: Life Beyond the Gene*. Oxford: Oxford University Press.

Rose, S. (2003b) Belief. Transcript of Radio 3 programme broadcast 23/12/03. http://www.bbc.co.uk/religion/programmes/belief/scripts/steven_rose.shtml. Last accessed 12 November 2004.

Rosenham, D.L. (1973) 'On being sane in insane places', *Science*, 179, 250–8.

Ross, R. and Fabiano, E. (1985) *The Time to Think: A Cognitive Model of Delinquency Prevention and Offender Rehabilitation*. Johnson City: Institute of Social Sciences and Arts.

Rossi, P.H., Berk, R.A. and Lenihan, K.J. (1980) *Money, Work and Crime: Experimental Evidence*. New York: Academic Press.

Rotter, J.B. (1975) 'Some problems and misconceptions related to the construct of internal versus external control of reinforcement', *Journal of Consulting and Clinical Psychology*, 43, 56–67.

Rowe, D. (1990) 'Inherited dispositions towards learning delinquent and criminal behaviour: new evidence'. In: L. Ellis and H. Hoffman (eds) *Crime in Biological, Social and Moral Contexts*. New York: Praeger.

Rowe, D. (2002) *Biology and Crime*. Los Angeles: Roxbury.

Rowe, D., Stever, D., Chase, S., Sherman, A., Abramowitz, A. and Waldman, I. (2001) 'Two dopamine genes related to reports of childhood retrospective inattention and conduct disorder', *Molecular Psychiatry*, 6, 429–33.

Rutter, M. (1971) 'Parent–child separation: psychological effects on the children', *Journal of Child Psychology and Psychiatry*, 12, 233–60.

Rutter, M. and Giller, H. (1983) *Juvenile Delinquency: Trends and Perspectives*. Harmondsworth: Penguin.

Rymer, S. (1993) *Genie: A Scientific Tragedy*. New York: Harper Perennial.

Saladin, M., Saper, Z. and Breen, L. (1988) 'Perceived attractiveness and attributions of criminality: what is beautiful is not criminal', *Canadian Journal of Criminology*, 30, 251–9.

Schore, A.N. (1997) 'Interdisciplinary developmental research as a source of clinical models'. In: M. Moskowitz, C. Monk, C. Kaye and S. Ellman (eds), *The Neurobiological and Developmental Basis for Psychotherapeutic Intervention*. Northvale: Jason Aronson.

Seager, J. (2003) *The Atlas of Women*. London: The Women's Press.

Segerstråle, U. (2000) *Defenders of the Truth: The Battle for Science in the Sociobiology Debate and Beyond.* Oxford: Oxford University Press.

Sennett, R. (1977) *The Fall of Public Man.* London: Faber.

Sharpe, J.A. (1995) *Early Modern England: A Social History 1550–1750*, second edition. London: Oxford University Press

Sharpe, J.A. (1999) *Crime in Early Modern England 1550–1750*, second edition. Harlow: Longman

Sheldon, W.H. (1949) *Varieties of Delinquent Youth.* New York: Harper.

Shute, S., Hood, R. and Seemungal, F. (2005) *A Fair Hearing? Ethnic Minorities in the Criminal Courts.* Cullompton: Willan Publishing.

Siegel, L. (1992) *Criminology*, fourth edition. St Paul, MN: West Publishing.

Simon, R. (1975) *Women and Crime.* Toronto: Lexington Books.

Skinner, B.F. (1974) *About Behaviourism.* New York: Knopf.

Slutske, W., Heath, A.C., Dinwiddie, S.H. and Madden, P. (1997) 'Modelling genetic and environmental influences in the etiology of conduct disorder: a study of 2,682 adult twin pairs', *Journal of Abnormal Psychology*, 106, 266–79.

Smart, C. (1976) *Women, Crime and Criminology: A Feminist Critique.* London: Routledge & Kegan Paul.

Smith, D. and Gray, J. (1983) *Police and People in London.* London: Policy Studies Institute (PSI).

Stangroom, J. (2005) 'Introduction'. In J. Stangroom, *What Scientists Think.* London: Routledge.

Steffensmeier, D. and Allan, E. (1996) 'Gender and crime: toward a gendered theory of female offending', *Annual Review of Sociology*, 22, 459–87.

Steffensmeier, D.J. (1978) 'Crime and the contemporary woman: an analysis of changing levels of female property crime 1960–1975', *Social Forces*, December, 566–84.

Steffensmeier, D.J. and Steffensmeier, R.H. (1980) 'Trends in female delinquency', *Criminology*, 18, 62–85.

Steinberg, L. and Morris, A.S. (2001) 'Adolescent development', *Annual Review of Psychology*, 52, 83–110.

Stevens, P. and Willis, C. (1979) *Race, Crime and Arrests.* London: HMSO.

Sutherland, E. (1949) *White Collar Crime.* New York: Holt, Rinehart and Winston.

Sutton, M. (2002) 'Race hatred and the far right on the internet', *Criminal Justice Matters*, 48.

Taylor, I., Walton, P. and Young, J. (eds) (1975) *Critical Criminology.* London: Routledge.

Taylor, J., Iacono, G. and McGue, M. (2000) 'Evidence for a genetic aetiology of early-onset delinquency', *Journal of Abnormal Psychology*, 109, 634–43.

The Social Exclusion Unit (2002) *Reducing Reoffending by Ex Prisoners.* London: HM Prison Service.

Thomas, W.I. (1907) *Sex and Society.* Chicago: University of Chicago Press.

Thomas, W.I. (1923) *The Unadjusted Girl.* Boston: Little, Brown.

Thornhill, R. and Palmer, C. (2000) *A Natural History of Rape: Biological bases of Sexual Coercion.* Cambridge, MA: MIT Press.

Tierney, J. (1996) *Criminology: Theory and Context.* Harlow: Longman.

Tolstoy, L. (1869/2005) *War and Peace.* Harmondsworth: Penguin Classics. (Translated by A. Briggs.)

Tooby, J. and Cosmides, L. (1992) 'The psychological foundations of culture'. In: J. Barkow, L. Cosmides and J. Tooby (eds), *The Adapted Mind: Evolutionary Psychology and the Generation of Culture*, 19–136. New York: Oxford University Press.

Tost, H., Vollmert, C., Brassen, S., Schmitt, A., Dressing, H. and Braus, D. (2004) 'Pedophilia: neuropsychological evidence encouraging a brain network perspective', *Medical Hypotheses*, 63, 528–31.

Trimble, J. and Fay, M. (1986) 'PMS in today's society', *Hamline Law Review*, 9, 1.

Vargha-Khadem, F., Cowan, J. and Mishkin, M. (2000) 'Sociopathic behaviour after early damage to prefrontal cortex', Presentation to the Society for Neuroscience, New Orleans, November.

Vines, G. (1998) 'Life sentence', *New Scientist*, 2162.

Wade, T.D. and Kendler, K.S. (2001) 'Parent, child and social correlates of parental discipline style: a retrospective, multi-informant investigation with female twins', *Social Psychiatry and Psychiatric Epidemiology*, 36, 4, 177–85.

Wadsworth, M. (1979) *Roots of Delinquency*. London: Martin Robertson.

Walklate, S. (2004) *Gender, Crime and Criminal Justice*, second edition. Cullompton: Willan Publishing.

Wall, D. (2004) 'Policing cyberspace: law and order on the cyberbeat', *Criminal Justice Review 2003–2004*, Centre for Criminal Justice Studies, University of Leeds.

Walsh, A. (2002) *Biosocial Criminology: Introduction and Integration*. Cincinnati, OH: Anderson Publishing.

Watson, J.B. (1925) *Behaviourism*. New York: Norton.

Weiner, J. (1995) *The Beak of the Finch: A Story of Evolution in Our Time*. New York: Vintage.

Wells, L.E. and Rankin, J.H. (1991) 'Families and delinquency: a meta-analysis of the impact of broken homes', *Social Problems*, 38, 71–93.

Werner, E.E. (1989) 'High-risk children in young adulthood: a longitudinal study from birth to 32 years', *American Journal of Orthopsychiatry*, 59, 72–81.

West, D.J. and Farrington, D.P. (1973) *Who Becomes Delinquent?* London: Heinemann.

West, D.J. and Farrington, D.P. (1977) *The Delinquent Way of Life*. London: Heinemann.

WHO (1997) *Poverty and Health: An Overview of the Basic Linkages and Public Policy Measures*. Geneva: WHO.

WHO (2002) *World Report on Violence and Health*. Geneva: WHO.

Williams, K.S. (2004) *Criminology*, fifth edition. Oxford: Oxford University Press.

Wilson, E.O. (1975) *Sociobiology: A New Synthesis*. Cambridge, MA: Harvard University Press.

Wilson, J. and Herrnstein, R. (1985) *Crime and Human Nature*. New York: Simon & Schuster.

Wisdom, C.S. (1989) 'The cycle of violence', *Science*, 244, 160–6.

Wright, R.A. and Miller, J.M. (1998) 'Taboo until today? The coverage of biological arguments in criminology textbooks, 1961 to 1970 and 1987 to 1996', *Journal of Criminal Justice*, 26, 1–19.

Yochelson, S. and Samenow, S. (1976) *The Criminal Personality. Volume One: A Profile for Change*. New York: Jason Aronson.

Young, J. (1971) *The Drugtakers: The Social Meaning of Drug Use*. London: McGibbon and Kee.

Zeleny, L. (1933) 'Feeblemindedness and criminal conduct', *American Journal of Sociology*, 38, 564–76.

INDEX